# A YEAR OF LIVING MINDFUL

## Seasonal Practices to Nourish Body, Mind, and Spirit

Randi Ragan

Notice:

The information, scientific studies, specific solutions, and opinions discussed in this book, while carefully researched, are for educational purposes only, and are designed to help you make informed decisions about your health and wellbeing. They are not intended as diagnoses, treatments for specific ailments, or replacements for the expertise of your qualified healthcare provider.

The use of any of this information without consulting a physician may be dangerous. The author accepts responsibility for any effects that may arise from the correct or incorrect use of information in this book. The health-related statements in this book have not been evaluated by the U.S. Food and Drug Administration.

Printed in the United States of America

First Printing, 2020

ISBN-13: 978-1-949001-60-0 print edition
ISBN-13: 978-1-949001-61-7 ebook edition

Waterside Productions

Waterside Productions
2055 Oxford Ave
Cardiff, CA 92007
www.waterside.com

# Contents

## Part 1 Everything Is Connected

## Part II The Four Seasons

### Spring

# Summer

# Autumn

# Winter

# Appendix

To the memory of my parents, Floyd and Jean

# Acknowledgments

I'd like to thank my husband, Richard, and my daughter, Olivia, who steady the oars on my boat and have made this journey possible. I very much appreciate Eugene Schwartz for his enthusiastic early support which helped this book see the light of day. My agent, Jill Kramer of Waterside Productions, gave great practical advice during all the ups and downs this book endured and is an expert in kind wisdom. Thank you to Terri Boekhoff for her editing talents extraordinaire. She helped me wrestle an unruly beast to the ground and not only tamed it, but made it sing in ways I never knew possible. I'm grateful to Celine Kwak and her beautiful art that graces these pages. Thank you to Caroline Pincus for her proposal writing talents and keen way of helping to hone a novice author's unwieldy ideas into understandable concepts. Her forthright guidance was a godsend. Much appreciation to early readers of the manuscript for their advice and assistance: Alex Schwartz, Kristina Coggins, Barbara Patrick and Kiki Giet. Thanks to Jennifer Louden for providing invaluable insight and resources all throughout this process. Gratitude to Justin Sachs of Motivational Press for rescuing this book when it had lost a home.

A very big thank you to the customers, therapists and technicians, vendors, consultants, benefactors, and fellow business owners who've been a part of my work with GreenBliss EcoSpa. This book is a direct result of my experience growing an idea from a corner of my living room to a now ten year endeavor and culminates in these pages. Thank you especially to Hope Malkan, Morgan Lawley, Kim Colwell, Alex Fallon, Alison Graham, staff and teachers of Silverlake Yoga, Center For Yoga and YogaWorks, and all the other bright and shining souls that have peopled my days before and throughout my experiences with GBES. Namaste.

*How we spend our days is, of course, how we spend our lives.*

—Annie Dillard

# PART 1

# EVERYTHING IS CONNECTED

# Introduction

## Make Meaning by Doing

. . . . . . . . . . . . . . . . . . .

There is a famous Zen proverb, "Before enlightenment: chop wood, carry water. After enlightenment: chop wood, carry water." This can be taken to mean that everyday tasking is the heart and soul of a life filled with purpose and meaning. The glue that holds our "aha" moments together can be found in the ordinary rituals that make up our lives and lifestyles. After all, the way we think about our lives affects how we live them.

Thinking about our lives and then living them more closely attuned to the rhythms and qualities inherent in the four seasons is the focus of *A Year of Living Mindfully*. For instance, taking the time to smell an early spring Meyer lemon and then using it in three or four different ways—for nutrition (its vitamin C helps fight a cold), flavor (it becomes an ingredient in a freshly made salad dressing), beauty (used in a brightening face mask), or cleaning (added to laundry for treating stains)—is the perfect example of seasonal living. This brings focus to the idea that a small yellow piece of fruit can be such an entirely handy tool in so many ways. It is truly a miracle of utility and sensory stimulation.

Other seasonal awareness might come through sensory experiences. You might appreciate how water jolts and refreshes on a hot summer day, how it soothes in a ritual bath, how it serves as a metaphor for fluidity and change when feeling overwhelmed and stuck. Noticing the scent of wood smoke and the taste of apples in autumn motivates cooking and baking more during those months, perhaps changing your dependence on packaged foods.

Our animal nature processes this kind of external information and registers it on our skin, in our blood, and deeply within our psyches. Our environment has the ability to alter how we structure our daily business in profound ways if we let it. We can take our cues from the colors and aromas of nature, from its tastes, textures, and sounds and create a richer experience of life to lift the mundane into something special. Doing this habitually allows our bodies, our basic internal chemistry, to begin to relax into an ancient and nourishing symbiosis with the rest of the natural world.

Through a mix of narrative, journaling exercises, guided meditations, rituals, and recipes, *A Year of Living Mindfully* interweaves seasonal themes into how-to tips for yoga, herbal healing, aromatherapy, diet and nutrition, natural beauty and self-care treatments, sustainable home living, and community activism. You will find creative and inspiring wisdom for exploring a daily life with poetic mindfulness and sensual awareness. It urges cultivation of a meaningful philosophy of life within the larger purpose of connecting to family, community, and the world at large for a complete holistic lifestyle practice.

How we feed and nurture our bodies, minds, spirits, and souls can be an art in and of itself. When this is done mindfully, the nervous system is soothed, stress abates, energy levels increase, and peace and contentment become something tangible we can feel and measure, rather than abstract concepts whose meanings most of us are grasping to define.

Seasonal, mindful living embraces a do-it-yourself ethic. No one can better provide the stuff of a balanced, healthy, and conscious life better than you. It is in the act of doing this daily tasking and ritual that we discover more about who we are and what meaning our lives hold. If we skip over those moments, then we miss creating our own wisdom traditions—the narrative of self that speaks about our lives, the stories of what is done every day, how it is done, the ingredients that are used, and the outcomes that are observed. The daily rituals become the process that forms the architecture of our lives. This is potent meaning through doing.

The prescriptions for "the daily doing" that I share in this book will help you to discover how the power of a holistic and harmonious lifestyle can be invigorating, joyous, awe-inspiring, soothing, delicious, and tasty. You will see this power ripple out patterns of real and lasting change, shift how you regard concepts of health and healing, and how you cope with and prevent stress. You will learn how to increase energy and vitality and find new ways to age naturally and gracefully, all while exploring the sensuality and healing benefits of food, plants, herbs, and aromas. You will find new and deeper connections to your body and physical self and learn how to move through all stages of life with curiosity and enjoyment.

By developing your own sense of style, routine, and rhythm using your mindful habits you will be set on the path of discovery to find and create more of them. Instead of consuming a ready-made formula or outsourcing these important components of your life to others, you will create a personalized way of being with them. The essence of a mindful lifestyle is a hands-on approach to using what is easily available to you; that is one of the paths to self-realization. Ingenuity, resourcefulness, passion, and thoughtfulness become part of the everyday vocabulary of action because you will have gained agency over your own life. You will become someone who knows how to nourish your soul with confidence, wisdom, and insight.

## ⌘ The Turning of the Seasons

The seasons are a central component of an ancient Native American symbol called the Medicine Wheel, which is the central organizing principle for *A Year of Living Mindfully*.

The Medicine Wheel's basic construct is a circle, or sacred hoop, divided into four parts that represent each season. Core themes are attached to each season: spring is transformation and inspiration/birth; summer is abundance and expansion/childhood; autumn is balance and intuition/adulthood; and winter is contemplation and resonance/wise elder. Each seasonal chapter's content reflects these themes: everything in the spring chapter is about renewal; summer is all high-energy and possibilities; autumn is about handling change with maturity and gratitude; and winter is about stillness and knowledge. Introductory passages for each season are designed to help readers connect to that season's themes, which stretch back to ancient and mythological lore in many cultures. If you take part in transformative and revitalizing activities in the spring, you're engaging in a theme that dates back thousands of years and you become part of the continuum.

You will be taken on a literal journey around the cycle of a year for in-the-moment sensual lifestyle experiences, as well as a figurative journey. This will serve to help you understand more of yourself through the Medicine Wheel's symbolic ages and phases: how to approach a dreaded task with a newborn's wide-eyed wonder, how to preserve energy and protect from burnout by keying into the slower rhythms of your inner elder, how to use the sense of balance and intuitiveness from a seasoned adult mind to take on a risky project. No matter what real-time age you are, the elements of the Wheel provide a rich tapestry of solutions for modern life conundrums.

In these ways the Wheel plays a number of different roles: it can be a tool for understanding our basic human psychology, a source of creative inspiration for daily problem-solving or a nature-based guide for efficient and wise use of resources. It emphasizes interconnection between all its components and was one of the first systems to promote the concept of achieving happiness through holistic living. At its heart the Medicine Wheel is a symbol of healing and interconnectedness, serving as a foundation for personal growth. It provides a focal point for making connections between Spirit, self, and nature—a tried and true formula for real and lasting health and wellbeing.

This, in essence, is a conscious, awakened lifestyle. Although the words holism and holistic mean *whole* in the semantic sense, they also call to mind the word *holy*. Living a holy life isn't necessarily just for religious leaders or ascetics who live on top of mountains. It's for anyone who regards life as containing the capacity for everyday holiness—the holiness of being fully alive and awake to potential and possibility. Treating each day as an opportunity for sacred and holy ritual, and immersing ourselves in rituals of holistic living, are central endeavors in the pursuit of a more meaningful life.

You will find that this book advocates for the priority of your self-care, equal to that of others. This becomes more difficult, of course, when you have children, parents, spouses, or other family members to care for. But good health and holism on all levels involves refreshing and invigorating ourselves inside and out on a continual, habitual basis if we are to be of any use to anyone else, let alone ourselves. The world around us benefits when we are each operating at our peak potential of our healthiest, calmest, most insightful, and feeling abundant within ourselves and toward others.

Undeniably, at the end of our lives two things will have had the greatest impact: how we've taken care of ourselves and how we've taken care of each other. It's all connected. *A Year of Living Mindfully* will show you how to make these comforting, reassuring nature-based connections and enhance your life immeasurably in the process.

# Chapter 1

## Your Essential Wellbeing Kit

. . . . . . . . . . . . . . . . . . . .

J ust as a mechanic has many different tools and methods for keeping your car running smoothly, this book contains dozens of different techniques and complementary mind-body therapies that have been proven throughout time to keep the human body healthy, happy, and balanced. This collection of therapies presents a wonderful array of choices for you to explore, each requiring varying amounts of time and involvement. You must find the methods that work best for you, given the stages and circumstances of your life.

The overarching seasonal theme is meant to further illustrate the concepts of the Medicine Wheel. Featured wellness practices are from many healing traditions around the world, and they are combined with discoveries from recent scientific studies that shed new light on common health issues making headlines today (such as detoxing, insomnia, depression, stress eating, sun exposure).

Sustained wellbeing is about being sensitively tuned in and present with your ongoing health maintenance. The practices ask that you do take some time to be with yourself on a deeper, more fully-engaged level, to tap into more of your own inherent wisdom and body intelligence. Healing is also about having desire and intention and those are yours and yours alone to cultivate.

## ⌘ The Medicine Wheel: A Circle of Holistic Wellbeing

It is significant that the Medicine Wheel is a circular shape. Circles have long been used as symbols in Native American teachings as they offer an ideal way to perceive how one form of life is completely interconnected and interdependent with all others. When these connections are recognized and honored they provide the highest form of harmony and balance within their systems. The whole systems approach of the Medicine Wheel is a perfect model for our exploration of the mind-body connection.

The Medicine Wheel dates back at least seven thousand years to the first known record of the North American Plains Indians. Various interpretations of the Medicine Wheel have circulated for the past one hundred years. It shares many traits with Tibetan mandala and Sanskrit chakras in its circular orientation and with philosophical traditions such as Traditional Chinese Medicine (TCM) and Ayurveda, the sister science of yoga. They have in common the idea that human behavior, health, wellness, and psychology find parallels in the qualities of elements in the natural world.

To help you nurture the healthy and balanced application of each of these energies, each seasonal chapter in this book will incorporate themes, activities, rituals, and recipes with which to coordinate this endeavor. There are also key words associated with each season and its energy, which can serve as a simple *mantra* or reminder of those concepts. Spring has *generate, begin, renew*; summer has *quicken, expand, flourish*; autumn has *mature, realize, fulfill*, and winter has *contemplate, stillness, release.* As you move around the Wheel throughout the year, these words are meant to encompass the kinds of energies already present in the natural world as it goes about its seasonal cycles evident in everything from the growth cycles of plants to the hibernation of certain animals.

(Note: I treat the term *Medicine Wheel* as a proper pronoun throughout this book. Native American spirituality is animistic, in that it assigns a spiritual essence to non-human entities (animals, plants, inanimate objects, phenomena). My usage is an attempt to honor that world view along with the concepts and practices conveyed to me by my teachers of the Wheel. My primary understanding of the Medicine Wheel came from a teacher with Cherokee heritage who was specifically charged with passing along the teachings to non-Native Americans at the behest of his teachers, one of whom was Navajo and the other Cheyenne. It is with the greatest respect for all the various lineages of Native American culture and traditions and their own interpretations of the Medicine Wheel that I share this material.)

## ⌘ Seasonal Health Practices

*Yoga, Meditation, Breath Work*

Throughout the book I'll be encouraging you to try some yoga practices. These practices were designed to be used by people at every level of familiarity with yoga—people who can already turn themselves into pretzels and rank beginners.

Why yoga?

Direct parallels can be drawn between the teachings of yoga and the teachings of the Medicine Wheel. They both advocate for daily, conscious inquiry into one's life and emphasize making connections between all the elements of the human condition—body, mind, spirit and emotion—for real and lasting wellbeing. As a practice steeped in habits, rituals, and ceremony there is nothing better than yoga to illustrate how beneficial this mind-body approach can be.

Yoga breaks up the patterns that bind us, transforming our energy. Like a psychic emery board it softens and smoothes down all the hard edges of life, which get expressed as anger, aggression, cynicism, disillusion, and hurt. While we are learning how to be fluid within our muscles and joints by practicing the physical poses, our *prana* (energy, *chi,* life force) is becoming more fluid as a result. This energized juice becomes a tonic for the nerves, the brain, and all the organs.

There are hundreds of yoga poses each with their own ability to illustrate a point or teach a concept on many layers with many interpretations. The yoga in this book is not meant to be a complete practice manual, but rather a highly curated sampling. I've chosen and arranged the yoga *asansas* (postures) to coordinate with the themes of our seasonal efforts.


## ⌘ Learning to Breathe

Vanda Scaravelli, a revered Hatha Yoga teacher from the mid-twentieth century, wrote, "There is great beauty in following, while breathing, the slow spreading of the lungs so delicate, and at the same time, so powerful, breathing life into all of us." Endurance in yoga, as in life, requires many things—strength, will, flexibility, relaxing into the present moment. The breath gives us a roadmap for endurance. We stay present with and are aware of the breath. We are supported in our efforts to endure. When we are off the mat we take the memory of our experience with us, within the breath. Whenever we are able to tune in to breath, it becomes the reminder of our practice—the experience of being in a moment of expansion and largesse with our existence.

The breathing exercises (*pranayama*) in this book, in addition to their purpose at hand (calming, energizing, balancing, warming-up), are meant to bring about an awareness of the larger function of mindfulness as it exists in your daily life. Your relationship to your breath is fundamental to this understanding. *Pranayama* will also help you focus and relax into the meditation exercises, finding in them a new relationship to stillness.

## ⌘ Healing Bodywork

Therapeutic massage and bodywork offer the profound, sometimes life-altering experience of the rituals of compassionate touch and all that that implies. As a pathway to understanding your personal mind/body/spirit balance this is a wonderful tool to assist you. So much of what we can understand about ourselves is often learned through the tissues of the physical body rather than intellectualized by the brain.

Massage is thought to be the oldest form of medical therapy practiced on the human body, dating back as far as 2700 BC. Ancient Egyptian tombs have been discovered adorned with images of figures being massaged. The different types of massage and the various techniques that encompass them stem from our most celebrated civilizations and their traditional beliefs: ancient Greece and Rome, India, China and Japan.

The particular modalities of healing bodywork featured in this book have been chosen to coordinate with seasonal themes so that you can continue to create an all-encompassing experience for yourself. The sensory elements of these experiences are heightened when blended with other seasonal components, such as aromatherapy and herbal teas.

## ⌘ Plant Healing: Aromatherapy, Herbs, Teas, and Tonics

*Phytotherapy* is the term referring to the medicinal use of plants or plant extracts. Most commonly herbalism has been the catch-all phrase to describe plant healing, but phytotherapy can also be applied to many of the plant-healing systems discussed in this book. The teachings of the Medicine Wheel recognize that plants offer extraordinary powers of healing for all living beings—not just humans. It urges communion and appreciation for their role in our existence from a very sacred perspective.

Working with plant healing also tends to bring about a more intuitive relationship between you and your body and its symptoms of illness or imbalance. Making connections between the root causes of these imbalances, rather than only paying attention to the symptoms, is an important first step in conscious self-care and holistic health and wellbeing.

The aromatherapy oils listed for each season in this book correspond to the themes and energies of that season. Purveyors of highest integrity harvest particular parts of a plant when they are considered to be at their peak for maximum results. All plants have peak-growth energy times during specific times of year, so I recommend particular oils to coincide with this energy for even stronger effects for healing.

The sections on herbs, teas, and tonics continue the exploration of plant healing by highlighting traditions that have achieved measurable success for people all over the world (Traditional Chinese Medicine and Ayurveda) and draw on folk medicine traditions from Europe, Japan, and the Americas. These are successful remedies known and used by millions of people and by naturopathic and homeopathic doctors, as well as other alternative health care practitioners.

While the essential oils I discuss are applied both topically (as a skin salve, for example) and internally (inhaled aromas), the herbal wellness in teas and supplements is taken internally and provides a completely different way of interacting with the plants' healing energies and properties than the oils.

Many of the herbs are meant to be taken in tea form, savored and imbibed by holding a hot mug between your hands, sipped slowly as you ritualize your engagement with them. "Tea time is me time." Often when we fall ill or get rundown we need some time to step out of our daily routines in order to properly heal and set ourselves back on track again. This can be a vital step in your healing process above anything else you might do. Take this precious time for yourself and consider how valuable it will be on all levels to savor and sip your cup of herbal tea, slowly and with deliberation.

## ⌘ Regarding Beauty Rituals

Plant-derived beauty ingredients to nourish skin, hair, and nails have been used by people all over the world for thousands of years because their effects are measurable and the rituals employing them are so deeply pleasurable. Every culture has beauty rituals for curing the consequences of lifestyle and aging and has known that plant textures and aromas (as well as the psychological benefits of engaging with them) are a great tonic for smoothing out the rough edges of life. We're lucky that we now find ourselves in a fantastic modern spa culture with an endless array of treatment and ingredient options. Time-out pampering is essential and one of the great pleasures of being human. But we can't always make the time or have the energy for these excursions, nor do we always have the budget.

The solution is simple and in keeping with our other efforts at conscious self-care. These sections of the book highlight effective and nourishing ingredients found right at our fingertips in our fridge and pantry with sensational sensory appeal.

If you only have time once a month to make something, a beauty ritual you stir up can have the power to feed the spirit in ways that assembly-line produced drugstore or department store products can never do. Our countenances glow from a love of life and a connection to our true selves, lovingly cherished and honored in our own rituals.

## ⌘ Focusing on Food

I love to eat, just like everybody else. Food is succor, food is sensual, food is *la vida*. Food occupies a particularly essential place in the discussion about mindful holistic living, health, wellness, and beauty. Food is spirit, home, and community and how we eat is a high form of ritual.

I like that it is a central tenet in both Buddhism and Yoga that the dining table can become a place of one's spiritual practice. Every time we sit down to a meal we can make the choice to eat as consciously and ethically as possible, a habit to strive for day in and day out. Food is a reflection of that holy endeavor—it nourishes us in our hard work to find grace, love, and a higher purpose.

The food sections and recipes in this book will show how easy it is to incorporate food that heals and inspires you, to keep you going in your quest for a healthier lifestyle, and to complement the other good and nourishing things you will learn to do for yourself. By continually making the connections between what we choose to eat and why we develop habits not only for our own health and for the compassionate welfare of all animals, but for the health of the whole planet. To this end, all of the recipes are vegetarian, with most being vegan; many are also gluten-free and sugar-free for those with special dietary restrictions.

I've provided a sample collection of recipes that highlight ingredients and techniques that hold thematically to everything else discussed in this book and can be dipped into as supplements to a reader's regular diet, whatever that may look like.

The aesthetic sensibility that inspired the recipes comes from cuisine found in health spas. For decades now, spas have been using food to heal, motivate, educate, and create deep sensory explorations that serve to seal in the experience of the time on the retreat, once back in everyday life. I want the experience you have making and eating the recipes in this book to give you the feeling that you are on a marvelous spa retreat in your own home each time you try one.

Most importantly, I've tried to create a selection whose first appeal is deliciousness. I hope you will come to believe cooking and eating consciously is worthy of your time and energy.

## ⌘ Connecting the Rest

There is nothing more sacred than the four walls of our homes that surround us day in and day out. All of our important activities and behaviors are brought to life within these dwellings and have profound lifelong effects on our psyches. We create and nurture our relationships to parents, siblings, lovers, spouses, children, friends, and even strangers here. All who cross the threshold and enter into our private living spaces are coming in contact with a very specific energetic expression of who we are and what is important to us.

The home and family sections of the book carry on the seasonal themes whether you live alone or with others and offer approaches to develop household habits which will support your personal efforts at conscious living. These are just a few out of many more potential topics that can be spun out of looking at your life this way. I hope these suggestions inspire you to notice how your personal transformations very much intertwine with and can positively affect the people and places directly around you, and that all of these things impact your wellbeing.

The community and world sections of the book briefly illustrate how the themes of the season can be applied to creating holistic health in our local communities and for a broader reach out into the world at large. The suggestions are meant to be simple and doable for busy people with busy lives, but hold the potential to be something larger, year-round, and continual should you wish.

It's also been proven that citizens who participate in making their neighborhoods better places to live not only reap the real-time benefits of that work (cleaner air and water, less crime, better schools), but their overall rates of life satisfaction and personal happiness are higher than people who never get involved. In this regard, our involvement with our community and world can even be thought of as self-serving.

Many of the challenges for finding personal joy and contentment discussed in this book are first-world problems; they affect people who have a roof over their heads, plenty to eat, and clothes to keep them warm and dry. We are the lucky ones. Unfortunately, our first world wealth is often tied to direct exploitation of third world resources and the people there who toil anonymously for us. It can be fairly paralyzing to realize this. But if we keep our eyes and hearts open to it, it also has the potential to be liberating. For example, using products that don't harm the environment in their manufacture or use, understanding the limits of natural resources and engaging in regular conservation to preserve them, and supporting locally made products to help grow your local economy organically, are good first steps. All our daily habits, when connected and added up, can and do have profound, planet-shifting effects for everyone's body, mind, and spirit.

Let's begin exploring a mindful year.

# PART II

# THE FOUR SEASONS

# The Four Directions and Seasons of the Medicine Wheel

**NORTH/WINTER**
**Element:** Air
**Human Aspect:** Mental
**Key Words:** Contemplate, Stillness, Release
**Season of Life:** Elders (Grandmother/Grandfather)
**World/Kingdom:** Animal
**Energy:** Receive
**Bodily Manifestation:** Breath, Lungs
**Time of Day:** Nighttime
**Heavenly Body:** Stars
**Earthly Manifestations:** Plains/Mesas/Winds
**Animal Totems:** Owl, Hawk, Eagle
**Human Manifestations:** Science & Math, Philosophy,
Religion, Abstract Learning
**Self Expression:** Wisdom, Knowledge, Harmony,
Resonance, Alignment, Logic

**WEST/AUTUMN**
**Element:** Earth
**Human Aspect:** Physical
**Key Words:** Mature, realize, fulfill
**Season of Life:** Adult Male/Female
**World/Kingdom:** Rocks, Minerals
**Energy:** Hold
**Bodily Manifestation:** Bones, Sexuality
**Time of Day:** Twilight
**Heavenly Body:** Earth
**Earthly Manifestations:** Mountains, Caves
**Animal Totems:** Snake, Horse, Deer
**Human Manifestation:** Magic, Duality
**Self Expression:** Intuition, Assessing,
Gathering, Balancing, Gratitude

The Great Mystery
The Void
The Cosmic Egg
The Seed of all Creation
The Center of the Universe

**EAST/SPRING**
**Element:** Fire
**Human Aspect:** Spiritual
**Key Words:** Generate, begin, renew
**Season of Life:** Newborn
**World/Kingdom:** Human
**Energy:** Determine
**Bodily Manifestation:** Blood
**Time of Day:** Morning
**Heavenly Body:** Sun
**Earthly Manifestations:** Volcanoes
**Animal Totems:** Butterfly, Dragonfly
**Human Manifestations:** Art, Writing
**Self Expression:** Inspiration, Illumination,
Purification, Transformation

**SOUTH/SUMMER**
**Element:** Water
**Human Aspect:** Emotional
**Key Words:** Quicken, Expand, Flourish
**Season of Life:** Children/Teenagers
**World Kingdom:** Plant
**Energy:** Give
**Bodily Manifestation:** Laughter/Tears
**Time of Day:** Noon
**Heavenly Body:** Moon
**Earthly Manifestations:** Oceans, Lakes, Rivers
**Animal Totems:** Whale, Dolphin
**Human Manifestation:** Music, Singing, Poetry
**Self Expression:** Abundance, Expansion, Joy, Generosity,
Spontaneity, Imagination

*I embrace emerging experience. I participate in discovery.*
*I am a butterfly. I am not a butterfly collector.*
*I want the experience of the butterfly.*

**William Stafford**

## Spring

**Element:** Fire

**Human Aspect**: Spiritual

**Key Words:** Generate, Begin, Renew

**Season of Life**: Newborn

**World/Kingdom:** Humans

**Energy**:  Determine

**Bodily Manifestation**: Blood

**Time of Day**: Morning

**Heavenly Body**: Sun

**Earthly Manifestations:** Volcanoes

**Animal Totems:** Butterfly, Dragonfly

**Human Manifestations:** Art, Writing, Language

**Self-Expression:** Inspiration, Purification, Illumination, Transformation

# Chapter 2

## Themes of the Spring Season: Generate, Begin, Renew

. . . . . . . . . . . . . . . . . . .

The beginning is here, the place of the newborn. The plant world is budding out and running sap again, the animal world is birthing its new generation. Spring is the raw, still forming time of year that is the gatherer of hope. We smell the fresh Earth coming alive and our bodies register a primeval zing of recognition. Our impulse is to generate—the key word for this position on the Wheel—and it creates new projects, new habits, new ideas for the coming year. We put the phrase "spring cleaning" in the forefront of our definition of what this season means and throw open the doors and windows of our homes as well as our psyches to release the pent up mustiness of winter; we shed layers of clothing, lighten our footsteps. Our health efforts require a cleansing and purification to symbolically reach a new place; this time of year we focus on blood and circulation as elemental in aiding the body's rejuvenation. On the Wheel, the east is represented by the element of fire, emblematic of transformation (fire burns wood into ash, iron into steel), illumination, and enlightenment. The east is home for Spirit, the determiner of energy. When Spirit is able to determine and generate the flow of energy, the dance has begun.

## ⌘ Stories and Rituals to Turn the Wheel

### The Myth of Ostara:  Goddess of Spring and Rebirth

The first harbinger of the season becomes the daily increase of light and the warmth it brings with it. The vernal (spring) equinox takes place when the day and night are the same length, usually around March 20-21. The ancient Romans, Persians, and Greeks celebrated the New Year at the spring equinox. Until the change in calendars in the Middle Ages, around 1600 or so, all of England, Scotland, and Ireland did as well.

On the Medicine Wheel, spring sits in the east, the place of dawn, the beginning of the new day. The Saxon goddess, Eostre (from whose name we get the direction *east* and the holiday Easter) is a dawn goddess. Her name is a derivation from the German word *Ostara*. The ancients in Germany named the spring equinox after Ostara, their goddess of spring, fertility, and rebirth.

According to myth, Ostara was a playful goddess whose reign over the earth began in the spring when the Sun King journeyed across the sky in his chariot, bringing the end of winter. Ostara came down to earth then with her animal consort, the rabbit. He accompanied her as she brought new life to dying plants and flowers. Both the rabbit and the other symbol of Ostara, the egg, are apt representatives of fertility and spring shenanigans in the animal kingdom.

On the Medicine Wheel, the beginning position, as in many traditions, is in the east. The alchemy of the east is the determiner of energy, the human world is here, and the spiritual aspect of the human condition is in the east. We generate what we think, decide, speak, and how we act upon the world around us from a spiritual foundation. Spirit directs us and begins our journey around the Medicine Wheel to show us how to live in balance and harmony.

### The Element of Fire and the Sweatlodge

Suitably, fire is the element for this direction. It gives us a very valuable concept with which to approach our understanding of this season; with fire, one is able to burn away all that is unnecessary and be reborn or transformed. Fire is a universal metaphor for purification, just as we use the literal power of fire for sterilization to burn away germs, illness, and disease. Fire is used alchemically to transform iron into steel. What goes into the flames comes out in a different form. Hindus burn their dead to hasten their transformation into their next life, so that they may be reborn anew. Hot saunas and steam rooms are used to purify and detoxify throughout many cultures.

The spiritual journey one undertakes during the sweat lodge ceremony is to enter it in one state and emerge out of it in another. In fact, the ceremony is meant to recreate the concept of the womb and to give the opportunity to be reborn, to come to a new realization, new vision, or new purpose for oneself. The ceremony is conducted in four rounds as the sweat lodge leader employs prayer, song, and chants to urge the participants onward in their journey of transformation. The four rounds are usually given over to the participant's relationship to self, family, community, and finally, the world at large.

The sweat lodge is an elegant model of a primeval experience that is intensely personal, yet paradoxically shared in the company of others. It's such a strong experience that it almost supersedes the need to talk about it when it's over. Similar to the experience of childbirth, one holds it in one's head while trying to process it through the sense memory of the body.

It was in sweat lodges that I learned how to give a heartfelt, spontaneous prayer. I heard it from anonymous fellow participants sitting in the dark with me. These were people whose names I never knew, and would never see again—strangers not on a train, but in a teepee—people who so completely poured their hearts out in extemporaneous speaking as to warrant some kind of award. The praying I came to know and love, something I hadn't understood before, was simply about verbalizing wishes and hopes to project them outward. Once out of our heads and hearts, they can collectively gather energy and travel into the firmament, to spread and grow, much the same way seeds are spread from wildflowers.

## HOW TO MAKE A SAGE BUNDLE FOR PURIFICATION

Using a sage bundle is a great way to create a tool for setting intention, clearing sacred space, and for beginning and ending a ritual. Making your own bundle exemplifies a hands-on approach which imbues your efforts with greater meaning.

White sage is the preferred plant to use, as it has a high oil content for a more pungent, impactful aroma. Our olfactory glands are in the oldest part of our brains that connect us to our primeval selves; the sense memories are ancient and can trigger deep psychological engagement.

When you harvest your sage, ask for permission from the "mother" plant (biggest plant in the family group) and then offer gratitude for the piece you take. This will surround your effort with the traditional respect with which Native Americans regard this plant.

Procure a three to four foot length of twine. Make a large, fist-sized bundle of the sage leaves (they can still be on their stems), and wrap the twine all around the bundle tightly. Hang upside down in a dry sunny spot for one week so that all the leaves inside the bundle have a chance to dry thoroughly.

Light one small corner of the bundle when you are ready to use it. Wave your hand or a feather over the bundle to get the smoke started, rather than blow on it, as your exhalation is considered to dilute the powers of the sage to cleanse and purify. Disperse the smoke around a space, room, object, or yourself by waving the sage bundle through the air, letting the smoke trail after the bundle. To extinguish, roll or crush the lighted part in a seashell (traditional native vessel for this purpose) or into the ground until the smoke stops.

### Spring Prayers

Our prayers and meditations, or simple wishes for the springtime, are about getting the chance to start over. We all want to be renewed, to experience the power of renewal. We all live with the collective results of our mistakes, rash and ill-informed decisions, disappointments, and unwise assumptions. A do-over is naturally seductive. As on our computers, the desire is to hit the big "refresh" button of life whenever we need it and have all the colors and shapes of our lives align the way they were meant to be. Spring offers that promise. The fresh newness of the scene outside the window invites it. Now is the time to seek out clarity, divest stagnant and old thoughts and old ways of being. It's the time to try new projects, open up to new possibilities, and new agendas determined with Spirit.

### My Spring Walk

The most fitting thing you can do to begin your relationship to new spring is to simply get out in it. You want to be able to notice all the details, treat yourself to the smells, the overwhelming fecundity of the season. Walk as much as you can and notice the difference between one day and the next all of the quick changes going on around you.

Here's a description of one of my walks:

⌘

On my spring walk this particular day I pass by a California black walnut tree, indigenous to just a few areas in Los Angeles County. We are lucky to still have several groves on my hillside. I look for old nutshells on the ground. My daughter showed me once how they look uncannily like a barn owl's face. I pick one up and put it in my pocket. I see the pair of nesting hawks that live on our hill, circling overhead. They catch the currents and float this way and that, barely making an effort with their own wing power. The hillsides are bright green, the wild grasses growing quickly before their time is up. Our rains came early and stayed strong all during the winter this year.

I head down a slope at the front edge of my hill. My sneakers sink into the earth, still damp from the most recent rains we had just a few days prior. The trail I'm following cuts crossways along the hillside and now I traverse an open field about one hundred yards long. I come upon a clump of some fried-egg poppies, surprising as it is early for them to be out. I suppose the spate of unseasonably warm days has seduced them to bloom.

These flowers are one of my favorite spring totems. They are more properly known as the Matilija poppy and grow both cultivated and wild around Southern California. Their stems are very tall and gangly, some up to eight feet tall, and they have a silvery, fringy-type leaf pattern up and down their stems. The money part though, is the bloom: a pure, round white collection of flat petals out of which pops the most insanely yellow gold, yolk-colored center. They look delicious enough to eat. I pick one in honor of Ostara—the egg flower for the goddess who loved eggs.

In the near distance, I can see the range of mountains that circle the eastern flank of Los Angeles, the San Gabriels. Their highest peak, Mt. Baldy, about thirty miles away as the crow flies, is completely covered in snow. It's the middle of March. I suddenly get a jumpy, nauseating feeling in my belly, and my chest cavity aches for a second or two; the stock physical reactions I still have when I think of my father being gone.

We had his funeral a couple years ago in the middle of March back in Texas. It was a brisk, windy, spring day. My hair kept blowing in my face while I was leading the graveside service. Every few minutes I would pull strands out of my mouth and eyes and shift my weight slightly, hoping for better stability. The funeral home had kindly laid Astroturf carpeting under the canopy where we were gathered, but it was doing little to keep me balanced and steady on my feet. The pointy, thin heels of my black pumps kept sinking down into the soft, March-damp dirt, much like the LaBrea Tar Pits must have claimed its beasts; one claw at a time.

I had wanted to make the service participatory and personal, so we read poems, took turns telling stories about my dad, and sang. The song my husband suggested to close the ceremony, and to which my family all agreed, was Louis Armstrong's "What a Wonderful World".

I felt this song perfect to capture the essence of spring and renewal. Even though it was a funeral, I didn't think it should be *all* about death and loss. I truly did feel it important to somehow convey the timelessness of the seasonal cycles, and how death (winter) is always followed by rebirth (spring). Nature renews, heals, and transforms; it is inevitable, and, hopefully, comforting.

Unfortunately, I can't now think about, or even hear the tiniest snippet of the song without bursting into tears.

Today on my walk, I think of this beautiful springtime song; it's still no different and I start bawling. As I wipe my leaky eyes and runny nose on my sleeve, I catch a movement out of the corner of my eye and notice a small brown rabbit making a dash for his burrow under a spindly sycamore tree—Ostara's consort. He scrunches himself into his safe haven and disappears. I look up and see the hawk couple wheeling off toward the other side of the hill. I come to the end of the trail, where it joins up again with the pavement, lining the way in front of the next block of houses. I quicken my steps so I can get home and start my new spring day. It is inevitable and comforting.

### Walking Wisdom from Thich Nhat Hanh

Hanh, the Buddhist monk and author, has a famous teaching about using walking for a specific kind of meditation exercise. It emphasizes the rewards of walking 108 steps slowly and precisely as a practice in mindfulness.

His instructions:

*Stand on one foot and be aware that it is resting upon the earth; see the great sphere upon which it rests. See it clearly—how wonderfully round it is. While walking, look down and anticipate the* ground where you are about to place your foot, and when you do, mindfully experience your foot, the ground, and the connection between your foot and the ground. Place your foot on the surface of the earth the way an emperor would place his seal on a royal decree.

A royal decree can bring happiness or misery to people. It can shower grace on them or it can ruin their lives. Your steps can do the same. If your steps are peaceful, the world will have peace. If you can take one peaceful step, you can take two. You can take one hundred and eight peaceful steps.

## THE POETRY AND SIGNIFICANCE OF THE NUMBER 108

108 is the number of beads on a *mala*, or Buddhist prayer "rosary." *Malas* are used to count mantras, and a mantra is a sound, syllable, word, or group of words that are considered capable of creating spiritual transformation.

**Harshad number:** 108 is a Harshad number, which is an integer divisible by the sum of its digits (*Harshad* is from Sanskrit, and means "great joy").

**Sun and Earth:** The diameter of the Sun is 108 times the diameter of the Earth. The distance from the Sun to the Earth is 108 times the diameter of the Sun.

**Moon and Earth:** The distance of the Moon from the Earth is about 108 times the diameter of the Moon.

**Heart Chakra:** The chakras are the intersections of energy lines, and there are said to be a total of 108 energy lines converging to form the heart chakra. One of them, *sushumna* leads to the crown chakra, and is said to be the path to self-realization.

**Sanskrit alphabet:** There are fifty-four letters in the Sanskrit alphabet. Each has masculine and feminine, *shiva* and *shakti*. Fifty-four times two is 108.

**Pranayama:** Yoga texts advise that if one is able to be so calm in meditation as to have only 108 breaths in a day, enlightenment will come.

> **Upanishads:** There are 108 Upanishads, texts of the wisdom of the ancient sages.
>
> **Marmas:** The energy intersections that form chakras, the "wheels" of life-force and energy in the body. There are said to be 108 marmas in the subtle body.

It's worth trying Hanh's exercise, as I think it certainly opens up a sacredness about walking that is good to have, no matter what pace or location your subsequent walks might take. Here's another thing to do: as a variation, set aside walking time for yourself, then pick any use of the number 108, and apply it to your walking efforts. Some examples:

⌘ Walk 108 days in a row (a little over three months, or the length of one season in the year, more or less) at the same time every day, 1:08 p.m.

⌘ Walk at 1:08 p.m. for 108 minutes (one hour and forty-eight minutes)

⌘ Walk 1.8 miles every day for 108 days

There is no right or wrong way, the intention should just be to remain in the present moment with your efforts and stay open to outcome. The beauty of taking a very simple thing like walking and then doing it at precisely the same time every day or walking for precisely the same amount of time every day is that it elevates it to another level. Actually, just doing *anything* with intention for 108 days in a row, is a remarkable setup. Engaging in a repetitive act, with discipline and focus, brings inevitable transformation. Your relationship to the activity will greatly change, your ideas about what you are getting out of it will change, and the sheer dedication to achieving a goal for a specific time, a specific count of numbers, will always lead you to fresh insights. Transformation comes with regular application.

### Writing Is in the East

This is where you can take advantage of journaling as a ritual experience. You can record your Spring 108 Walking Journeys to honor writing, an attribute that is in the east on the Medicine Wheel. Surely the Wheel offers this as a clue about the abilities of writing to illuminate and transform both the writer and reader. Note your thoughts, observations, challenges, and victories in keeping to your 108 set. Perhaps make notations or drawings of what you observe differently on each walk, as the landscape in springtime is also undergoing transformation at the same time that you are.

Keeping a journal dedicated to your progress through this book would be an excellent investment for the future. The great thing about journal writing is that it takes no skill or formal training; it is simply a way to connect to and nurture insightful thinking. There's no format you have to follow, no grade you're going to get in the school of self-actualization. It will help you remember your insights before they slip away; they are fleeting, and are currency to spend later when you are in periods of self-doubt, confusion, or angst. Recording what you experience, imagine, dream, and act on in your everyday life has immeasurable value. These are your own stories, after all, and form the narrative to your travels.

### *Your Own Bodhi Tree*

For another experience conducive to spring's energies, here is a variation on a Native American rite of passage ceremony. It's a simple way to pause and take stock of where you are now versus where you want to go in your life. I think these are questions a lot of us ask ourselves on our birthdays or maybe they help us to arrive at our traditional New Year's resolutions. But by asking them in the context of your new relationship to spring, you are particularly primed for a fresh start. It is a great way to understand the dynamic of the Wheel's energy in the East: determine with Spirit your course of action and begin generating all the new things you are inviting into your life.

I think of this ritual as an adult version of the daydream time a tree-sitting child might do. To Native Americans, as with other shamanistic cultures, this magical sense of wonder and acceptance of other realities is something that is not just the territory of childhood, but can be a guiding force all throughout life.

There is a long and sacred history of people all over the world getting wisdom and guidance from trees. Buddha received his visions from sitting under the Bodhi tree. Ancient Druids (*druid* being the Celtic word for *oak*) regarded a whole range of trees to have specific powers and purposes. Besides the oak (naturally), the rowan, ash, and hazelnut trees play a huge part in the telling of their history. The Tree of Knowledge is a main Bible story and the Hindus have the banyan tree at the center of their creation myths.

So how does one begin to communicate with a tree? I think it first starts with creating empathy for anything in nature with which you want to communicate. Perhaps see it in your mind as having a persona. Maybe come up with a list of the tree's attributes that have resonance for you: strong, wise, enveloping, silent, for example. By using your imagination and visualizing its qualities, you'll be inviting a different perspective about it.

In preparation and for general cultivation of your new relationship to trees, now would be a great time to get your own copy of Peterson's *Complete Field Guide to North American Trees*. It's a small investment which fits easily into a pocket and will pay big dividends in your quest to cultivate a deeper relationship with the nature around you. (While you're at it, get the editions for flowers, butterflies, and birds. You won't be sorry.)

## THE FLOWERING TREE MEDITATION

You might want to combine the peace-in-every-step walking meditation described earlier as a prelude to sitting with your tree or maybe opt to just start the ritual with a nice meditative walk on a lovely spring day. Bring your journal, a sage bundle, and a small pouch or bag of pure loose-leaf tobacco (a traditional Native American plant offering).

This meditation requires that you find a beautiful tree in a fairly secluded area so that you are relatively alone with it. Your tree should be big enough to sit under—the older the better and ideally, one with which you already have a relationship. But it's perfectly alright to walk around and find one just for the purpose of this exercise. Notice what attracts you to your tree: is it the height, the shape of the leaves, the smell? Is it a fruiting tree with new blossoms, a deciduous, or an evergreen?

Walk around the base of the tree using your sage bundle to make a smoke circle; then extinguish it. Determine the cardinal directions, then sit on the east side of the tree with your back pressing up against the trunk. Feel the coarse texture of the bark through your shirt. Notice the thickness of the trunk, the way the branches grow overhead, and the leaf canopy. Center yourself in silence.

When you feel ready, these are the questions to ask for each direction:

**East:** Who am I? (What ideas have brought me liberation?)

**South:** Where have I come from? (What beliefs have I outgrown; what are my achievements?)

**West:** Where am I now? (What is my daily purpose?)

**North:** Where am I going? (What are my unfulfilled goals and desires?)

Take as long as you need to mull over your answers. Write down whatever comes up. Stay with each direction until you feel an overwhelming need to move to the next side/direction of the tree. Ask the tree for help with your answers. It's holding wisdom in its sap. Listen very closely for the leaves to whisper out clues.

When you've finished, take out your tobacco, and sprinkle it around the base of the tree in a circle going clockwise. As you do this, express your thanks to the tree for all that it has given you.

# Chapter 3

## Essential Spring Health Practices

. . . . . . . . . . . . . . . . . . . .

On the Wheel, the physiological system (bodily manifestation) associated with the east and spring is that of the circulation (blood) system. Our blood is the transporter of oxygen and nutrients to everything else in our body. It is the foundational element to carrying away debris and toxins from the organs, glands, and tissues.

### *Everyday Detoxifying Habits*

One of the most common approaches to wellness associated with spring, is that of detoxification. Detoxification is a way to clean out all the collected waste matter, environmental pollutants, and residue from medicines/drugs, alcohol, and just plain bad habits that can accrue and become trapped in our bodies. For thousands of years, body purification has been a part of our rituals for health and wellbeing throughout all ages and cultures. It was used in ancient times as a way to reconnect with the divine. Today the word *detox* is being used more as a verb. It is a hot topic for debate and discussion and has become its own industry worth hundreds of millions of dollars—including the requisite charlatans and scam artists ready to take advantage of a public desperate for a quick solution.

Some people believe that even the term *detoxification* as a concept, an action one can undertake as a health practice, is misleading and incorrect. Many physicians who practice allopathic medicine will insist that the body has evolved its own systems of detoxification that work very well on their own to rid the body of accumulated matter that it can't use (through sweating and the natural functions of the liver, kidneys, and colon). While this may have been true up to a certain point in our collective human history, I don't think it is absolutely true anymore. Our modern exposure to environmental and chemical overloads has altered our natural ability to rid the body of toxins in ways we can no longer deny.

Randall Fitzgerald has a great overview of this in his book, *The Hundred Year Lie,* and his Slippery Slope Index. The index lists in a timeline format when manmade chemicals in our environment, in our foods, and medicines were introduced over the last one hundred years, as well as the public health consequences that have subsequently been documented as a result. Through Fitzgerald's findings (as well as through many, many others') it is safe to say that it is a medical, biological, empirical fact that we store these chemicals in our bodies. The only question is to what degree and that is dependent largely on where we live and what our cumulative daily health habits are.

Fitzgerald has this to say about detox:

⌘ It is not about any miracle potion you can ingest; it is also about what you *stop* ingesting and it's a frame of mind.

⌘ There truly is no "quick fix," so nothing you do is going to have any lasting effect on your health (nor your toxic load) if it is just done for a few days and you then go back to eating the standard American diet and living the standard American lifestyle. To truly detox you need to make changes to your diet and lifestyle that are both major and lasting.

⌘ But if you *are* prepared to make those changes there is a great deal you can do to help your body lighten its toxic load to the point where you will notice marked improvements in your health, wellbeing, appearance, and quality of life.

Habits. How do we cultivate good habits? Taken a step further, this concise bit of advice commonly attributed to Lao Tzu always appealed to me:

> *Watch your thoughts, for they become words.*
> *Watch your words, for they become actions.*
> *Watch your actions, for they become habits.*
> *Watch your habits, for they become character.*
> *Watch your character, for it becomes your destiny.*

Our lives are a process, and watchfulness, a form of mindfulness, is paramount. One must undertake to be a fearless and brave leader of one's self throughout the process of one's life. It's an ongoing effort, with ups and downs, failures and successes. Diligence, compassion, and forgiveness are necessary ingredients in the mix. Everyday habits become transformative.

*Cultivating Regular Detox Practices*

Here are some simple, everyday habits that will help move you toward a lifestyle ingrained with positive, detoxing habits:

- ⌘ Drink lots of filtered, purified water each day. There is nothing that you can do for yourself physically that is simpler or more important.

- ⌘ Eat plenty of fiber, including brown rice, oatmeal, and organically-grown fresh fruits and vegetables. Beets, radishes, artichokes, cabbage, broccoli, chlorella, and seaweed are excellent foods for stimulating the liver and cleaning out the bloodstream.

- ⌘ Cleanse and protect the liver by drinking green tea and by taking herbs such as dandelion root, burdock, and milk thistle.

- ⌘ 500–1000 mg of vitamin C a day will help the body produce glutathione, a liver compound that stimulates cleansing.

- ⌘ Visit saunas regularly so your body can eliminate wastes through perspiration. Try going to ethnic enclaves in your city for some of the best of these kinds of inexpensive experiences: Russian, Turkish, and Korean traditions have beautiful histories of working with sauna heat for everyday detoxing.

- ⌘ Exercise for at least thirty minutes every day; enough to elevate your heart rate and break a sweat. Choose anything that gives you enough pleasure that you will keep doing it on a regular basis and include variety.

I have another way to think about bringing new lifestyle habits in to replace old ones; I think of it as flooding out bad habits with better ones. It calls to mind the method in which cranberries are harvested. For hundreds of years they had to be handpicked, a very laborious and time consuming process. Then someone figured out that because the bushes are always situated in a bog, the area could be flooded with water during harvest time. The water loosens the berries and the farmers wade into the bog, thigh deep in a crimson pond, to corral the fruit with large brooms quickly into catch nets.

Flooding your life with good habits then gradually scooping up less desirable ones and corralling them into insignificance seems infinitely more manageable than setting out to break them one by one.

## DRY BRUSHING FOR NATURAL DETOXIFICATION

Here in Los Angeles, we are blessed with a large Korean community that has gifted us with their tradition of spa going. In Korean culture, bathing and cleanliness represent the spiritual experience of washing and purifying the soul. At the centerpiece of this approach to health and wellness, is the prescriptive treatment of the Akasuri body scrub or Korean-style red scrub. If you aren't lucky enough to have a Korean spa in your town, you can still experience the health benefits and wonderful, soft skin that a technique called *dry brushing* will give you. Variations of this treatment can be found at every spa around the world in their efforts to pamper and rejuvenate their clients, but it's something so deceptively simple that you can do it yourself at home.

### Why Dry Brush?

Dry-skin brushing increases circulation to the skin, encouraging the body's discharge of metabolic wastes, which greatly aids the lymphatic drainage of the entire body. When the body rids itself of toxins, it is able to run more efficiently in all areas. Dry skin brushing rejuvenates the nervous system by stimulating nerve endings in the skin and helps the skin to absorb nutrients by eliminating clogged pores. Healthy, breathing skin contributes to overall body health.

## How to Dry Brush

Select a long-handled, natural-bristle brush or loofah. Begin brushing your skin in long sweeping strokes starting from the bottom of your feet upwards, and from the hands towards the shoulders, and on the torso in an upward direction. *Always brush towards the heart.* Try and brush several times in each area, overlapping as you go. Focus on the armpit area and sides of the neck, as both of those places contain a large grouping of lymph nodes. Focus on the lower belly, (colon area) and lower back (kidneys) as those are the other key components in your body's elimination system. Avoid tender or sensitive areas (nipples; cuts, bruises). Start out with gentle brushing energy and work up to a more vigorous one after your skin becomes used to it. Each session shouldn't take more than five minutes if you are in a hurry, longer if you have the time to luxuriate in it.

Try following your dry-brushing session with an extremely hot shower session, then dial the water setting all the way to cold for as long as you can stand it. You've just given yourself a first rate, homemade spa treatment.

## Conquering Spring Allergies

The biggest spring-allergy trigger is pollen—tiny grains released into the air by trees, grasses, and weeds for the purpose of fertilizing other plants. When pollen grains get into the nose of someone who's allergic, they send the immune system into overdrive, causing increased allergy symptoms: stuffy nose, ears, and sinuses, inflamed eyes, headaches, sore throat, and difficulty breathing. The mucus-producing processes of the immune system are on alert to attack innocuous invaders such as springtime pollens. Antibodies—substances that normally identify and attack bacteria, viruses, and other illness-causing organisms—attack the invaders, which leads to the release of chemicals called histamines into the blood. Histamines trigger the allergy symptoms.

Many of us (myself included) have been severely affected by seasonal allergies; some unfortunate folks experience them year round. Mine were so bad they led to asthma attacks and a few trips to the emergency room for adrenaline shots as a child. I outgrew the original severity, but was continually plagued with symptoms for many years. I noticed that the symptoms reoccurred during times of stress and uncertainty. They spiked in a work situation once and I could not breathe.

In desperation, I tried every traditional, drug-based therapy (both over the counter and pre-scription). Without a doubt, it's exhausting to have to sleep upright and it's an extremely scary feeling to be sucking on your steroidal inhaler and not getting any relief. Gradually, as I became aware of more natural ways of taking care of myself (with diet, acupuncture, and herbs) and started seeing results, it was unbelievable to think I had once thought it was my lot to live with steroidal inhalers.

There are other causes of allergies, of course, having nothing to do with pollen. They are due to indoor toxins (cleaning chemicals, chemicals in carpets, paints, furniture glues, and resins), outdoor toxins (factory and automobile exhaust, pesticide sprays), and myriad other environmental chemicals. We can't all walk around wearing gas masks and yet it's a miracle to me that not every single one of us is in a heightened state of allergy-induced trauma. But we do have epic proportions of kids with childhood asthma and allergy-induced asthma in people of all ages, along with the use of drugs to combat them.

Some allergy suffering doesn't have to be chronic and inevitable; it can be prevented or at the very least reduced through some fairly simple daily health habits.

⌘ **Yoga:** Through relaxation, the nervous system can tell the immune system to settle down and stop attacking the foreign bodies, which are naturally cleared out in a non-allergic person by sneezing once or twice a day. When the immune system backs off, inflammation and mucus decrease and symptoms diminish. Practicing any yoga posture in a relaxing way with slow, deep breathing and the intention to let go and relax the nervous system can be very beneficial in decreasing the symptoms of allergies.

⌘ **Nasal Wash:** Use a neti pot—devised by the ancient Ayurvedics—to cleanse your nasal passages. Nasal washing thins the mucus in the nasal cavity, which makes it flow more easily out of the body and removes bacteria, allergens, and other irritants that cause problems. The job of the nose is to moisten the air for the lungs. It's important for water to be in the air for the lungs to function.

When the nose becomes inflamed from allergens or even colds, the inflammation decreases moisture, causing the nose to get dry. When the nose gets dry, the brain pumps more mucus to keep the air sent to the lungs moist. Adding water to the surface gives the nose the ability to add water to the air, which calms the brain and lowers inflammation.

⌘ **Probiotics:** Studies are looking at whether probiotics might help asthma and allergy sufferers, by switching off an inflammatory response in the intestine. Research shows people with allergies have lower levels of healthy gut flora and are overrun with bad bacteria.

Probiotics are good bacteria that can be taken as a supplement, which helps to reset the bacteria balance, providing a protective barrier in the gut. Immune responses are a balance between *go* and *stop* responses. Go responses cause inflammation that are necessary to eliminate infections. However, without stop responses, inflammation continues resulting in an inflammatory disease. Probiotics help the immune system to develop stop responses, so that you don't overreact to something harmless like food or pollens.

Make sure you are taking one that can withstand stomach acids during digestion; these will have an *enteric* coating. Probiotic supplements can take between *eight and ten weeks of daily use* to change the environment of your gut for you to notice a difference, so be diligent and patient.

Note: Chlorinated water can contribute to probiotic depletion in the body, so install water and shower filters throughout your home.

## *The Health Benefits of Fermented Foods*

Cultures around the world have been eating fermented foods for years, from sauerkraut in Eastern Europe, to kimchi in Korea, to yogurt in Bulgaria, and miso in Japan. Many of these traditions were brought to this country by early immigrants where they thrived and spread. But the amount of probiotic nutrients and beneficial enzymes available in the current American diet has declined sharply over the last few decades as pasteurized milk has replaced raw, pasteurized yogurt has replaced homemade, vinegar-based pickles and sauerkraut have replaced traditional lacto-fermented versions, and highly-processed foods have overtaken everything.

Fermented foods have been through a process of lacto-fermentation in which natural bacteria feed on the sugar and starch in the food creating lactic acid. This process preserves the food, and creates beneficial enzymes, B vitamins, omega-3 fatty acids, and various strains of our friends, the fabulous probiotics.

Natural fermentation of foods has also been shown to preserve nutrients in food and increase digestibility. This, along with the bevy of probiotics created during the fermentation process, could explain the link between consumption of fermented foods and improved digestion, improved bio-availability for nutrients to the immune system, decreased allergies in people susceptible to them, and a reduced risk of certain cancers which are thought to be triggered by chronic inflammation.

The easiest way to consume natural probiotics (you can't overdose!) is through foods that have been clearly marked as being naturally fermented. The highest quality yogurts, kefirs, and sauer-krauts should not have added sugars and other fillers, and the krauts should not have vinegar as one of its ingredients (cabbage and salt should be all). High quality miso, kimchi, and kvass (fermented beets) should also be sought out. Try to find brands made locally or by small producers that still use traditional methods to ensure the integrity of their food product. Farmer's markets in ethnic enclaves are a great source.

Traditional Chinese Medicine advises adding sour-tasting foods to your diet in order to keep a healthy liver. Include citrus fruits (sprinkle lemon in your water and on your veggies, raw or cooked), and apple cider vinegar (good for balancing pH)—try two tablespoons in a glass of water or use with olive oil on your salad. The sour flavor is associated with the liver and it enhances bile flow, which supports natural liver detoxification.

## ⌘ Yoga, Meditation, Breath Work

This season we are activating our spiritual energy and beginning to see how its innate fire is transforming the very essence of who we are and how we want to be in the world. Yoga, as a spiritual practice, is perfectly equipped as the vehicle with which to further explore these transformations in our bodies. As yoga poses are prayers made with the body, they can be ones of supplication in which we humble ourselves before the magnificence of the universe; they can be of reassurance, helping us to tap into inner strength we didn't know we had, or they can be expressions of delight and humor, as we exalt in the pure joy of being alive. Just as the sweat lodge is a vehicle for transformation, yoga also shepherds us through that process.

Each time you stand on your yoga mat you can transcend the ordinariness of your day and link to an ancient sacred ritual. Dealing with our physical limitations (and we all have them at one time or another) and coming up against our natural mental resistance (to get started, to stay with it, to keep going), is a constant interplay between will and surrender. This becomes a huge metaphor for the push-pull reflex inherent in our dualistic nature as humans. Ultimately, practicing yoga consistently helps us overcome this reflex and to relax into acceptance and non-judgment, which begets flexibility of thought, word, and deed; for me the most important aspects of why I practice yoga.

### Surya Namaskar A (Sun Salutation 'A' Sequence)

In many Hatha yoga circles and classes, 108 Sun Salutations (*Surya Namaskar*) are done as a ceremonial offering to mark the seasonal changes at the equinoxes and solstices. Ideally this practice is done at sunrise. It's about a two-hour experience or roughly one salutation a minute. The sequence is composed of linked standing, squatting, lunging, and stretching poses designed to give a complete workout to all the major muscle groups in the body and to bring one into a dynamic communion with the breath cycle, an illumination of Spirit active within us.

Learning about the Sun Salutation is a great way to dive into yoga if you've never tried it.

Technically it is not difficult to perform a Sun Salutation or ten or twenty with a little bit of conditioning. The challenge, of course, comes in the perseverance of staying with it when fatigue sets in on your way to the 108. Let's face it, 108 is a big challenge. The other option, if you aren't quite up to *full* salutations, is to do half salutations for now.

Here's a chart showing the sequence (start at the top of the chart). The easier version is a half *Surya Namaskar* and leaves out positions 5,6,7, and 8. Like any choreography, the more you practice, the more automatic the dance-like steps become.

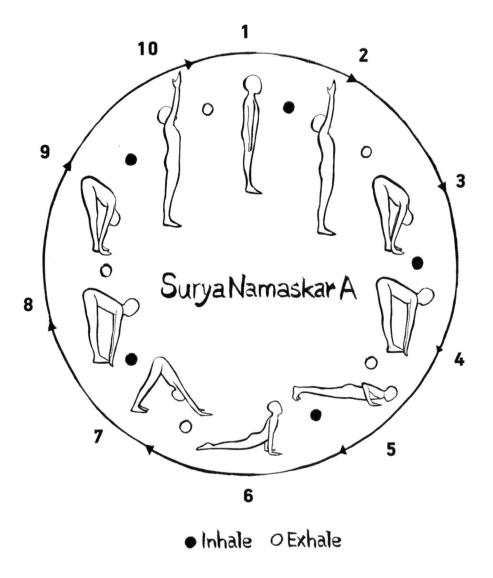

Surya Namaskar A

● Inhale   ○ Exhale

Tips for practicing the Sun Salutation:

⌘ Practice on an empty stomach or at least two hours after eating.

⌘ Practice on a mat for better traction.

⌘ Start with your hands pressed together in prayer position in front of your heart, thumbs touching your breastplate. This is a way of honoring the ancient yogis and is the **Atmanjali Mudra** (Reverence Seal, see page 253). Since the sequence is, in essence, an honoring of the light shining on you from the sun, as well as the light of your insight, it's important to practice Sun Salutations in a spirit of devotion. Make each movement as mindful and precise as possible, especially as you near the end of your rounds, when fatigue can lead to sloppiness.

⌘ Keep breathing through your nose, lips together, jaw relaxed.

⌘ Step or hop to the BACK of your mat to get from position 4 to position 5, and then step or hop to the FRONT of your mat to get from position 7 to position 8.

⌘ Lay down on your back and rest after you are finished with however many salutations you did in your practice until you are thoroughly conditioned. If you've done 108, then lie down anyway to set the devotion into your being.

## CELEBRATING THE NEW YEAR'S SUN WITH THE GAYATRI MANTRA

It is so beautiful to be doing this while you watch the world in front of you go from the grey light of pre-dawn through all the permutations of rosy yellow to a full, bright, golden morning. I can't think of a more apt tribute to our theme of transformation, illumination, and new beginnings.

At dawn on the Spring Equinox (our "new" New Year's Day), face the east and do some Sun Salutations.

### Add a Chant

Bring more energy to your Sun Salutations by saying this mantra before and after you practice your salutations. Called the Gayatri Mantra (*gayatri* comes from a root word meaning *sing*), it's considered among the most powerful of the yogic incantations. In the yogic tradition, light equals knowledge. This particular mantra is about linking the sun with your thoughts and enlightening yourself by means of higher knowledge. First recorded in the

Rig-Veda, the ancient Hindu scripture dating back more than 5,000 years, the Gayatri Mantra is a perfect prayer for sunrise.

**Chant:** Om bhur bhuvah suvah

**Pronunciation:** Om boor boo-vah-ha soo-vah-ha

**Translation:** Om, earth, atmosphere, heaven


**Chant:** Tat savitur varenyam

**Pronunciation:** Tut sah-vee-toor vah-rain-yum

**Translation:** May we meditate on the radiant light


**Chant:** Bhargo devasya dhimahi

**Pronunciation:** Bar-go day-vass-yuh dee-ma-hee

**Translation:** Of that brilliant creator


**Chant:** Dhiyo yo nah pracodayat

**Pronunciation:** Dee-yo yo na-ha prah-cho-die-yot

**Translation:** Who may guide our thoughts

## Triangle (Trikonasana)

I love this pose for many reasons, but in particular because it is the perfect pose to activate the liver and help it to function better, a hallmark of our springtime cleansing efforts. Bending to one side in *Trikonasana*, will compress and massage stagnate and clogged energy channels in the liver and gallbladder, forcing toxins out. Then turning around and bending to the other side will open the area to let flow in freshly oxygenated blood.

When the body assumes this pose in *Trikonasana*, its natural inclination is to expand to all three corners and open up toward them. As you stretch and reach to fill in the outermost points of your triangle, feel the way the top side of your waist is slightly rotating. That's the action which is stimulating the liver. Make sure you are inhaling deeply to help bring fresh oxygen into the body, and then exhaling thoroughly to release everything from your cleansing efforts.

Tips for Practicing *Trikonasana*:

⌘ Place your feet three and a half to four feet apart (it is usually wider than you think) with your heels in line and your feet parallel to one another.

⌘ Try to avoid collapsing the chest and front body downward; keep them elevated.

⌘ Extend through the crown of the head and energetically move the hips and tailbone in the opposite direction. Think about stretching your side body so that both sides are equal in length.

⌘ Remember to be very mindful and intentional with your lower body. Push down through all four corners of your feet.

⌘ Engage the thigh muscles, microbend the front knee, and press firmly into the front foot to avoid hyper-extending at the front knee joint.

⌘ If looking up is uncomfortable or if you have neck issues, turn your gaze down to the floor and consciously relax your neck. Then try shifting your gaze upward slowly.

### Twists: Wringing Out Toxins

Twists are not only an excellent way to wring out bodily toxins, but they can also help you to detox from overindulgence in emotions—anger, fear, sadness, guilt—that can accumulate when we are coping with the stuff of life. The liver is associated with holding anger, hence we have as a figure of speech, "my bile is up" as a way of describing intense anger. Yogic twists will help you to make space inside yourself so that you can breathe out what is not serving you and not working for you anymore.

Indian yoga master B. K. S. Iyengar describes twists as a squeeze-and-soak action. The organs are compressed during a twist, pushing out blood filled with metabolic by-products and toxins. When we release a twist, fresh blood flows in, carrying oxygen and the building blocks for tissue healing. From the physiological standpoint, twists stimulate circulation and have a cleansing and refreshing effect on the torso organs and associated glands. Our modern, sedentary lifestyle has the ill effects of compressing and compacting our spine, as does plain old bad posture. Even something as innocuous as continually tight and restrictive clothing can squish the inner organs and deplete their full functioning.

All these poses require an easy sense of Iyengar's wringing the spine out like a sponge. Use your hands and arms to gain traction against your legs and the floor to deepen the twist. Emphasize your exhales as a way to release the resistance in the body, but also to help push out stagnant emotions. With each inhale you bring cleansing air and thought into the body and begin the squeeze and soak action again. Stay for up to two minutes on each side.

## ⌘ Breathwork

### *Breath of Fire (Kapalabhati)*

Learning how to breathe deeply is a must for physical cleansing and health. But breathing exercises also form the foundation of many ancient practices that promote a deepening of consciousness, such as meditation, mindfulness, yoga, and chi gong. In the Middle East the word for breath (*ruach* in Hebrew and *ruhain* in Aramaic) also means *"Spirit."* The way in which we breathe is also the way in which we embody Spirit.

Deep flowing breath is a sign of health, balance, and fullness of spirit. Short, shallow breath indicates stress. Breath is the simplest, most direct way to focus one's energy and to connect with the center of awareness. By changing the way we breathe, we can change emotional and physical states. Unhelpful feelings and emotions can be released and cleared out of the body by working with the breath.

*Kapalabhati* is a yogic technique of rapid diaphragmatic breathing. It has a remarkable effect as a de-stressing tool and clearing the mind of negative emotions. In fact, the Sanskrit words *"kapal"* means the skull and *"bhati"* means polishing or shining. *Kapalabhati*, as the name suggests, is a method to make the head "sparkling clean" and devoid of toxins.

If you're suffering from cardiac problems, severe respiratory infection, high blood pressure, diabetes, or abdominal ulcers it is advisable to consult your health care provider first.

Although the cleansing breath is remarkably simple, it is important that it is done properly.

⌘ Sit in a comfortable position with your spine erect. You can sit either cross-legged or in any position that you feel comfortable. Breathe normally for about a minute. Once composed, you can begin.

⌘ First, stick out your tongue and pant like a dog, emphasizing your exhales. Then close your mouth and continue, only now the breath is through the nose, still emphasizing the exhales.

⌘ Keep going and gradually speed up the exhales a bit. The air should be exhaled completely from the lungs with a sudden, vigorous stroke while simultaneously drawing inward with the abdominal muscles.

You might feel a little dizzy or lightheaded after you do this exercise. This is normal if you aren't used to this much oxygen flooding your brain. Stay seated until the sensation has passed.

This exercise should be done in three rounds, each taking about a minute. A little rest can be taken in between the rounds at your convenience. Throughout the exercise, the chest should be kept still, without expansion or contraction. Only the diaphragm is used for breathing and not the upper chest.

Some of the benefits attributed to *Kapalabhati* are:

⌘ **Physiological**: The heat generated has powerful effects on the respiratory system as it purifies the nasal passage and the lungs. Even in cases of asthma, it tamps down spasms in bronchial tubes. It stimulates the digestive organs and the circulatory system and it increases the exchange of gases in the lungs—there is large-scale elimination of carbon dioxide and a huge absorption of oxygen.

⌘ **Mental/Emotional**: As with anything that floods the brain with copious amounts of oxygen, you'll feel calmer and less tense, peaceful and more relaxed. This is stress-busting on an immediate level.

## ⌘ Healing Bodywork for Spring

Most people are familiar with the body's vessel system that carries blood to and from the tissues, but few understand that there is another equally vital system of vessels that removes cell wastes, proteins, excess fluid, viruses, and bacteria. The lymph system picks up fluids and waste products from the spaces between the cells and then filters and cleans them. The lymphatic system returns about 3.17 quarts (3 liters) of fluid *each day* from the tissues to the circulatory system.

There are over six hundred lymph nodes throughout the body, with the majority of them located in the neck, groin, and armpits. Lymph fluid is transported through vessels via the squeezing action of their neighboring skeletal muscles. This is why exercise is such a good tonic for sluggishness and for keeping energy levels up. By exercising (any kind, any time) regularly, you are helping your lymphatic system to do its job better.

When the lymph system works well, we feel healthy and have a strong defense against illness. When it's sluggish or blocked we can have swelling, feel tired, and be more susceptible to colds and infections.

## Lymphatic Massage

A customized form of bodywork, this type of massage can help your body in clearing sluggish tissues of waste and swelling, and is an excellent adjunct to the rest of your springtime cleansing efforts. Though lymph vessels are found throughout the body, most of them—about seventy percent—are located just below the skin. By using very light pressure in a rhythmic, circular motion, a massage therapist can stimulate the lymph system to work more efficiently and help it move the lymph fluids back to the heart. Furthermore, by freeing vessel pathways, a lymphatic massage can help retrain the lymph system to work better for more long-term health benefits.

### SIMPLE LYMPHATIC DRAINAGE

Sit comfortably and erect in a chair, feet flat on the floor.

Place your fingers, relaxed, at collarbones, just inside the bone. Gently press in and down, pulsing 25 times.

Place your peace fingers, relaxed, on either side of your neck right under your ears.

Gently move the skin in a downward motion toward the collarbones.

Repeat ten times by gradually positioning your fingers lower and further down from your ear, and moving more toward the back of your shoulders.

Place fingers at the top of your shoulders on either side of the neck.

Gently massage by bringing the skin closer to the collarbone.

Repeat ten times.

### Lomi Lomi Massage: Energetic Detoxing

Lomi Lomi massage is the perfect vehicle for addressing emotional energy blockages and helping to release them in a very gentle and loving manner. First practiced by ancient Polynesian healers, its philosophy states that every single thing in the world seeks harmony and love.

Broad stokes, gentle stretches, and joint rotations are applied by the practitioner to release energy trapped in the joints. Lomi Lomi technique covers a broad area of the body and works the muscles, often simultaneously to encourage the continuous flow of love and harmony and to wash harmful thoughts, patterns, memories, and behaviors out of the cells of our bodies to make way for more beneficial modes of thought. Once positive energy is permitted to flow unhindered, the healing is accomplished.

Before a Lomi Lomi massage begins, the massage therapist will say a quiet prayer to request effective healing. It's also common for the therapist to hum or chant during the massage.

Authentic Lomi Lomi requires traditional training by the student who studies with the elder teacher for several years. Most traditional practitioners of Lomi Lomi find it virtually impossible to work within a spa or massage office setting and instead prefer a home visit. Be sure and ask detailed questions about your practitioner's training if you are seeking out a traditional Lomi Lomi experience.

## ⌘ Plant Healing for Spring: Aromatherapy, Herbs, Teas, and Tonics

### Aromatherapy

Working with aromatherapy during this season of cleansing and detoxifying, presents many choices. A quickie treatment is to put a few drops on a tissue or cloth handkerchief and hold it under your nose. Try placing a couple drops on your yoga mat before practice or pillowcase right before you go to sleep.

Another effective way to use essential oils, is by bathing in them. You only need to use five or six drops of oil in a medium-sized bath of water. No other ingredients are necessary (soaps, bath and shower gels, bombs) and may, in fact, interfere with the work of the essential oils. Drop them into a clean tub of warm—not hot—water. You should save your body scrubbing and soaping off for another bath. Let the oils stay on your skin for as long as possible.

⌘ **Helichrysum** *(Helichrysum italicum)* is harvested mostly around the Mediterranean region, and has a ball-shaped golden flower with a pungent, curry-like smell and a faint honey sweetness. Greek in origin, *(helios* sun and *chrysos* gold), the oil supports the "I Am" consciousness and is a great aid in meditation when one wishes to contact their higher knowledge or when seeking their karmic path. It stimulates the right hemisphere of the brain, which enhances artistic and creative expression, aspects of human manifestation found on the Medicine Wheel in the east. It has been found to be beneficial in clearing stagnation in the liver, as well as supporting the lymphatic system. In France, it is widely used for  respiratory issues, such as asthma and bronchitis. This oil also provides relief from fever and other general states of inflammation and gently soothes the body when a few drops are added to a cool cloth pressed on the forehead or pulse points of the body. It has cytophylactic properties, in that it encourages recycling of dead cells and production of new cells. This property can be particularly beneficial for skin care as an ingredient in rejuvenating facial oils. Add two to three drops to a teaspoon of carrier oil, such as coconut or olive.

⌘ **Juniper Berry** *(Juniperus communis)*: In Chinese five-element acupuncture, spring supports the liver and gall bladder meridians. Juniper is recommended to detoxify both the liver and gall bladder, bringing balance and harmony to the body. Juniper also protects against infection and is a perfect defense against those lingering winter colds and flu. It stimulates the immune system to bring rejuvenation and vitality to the body after months of hibernation and stagnation. Juniper is renowned for its diuretic and detoxifying properties and will help to eliminate toxic wastes and release sluggish body fluids. This powerful oil is a purifier and it helps avert nervous tension. Juniper essential oil is an antiviral, antiseptic, diuretic, and can help relieve pain and expel uric acid from the system. Its spicy aroma helps to strengthen and fortify the spirit during times of low energy, anxiety, and emotional overload. As it detoxifies the body, juniper can also detox the mind. (Avoid rubbing directly on the skin as it can be irritating for some people. It should be avoided during pregnancy.)

## Herbs, Teas, and Tonics

The remedies for spring have straightforward purposes: to cleanse and strengthen the blood, fight allergies, decrease inflammation, and to cleanse and strengthen the liver.

- ⌘ **Chrysanthemum** (*Chrysanthemum indicum*) is a bittersweet herb that has an affinity for the liver. This herb is said to calm the liver and resolve toxicity. In Traditional Chinese Medicine, if you are feeling a bit on edge and hot tempered chrysanthemum tea is prescribed. Brewing the flowers in the form of a tea requires steeping them in hot water for about five minutes. The aroma is gently floral and the smell is instantly calming.

- ⌘ **Dandelion** (*Taraxacum officinale*) is a common meadow herb of the *Asteraceae* or sunflower family. It has been used for centuries by herbalists for general detox. Dandelion is a powerful restorative to the liver, purifies the blood, and increases bile production. It reduces serum cholesterol and uric acid levels and improves the functioning of the kidneys, pancreas, spleen, and stomach. The young leaves of the dandelion in spring are somewhat bitter, but chewing on them (indeed, anything bitter) stimulates bile production and the liver starts to purge.

# THE OFFICIAL REMEDY FOR DISORDERS

*By Euell Gibbons*

(Excerpted from *Stalking the Wild Asparagus*, 1962)

Ancient herb doctors dug up the perennial roots of the dandelion, which could be obtained even in midwinter. These were washed then the juice was expressed from them and given to the sufferers. When this was done the patient always improved. Then, in early spring he was advised to eat raw as many of the first young dandelion leaves as he could consume. This healthful salad soon restored him to health and vigor. I do not think it is an exaggeration to say that this vitamin-filled wild plant has, over the centuries, probably saved a good many lives.

But how the mighty have fallen! This herbal hero, one of the most healthful and genuinely useful plants in the material medica of the past, is now a despised lawn weed. Now that supermarkets sell green vegetables throughout the winter and the druggists are vending tons of synthetic vitamins, we no longer need to depend on the roots and leaves of this humble plant to ward off sickness and death, so we have turned on the dandelion. Every garden-supply house offers for sale a veritable arsenal of diggers, devices and deadly poisons, all designed to exterminate this useful and essentially beautiful little plant which has so immensely benefited the human race.

I learned to love dandelions when I was a small child. Not only did I enjoy the delicious dandelion greens my mother gathered and prepared, but the bright yellow flower, with its wonderful composite construction, fascinated me. I never believed that spring had really come until I saw the first dandelion in bloom.

⌘ **Milk Thistle** (*Silybum marianum*) has been used medicinally for over two thousand years, most commonly for the treatment of liver and gallbladder disorders. It is the most researched and best understood of all the medicinal herbs. Study after study has confirmed its ability to protect and actually rejuvenate the liver. The best proof: people who have accidentally ingested the very fatal death cap mushroom (which poisons by attacking the liver) have been saved by taking milk thistle as an antidote.

⌘ **Turmeric** (*Curcuma longa*) is in the rhizome family of roots, and is related to ginger. It is a spice that has been a vital part of Chinese herbal and Ayurvedic medicine for centuries. It's what gives curry powder its distinctive golden, yellow color. It has traditionally been used for liver ailments and as a digestive aid by traditional herbalists, but has recently become popular in the Western world due to its multiple health benefits from its anti-inflammatory, antioxidant, and antibacterial properties. German researchers found that when turmeric was taken with milk thistle it increased bile flow about six times more than when the herbs were used without it. There have been warnings about several brands of turmeric containing high lead levels so make sure you buy a reputable brand.

May your springtime health practices move you forward into the coming year with clarity, rejuvenation, and purpose.  But know that revisiting these essential practices can be done throughout any season, as needed.

# Chapter 4

## Healing Beauty Rituals for Spring

. . . . . . . . . . . . . . . . . .

Hopefully, you've been able to alter your wellness habits a bit to incorporate a few spring cleaning suggestions and regular, everyday detoxing. If this is something new for you then you may have noticed your face going through its own little detox as well. Those with fair skin may flush and show a rosacea-like rash until the body is cleansed, others may suffer occasional breakouts and eruptions as the body discharges its wastes. This is a temporary reaction. Your skin, as your largest organ and the most accurate indicator of your internal states of being, will settle and definitely improve its quality as you experience longer periods of conscious wellness.

I find it inspiring and uplifting to incorporate what's happening in nature all around me in spring, to create treatments to nourish my skin in the same way. The same foods I crave to eat to feel lighter and fresher internally can provide the same benefits for my face and body when applied topically. I smell their light, delicate aromas and touch the various textures of their leaves. The just-minted feeling of the new permeates the energy around my plants. To take in this energy through my mouth and skin is a symbiotic ritual of communion; this is my religion. It is simple, straightforward, and here at my fingertips. The beauty of the plants gives me beauty; I wear spring on my skin.

### How to Love (Clean) Your Face: A Meditation on Acceptance

When my daughter was small it used to amaze me the amount of *schmutz* that landed on her little face. She was in the enviable mode of being unaware of what was on her face. The more that was there, the more immersed I knew she had been in her activities. I was drawn to her face like a moth to a flame. My instinct was to tidy it all up, much like a mother cat's ritual of washing her kittens laboriously with her paws and rough tongue. I wanted to clean, not in the quest to make my child's face a canvas of perfection, but to engage in the ritual itself. I groomed out of love of being close enough to her to feel her sweet breath on my face, to smell her child's smell of fresh grass and brown sugar, to see stray beads of sweat sparkle on her upper lip. I wanted to take a bite out of her, she was so delectable.

Wouldn't it be great to approach the scrutiny of our own faces with as much love, tenderness, and non-judgment as the gaze we cast upon a child's face? It's easy to get caught in a self-critical place. We find flaws with the basic shape and arrangement of our features, we compare ourselves to airbrushed celebrities, we panic at seeing ourselves age. The result of this relentless inspection, is that anything will look distorted if stared at in a mirror long enough. Other than reducing the time we spend in front of mirrors, maybe there is another way to find more graceful acceptance and less disappointment with what we see when we do look.

We learn from Buddhist philosophy that a mundane routine can be elevated to a spiritual exercise if practiced with right intention and focus. This everyday ritual of self-care can become an exercise in loving kindness toward ourselves. Transformation from critical appraisal and worry about gravity's effects starts with gratitude about what we have, instead of what we wish we had. We experience the miracle of our face and its components (eyes, nose, mouth, ears) because we are conscious caretakers of them.

If you're burdened with a complicated routine consisting of several steps, multiple products, and a drawer or cabinet overflowing with other partly used products that you never use, now is the time to simplify.

It's only necessary to wash your face once or twice a day; use a lighter rinsing cleanse for morning and a more thorough regimen at night before you go to bed. Over-washing can strip beneficial oils and dry out already dry skin. In acne prone skin, when the natural oils in the skin are constantly removed and dried out, the sebum glands react by producing more oil.

Other tips:

⌘ Use a very pure, organic face cleanser, with as few ingredients as possible.

⌘ Never use hot water, keep the temperature to lukewarm. Hot water might dry your skin too much.

⌘ Use a light touch with a couple of fingertips (middle and ring fingers are weaker, so you will tend to use less pressure) to massage your cleaner all over the surface of your face. If using a cotton ball, use short, gentle swipes in all directions to cover the surface. Take about thirty to forty-five seconds to do this.

⌘ Avoid heavy, pulling, downward actions with your massage touch. Emphasize upward, light, lifting strokes to keep from disrupting skin's elasticity.

⌘ Avoid using a thick washcloth (too rough on the skin), as well as loofah-type sponges. Your own hands and fingers are best. Thin, porous cotton cloths are next best.

⌘ If dealing with acne breakouts, be especially gentle around the inflamed areas.

⌘ Thoroughly rinse all the cleanser off (leaving cleaner residue can also clog pores); four or five splashes with cool water helps to close your pores.

⌘ Gently pat your face dry with a soft, clean towel.

### Parsley Mint Face Wash

Parsley increases blood circulation to the skin and helps purify it. Other than stimulating, soothing, and cleansing skin parsley is a source of remarkable skin nutrition as it is rich in vitamin C, pro vitamin B5, and chlorophyll—all great skin rejuvenators and nourishers. Mint is high in vitamin A and calcium and its aromatic qualities are uplifting.

2 cups boiling, purified water

2 generous fistfuls flat-leafed parsley

7-10 large mint leaves

1. Make an infusion by pouring water over parsley (stems, leaves and seeds—no need to separate) and mint leaves.

2. Let it cool, strain, and put in a glass jar, cover tightly. Store in fridge for up to a week.

3. Wash the face with a cotton ball dipped in the parsley mint infusion, or soak a thin cotton washcloth in the infusion and press against your face. Let the infusion soak into your skin. Rinse with lukewarm water. Follow with moisturizer.

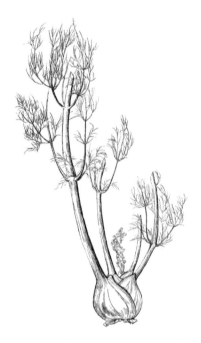

### Fennel Thyme All-Purpose Face Toner

In Greek myths it was said that intelligence came from the gods and reached humans through a fennel stem. Fennel has been considered to have magical characteristics wherever it has been cultivated. As one of the ancient Saxon people's nine sacred herbs, fennel was credited with the power to cure what were then believed to be the nine causes of disease. It was also draped over doorways to protect from evil spirits and the seeds stuffed in keyholes to keep ghosts from entering the room.

Fennel has been used throughout history as an aid to digestion or as a slight diuretic. As an infusion, fennel seeds can be gently cleansing and toning for the skin and they can help reduce puffiness and superficial irritation. Thyme, which is used in natural antiseptic preparations, is a good astringent (cleans and clears tissues, as well as constricts the pores).

2 sprigs fresh thyme, crumbled (or ½ tablespoon dried thyme)

2 teaspoons dried or fresh fennel seeds, crushed

½ cup boiling water

Juice of half a lemon

1. Mix the thyme and fennel seed in a bowl and cover with boiling water. Add lemon juice and steep for fifteen minutes.

2. Strain the infusion and store the liquid in a glass jar in the refrigerator. Will keep up to five days. Shake to mix thoroughly before using.

Because this mix is very gentle, it can be used each morning and evening as a toner to reset the ph balance of your skin. If you can put it in a bottle with a spray attachment, mist on the skin, and let it stay—do not rinse it off. If you are using it as a cleanser, apply to a cotton ball and swab your face and neck then rinse with lukewarm water.

## Strawberry Revitalizing Face Mask

Yogurt is a wonderful beauty ingredient. The lipids in the milk, which are essentially fat, work wonders to plump up depleted skin. The lactic acid in yogurt soothes, softens and tightens the skin and refines the pores. Because it is a fermented product, the natural antibacterial and antifungal properties get rid of germs and other bacteria that can cause breakouts and disruptions.

Strawberries are a member of the rose family and contain salicylic acid (a key ingredient in over the counter and prescription acne medicines), which rids the skin of dead cells, allowing it to absorb moisture more efficiently. Strawberries also have a mild bleaching effect on the skin and help prevent and heal blemishes.

Note: It's important to source organic strawberries since you are putting them on your face to heal it; strawberries are a food crop with one of the highest concentrations of pesticide residues.

1/4 cup plain, full fat yogurt (the thickness of unstrained Greek-style yogurt is preferable to a thinner-type yogurt, as it is easier to apply as a mask; vegan yogurt can be substituted)

1/4 cup mashed fresh strawberries

1 tsp. honey

1. Blend all ingredients either with a fork or a quick pulse in a blender, until a smooth paste.
2. Apply evenly to clean, dry face. Let set for at least ten minutes; longer if you have the luxury. Rinse well with lukewarm water and pat dry.

## Lemon Face Paste

Lemons is the go-to beauty ingredient for so many purposes with its high vitamin C content, as well as other beneficial nutrients (folate, potassium, calcium). It's a natural lightener of age spots or sun spots. This recipe is a perfect refresher for nourishing the skin and tightening pores.

1 egg white

¼ cup, freshly squeezed lemon juice

1. Combine lemon juice and egg white. Beat vigorously with a fork.

2. Use a large, natural bristle cosmetic brush to dab on the paste. Let it dry for 20 minutes. Rinse with lukewarm water and pat dry.

### Natural Mouth Hygiene

⌘ Flossing: Regular, effective flossing keeps bacteria from migrating to the digestive tract and causing inflammation, which has been linked to allergies, as well as a host of other chronic ailments.

⌘ Teeth Whitening: Mix equal parts salt and baking soda in a ceramic or porcelain dish. Wet toothbrush and dab into mixture, then scrub teeth. Salt is a wonderful exfoliator so it removes coffee, tea, and food stains, and baking soda is a gum protector. Additionally, the alkaline ph balance of baking soda neutralizes the acids in the mouth that can cause bad breath and tooth decay.

⌘ Mouth rinse for bad breath: Parsley is a great solution for bad breath. Boil two cups of water and pour over five or six sprigs of parsley, coarsely chopped, and two or three whole cloves or a quarter teaspoon of ground cloves. This mixture should be stirred occasionally while cooling. It should then be strained into a glass jar with a tight fitting lid. Use as a mouthwash or gargle several times a day.

### The Case for a Chemi-Free Mani Pedi

Think about the chemical soup your body can absorb during a regular mani or pedi: first the polish remover (typically made of acetone—a strong, chemical solvent used to break up the composition of plastics and paints), then a cuticle cream (most contain ingredients like triethanolamine, an emulsifier). Paraffin dips use wax that is a by-product of petroleum. Polishes can contain formaldehyde, DBP, and tuolene—all very potent chemicals that have been linked to cancer, developmental/reproductive toxicity, and allergies.

Creating a home mani/pedi ritual for yourself is a great way to lighten your chemical exposure and be kinder to the Earth. Or seek out salons with more eco-friendly services.

There are many options for polish available at health food stores and natural beauty apothecaries, as well as online. Known as the *three-free* polishes, they have had the formaldehyde, DBP, and tuolene removed and last just as long as any other conventional brand, without chipping or peeling.

# Chapter 5

## Spring Kitchen Rituals: Food, Nutrition, Recipes

. . . . . . . . . . . . . . . . . . .

The tiniest, tenderest shoots of spring begin to poke their heads above the soil and tempt us with their light, delicate flavors. When you begin to tune in to the natural world by noticing which parts of the plants are eaten at which time of the year, as well as their texture and shape, then you are truly a seasonal voyager. Spring plants are in the paler, chartreuse end of the green palette (peas, arugula, fennel, asparagus) and we eat the lacy, delicate leaves, stalks, and tops of the plants this time of year more than the roots. Strawberries, lemons, lettuces are more fragile than the hearty weight of gourds and squashes which come into season when it's colder and we need their supporting nourishment. Seasonings are minimal to enhance the delicate aromas and tastes on our plates. The tentative first steps of nature urge us to go lightly, gently, and easily as we too find our footing with this new season.

### THE SACRED RITUAL OF FOOD PREPARATION

Often we are in such a hurry to throw together something on a plate, pressed to just get fuel in our body, we skip over the importance of using our daily interactions with our nourishment as a moment which can absolutely elevate the energy of body, mind and spirit in an instant.

Cristina Urioste, owner of Rasa Foods in Los Angeles, is a chef trained in Ayurvedic health principles with whom I have worked on my yoga retreats. She has shared with me her approach to food preparation and eating:

⌘ Every time you cook and eat a piece of food you have an energetic relationship to it, so never make food while in a bad mood or angry. Your emotions go into food and are stored in the body of the people eating it. Cook with love and openheartedness.

⌘ Don't take in negative information from watching TV, listening to radio news, or from violent programs while you cook. Instead listen to beautiful music or sing as you cook, or notice the sounds of the environment around you, if alone. While cooking with others, engage in respectful and loving conversations.

⌘ Make mealtimes sacred and peaceful—take the blessing of the food into the body with each bite.

⌘ Recycle leftovers and waste. Consider this part of your meal to be as important as the others. Try to throw away as little as possible out of respect for those who are hungry in this moment.

### Kale Lemon Ginger Smoothie

I think it's safe to say kale is definitely having a moment, a prolonged moment. One that I hope never fades. Other than having several shapes and textures which feel and taste exquisite, kale is a nutrient powerhouse for its high sulfur content and isothiocyanates (ITC) from glucosinolates, which aid in the body's detoxification process. Additionally, it's a superstar for antioxidant vitamins A, D, and E.

This kale drink has a spicy, energizing kick from the ginger-lemon combo, which are blood purifiers. The dates and mango add a creamy texture that when blended together, makes a delicious sweet treat.

2 cups kale leaves torn into small pieces

3 dried dates, pitted

1-inch piece fresh ginger root, peeled

Juice of 3 lemons

½ cup frozen mango chunks, more for extra creaminess

1–2 cups purified water or coconut water, depending on your preferred consistency

1. Blend all together until smooth and creamy.

2. Makes one large, 16-ounce serving.

## Super Veggie Smoothie

Wild ancestors of the carrot most likely came from Afghanistan, which remains the center of diversity for the wild carrot today. Carrots support healthy liver, nails, skin and hair. The beta carotene in carrots cools the blood, and has a noticeably cooling effect in the eyes, which can feel inflamed, itchy and irritated when the body releases fats during a cleansing effort. The beautiful frothy tops are packed with potassium and chlorophyll.

Radish, garlic, and beetroot cleanse the liver and gall bladder, the organs and tissues that are working hard to break down stored fats, oils, and sugars. The pigment that gives beets their bright color helps to neutralize the toxins from alcohol and balances blood chemistry.

Basil is a good source of vitamin A, which keeps free radicals from oxidizing cholesterol in the blood stream, preventing the cholesterol from building up in the blood vessels. Magnesium is also present in basil. This essential mineral helps the heart and blood vessels to relax, improving blood flow.

6 carrots (with tops if possible)

1 or 2 radishes

1 beet, cut into pieces

1 soft avocado

1 clove of fresh minced garlic

5–7 basil leaves

¼ to ½ cup of fresh squeezed lemon juice

1 lemon slice (to squeeze at end)

1–2 cups purified water (more for a thinner consistency)

1. Blend all ingredients together until smooth.

2. Squeeze an extra dash of lemon into the drink for brightness, a sprinkle of cayenne for kick.

### Cilantro Detox Pesto

Cilantro is the Spanish word for coriander leaves. It is a member of the carrot family.

It is thought that the leaves of the cilantro plant can accelerate the excretion of mercury, lead, and aluminum from the body. This delicious herb can greatly contribute in the detox process.

Make sure your leaves are highly aromatic; if there is no aroma, there is less taste.

1 generous handful fresh cilantro leaves (a good packed cup)

1 generous handful fresh basil

½ cup of raw almonds

1–3 cloves of garlic (depending on your tolerance for eating raw garlic)

Juice of half a lemon

2 tablespoons of olive oil

½ teaspoon sea salt

1. Combine all ingredients, except oil, in a food processor or blender until nuts are well integrated. With motor running, pour in oil and process until you get a smooth paste (you can make the paste less lumpy by adding hot water).

2. Spread on toast, fresh bread, crackers; or toss with fresh cooked organic pasta, udon, or soba noodles.

### Casbah Cauliflower Salad

Many people do not understand and appreciate cauliflower—outright abhorring it, while others adore it. It's a cruciferous veggie and a cool weather descendant of the cabbage that flowers in the spring. It contains glucosinolates, the sulfur-containing compounds that activate the body's detoxification system.

This recipe dispels the usual prejudice against cauliflower's blandness by emphasizing other flavors from our seasonal health arsenal with exciting Moroccan flavors that anyone can love.

Small head of cauliflower, rinsed and cut into small pieces (about 3 cups)

½ cup chopped, fresh spearmint

½ cup chopped fresh cilantro

½ cup chopped raw cashews

¼ cup dried figs or dates, chopped

*Dressing:*

¼ teaspoon ground cayenne pepper

¼ teaspoon ground black pepper

¼ teaspoon turmeric powder

½ teaspoon sea salt of high quality

Juice of one whole lemon (preferably Meyer)

½ cup virgin, unprocessed coconut oil

1. Combine veggies and fruits in a salad bowl.

2. Combine dressing ingredients in a small mixing bowl and whisk briskly.

3. Toss salad ingredients with dressing to coat well.

### Asparagus Mint Salad

Asparagus contains high levels of the amino acid asparagine. This serves as a natural diuretic, which not only releases fluid, but helps rid the body of excess salts which can cause edema or swelling. This is especially beneficial to people with high blood pressure. Asparagus is also a very good source of fiber, folate, vitamins A, C, E, and K and is ranked as a top veggie for containing a high level of antioxidants.

I like this recipe because it calls for shaving the asparagus stalks for a different kind of texture on the plate and employs a simple dressing to let its flavor shine.

1 bunch asparagus

1 handful toasted, crushed almonds or hazelnuts

1 tablespoon chopped mint

3 tablespoons freshly squeezed lemon juice

2 tablespoons Sherry vinegar

1 teaspoon raw, organic honey

3 tablespoons extra virgin olive oil

1. Using a vegetable peeler, shave the asparagus lengthwise to create strips. Toss with the nuts and mint.

2. Wisk together lemon juice, vinegar, honey, and olive oil.

3. Pour over asparagus and mix with salt and pepper to taste.

### Fennel and Meyer Lemon Salad

Rich in phytonutrients, fennel seeds and roots unclog the liver and spleen, helping to eliminate toxins from the body. This recipe captures the bright licorice tones of fresh shaved fennel and marries it with our spring standby, the Meyer lemon. In this instance, the whole glorious fruit is showcased, not just the juice.

2 fennel bulbs

2 Meyer lemons

½ cup toasted sunflower seeds

1 large bunch arugula tossed with a drizzle of olive oil

½ teaspoon salt, plus more to taste

1. Cut fennel bulb in half lengthwise. Lay halves cut-side down and use a sharp knife to slice crosswise as thinly as possible (or use mandolin). Put fennel in a medium bowl.

2. Cut off and discard ends of lemon (cut enough so you can see fruit, not just the white pith). Put the fruit cut-side down and with a sharp paring knife cut off and discard the peel and pith. You should be left with a piece of fully peeled (no white pith remaining) lemon.

3. Add lemon sections to fennel. Add the sunflower seeds. Toss. Sprinkle with salt and toss to combine. Taste and add more salt to taste if you like.

4. Spoon over bed of plated arugula.

### Lemon Herb Quinoa with Hemp Seeds, Spring Peas, and Basil

(adapted from Gena Hamshaw's *Choosing Raw* blog)

Get your protein on with the double whammy of quinoa and hemp seeds in this dish. Both have a complimentary "nuttiness" to them and serve as a perfect backdrop to a couple of our spring friends (peas and basil). Fresh peas are one of the most nutritious leguminous vegetables around, rich in health benefiting phyto-nutrients, minerals, vitamins, and antioxidants. The dressing is an outstanding blend of salty tart and sweet, proving once again that fresh vegan eating need not be boring.

1 cup quinoa, dry

2 cups water, cold

1 cup green spring peas (fresh or frozen)

¼ cup fresh basil, finely chopped

¼ cup shelled hemp seeds

2 tablespoons olive oil

2 tablespoons fresh squeezed lemon juice

1½ teaspoons maple syrup

Salt and pepper to taste

Pinch garlic salt (optional)

1. Rinse quinoa in a mesh strainer with cold water. Transfer to a pot and add the water and a nice pinch of regular or garlic salt. Bring to a boil.

2. Reduce heat to a simmer, and leave the lid of the pot slightly ajar while cooking. Simmer for about 15 minutes or until quinoa is plump, the water is absorbed, and you see the tiny little outer casings of the quinoa grain coming loose in the pot. About 5 minutes before you pull the quinoa off the stove, stir in the peas.

3. Remove quinoa and peas from heat and let sit, covered, for 5 minutes or so. Fluff with a fork and set aside.

4. Mix quinoa-pea mixture with basil, and hemp seeds in a large bowl. Whisk together the oil,

lemon juice, maple syrup, sea salt, and black pepper. Pour over the quinoa salad mixture, and serve warm or cold.

## Detox Spice Mix

I've run across variations of this recipe in many places over the years. It's an Ayurvedic tradition to have a jar of this mix as a staple in the pantry and to use as an everyday seasoning and flavoring component with added health benefit from the herbs.

1 teaspoon turmeric

2 teaspoons ground cumin

3 teaspoons ground coriander

4 teaspoons ground fennel

1 teaspoon dried minced garlic

¼–½ teaspoon sea salt

½ teaspoon ground peppercorns

1. Mix the spices together and store in a clean glass jar.
2. When you are cooking a meal, place a small amount of oil in a frying pan and heat gently on low to medium.
3. Add detoxifying spice mixture, measuring out one teaspoon of spice mixture per serving of vegetables. Sauté spices until the aroma is released, but be careful not to burn.
4. Add to rice, couscous, quinoa, bean and lentil dishes, stir fried, or steamed vegetables. It also works well as a base for vegetable soups: lentil, potato, cabbage, or beet.

## Spring Cleansing Kitchari

Kitchari (pronounced kitch-a-ree) is a staple comfort food of India. The word *kitchari* means *mixture* or *mess* as in "mess of pottage" or "mess of stew" or porridge. The main ingredients are rice and mung beans, to which a variety of spices and other vegetables may be added. In Ayurveda, rice and mung beans are considered extremely easy to digest, believed to purify and cleanse the body of toxins.

Kitchari fasting is actually a mono-diet, which means the body receives a limited diversity of food and therefore needs to produce a limited number of digestive enzymes. The work of the digestive system is lessened, allowing for greater healing and cleansing to occur.

4 tablespoons olive or coconut oil

1 teaspoon whole or ground cumin seeds

1-inch piece fresh ginger, peeled and finely chopped

2 black cardamom pods

½ teaspoon turmeric

1 tablespoon ground coriander

½ teaspoon fennel seeds

½ teaspoon ground black pepper

Pinch of cayenne

1½ teaspoon salt (to taste)

1 cup split mung dal beans (soaked 6 hours or overnight)

½ cup basmati rice

Salt to taste

About 5 cups water

1. Heat oil in a large heavy-bottom saucepan casserole over medium heat. Add cumin seeds. As soon as you smell the fragrance of the cumin seeds, add the ginger, cardamom pods, garlic, and turmeric. Stir and saute for 1 minute.

2. Add the mung beans and rice. Sauté for about a minute or two.

3. Add salt and water and bring to a boil. Cover, turn heat to low, and cook for 30 minutes, stirring now and then to prevent sticking.

4. Uncover and check to ensure that the rice and mung beans are thoroughly cooked. Let cool for 15 minutes, then serve.

5. Optional: top with chopped cilantro or a dollop of plain yogurt, regular or vegan.

# FASTING AS SPIRITUAL PRACTICE

Our everyday pop culture is made up of fads and trends that are generalized and diluted for easier mass consumption. The recent fads in the last several years involving fasting fit this latter category for me. Our relationship to food and body image, sustenance and nourishment, is very complex and complicated. What is one to make of a culture that has epidemics of both teenage girls starving themselves literally to death and a rising obesity rate that is plunging our country's health care resources into bankruptcy?

Addressing these myriad issues requires more thoughtful deliberation than our busy and distracted culture has time for (perhaps that's *why* we are starving and obese at the same time). Any ritual that begs a spiritual context, such as fasting, when plunked down in the middle of our secular society, runs the risk of being nothing more than a goal of "fitting into skinny jeans" and "losing unwanted belly fat" or worse, mitigation against too much "partying."

Instead, the context, when approached as a means for spiritual transformation, requires we delve into the basic philosophies we construct for ourselves. After all, what connects us more closely to our ordinary material lives than hunger and the satisfaction of hunger? All religious traditions use feasting and fasting to infuse adherents' lives with something special and spiritual—Yogic, Buddhism, Judaism (Yom Kippur), Christianity (Lent), and Islam (Ramadan). Often, fasting is associated with the desire to experience new revelations out of the temporary discomfort of doing without. In the Yoga Sutras (yogic scriptures), it is noted that the more one indulges the senses, the more they make their demands. Fasting helps to cultivate control over the senses, sublimate desires, and guide the mind to be poised and at peace. Fasting can help that process of transforming desire to wisdom by subduing the body's coarse desires.

Absent a dedicated spiritual or religious focus, fasting can help us to see how so much of our time and energy is spent in procuring food, preparing, cooking, and eating it. Living with time rearranged around an all-encompassing activity offers big insights. Many people find that the most profound insights occur while coming out of the fast, not just during. Physical, emotional, and spiritual changes may also be experienced in the days and weeks following.

### *Strawberry Rhubarb Crunch*

In Traditional Chinese Medicine, rhubarb's vitamins and natural compounds are used for their powers to cleanse the body of toxins. Eaten raw, the sour nature of the rhubarb stimulates the saliva glands which stimulate bile production and liver detoxing.

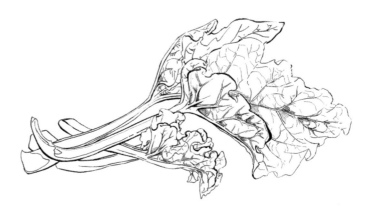

Even though rhubarb is considered a vegetable, it is most often treated as a fruit. Oddly, the leaves are poisonous, but the stalks are packed with antioxidants, fiber, and calcium (just be sure and cut well below the leaf).

This deceptively simple compote has a hidden element of fresh rosemary. This dish captures the classic combo of sweet and tart and sets it off with oaty goodness.

2 cups of diced rhubarb stalks, leaves removed

2 cups of sliced strawberries, hulled and trimmed

½ cup raw honey or 3 tablespoons agave nectar

1 tablespoon fresh rosemary, chopped

½ cup uncooked oats

½ cup raw almonds, lightly toasted

3 dried dates, pitted

Pinch cinnamon

Pinch salt

1. Combine the rhubarb, strawberries, sweetener, and rosemary in a pot and cook over low heat until the fruit is very soft.

2. Transfer to a tightly sealed container and refrigerate overnight or at least 6 hours to allow the honey and rosemary to infuse the fruit properly.

3. For the topping: Put the almonds into a food processor or blender and chop into small bits, but stop before they turn to powder. Add the rest of the ingredients and pulse just enough to create a course blend.

4. Spread the oat/nut blend on a cookie sheet and toast in a 400-degree oven for 15 minutes, or until crispy.

5. Spoon the hot, toasty oat and nut topping over the compote.

# Chapter 6

## Spring in Your Home and Family

. . . . . . . . . . . . . . . . . .

One of my favorite retreat locales is the Zen Mountain Center in Idyllwild, California. When teaching, I led several years of yoga retreats there. High in the San Jacinto mountain range that rings the Palm Springs desert area, this retreat center is the very model of Zen simplicity in action. It was here that I was first exposed to the aesthetic of Zen housekeeping.

The approach to keeping things clean, is gentle, laid back, and pursued, like all things Zen, as a ritual part of spiritual practice. Cleaning can be meditation in action, just like praying. A ritual to tidy up your space, purify, and bless it can be made with each cleaning session you undertake. Using non-toxic, chemical free cleaning solutions is also the very soul of a sustainable home ritual.

### Why Clean Green?

Many of the antibacterial products heavily marketed and expensively packaged for consumers, clean no better than soap and water. They can also breed some forms of super bacteria that become resistant to regular cleaning with soap and water. A key component of many anti-bacterial soaps and cleansers is triclosan, which is increasingly linked to a range of health and environmental problems, from skin irritation, allergy susceptibility, and dioxin contamination to destruction of fragile aquatic ecosystems. The contents of many chemical cleaners leave residues on surfaces and toxins in the air and then later leach into the environment and ground water.

Many common major brand cleaning ingredients have dangerous or even fatal effects on human health. Ingredients that you should avoid in your cleaning products are ammonia, formaldehyde, hydrochloric acid, sodium hydroxide lye, paradichlorobenzenes, butyl cellosolve, and ethanol.

*Green Cleaning Solutions*

These are the essential products to have in your green-home cleaning cupboard. They are cheap, natural, and easy to buy:

⌘ Baking soda—natural deodorizer and lightly abrasive

⌘ Lemon juice—wonderful de-greaser, deodorizes

⌘ White distilled vinegar—all round great cleaner

⌘ Grapefruit seed extract—amazing antibacterial and antimicrobial properties, making it indispensable

⌘ Salt—super cleaner and degreaser

⌘ Liquid soap—read the label carefully. The contents should be a natural plant oil such as olive or coconut, or a vegetable-derived glycerin base. Kinder to you and the environment

⌘ Essential oils—as natural air fresheners, they are unsurpassable. Lavender and tea tree oil have antiviral, antifungal, and antibacterial properties. Try to use organic if possible. Note: Essential oils must be used with caution. They should never be ingested and for the most part should not be applied directly to the skin

## ALL-PURPOSE RECIPES FOR MAKING YOUR OWN CLEANERS

### Baking Soda

Mix ¼ cup baking soda in a spray bottle of water to use as general cleaner. The next time you do laundry, try adding ½ -1 cup to your load to deodorize. Before you vacuum, sprinkle it on your carpet as a deodorizer.

### Antifungals/Disinfectants

To keep mold at bay and to disinfect countertops and toilets, add 1 or 2 teaspoons of tea tree oil to 2 cups of water in a spray bottle, or 20 drops of grapefruit seed extract to 1 quart of water.

### No-Streak Glass Cleaner

For sparkling mirrors and windows, combine ¼ cup undiluted white vinegar, 1 tablespoon cornstarch, several drops of your favorite essential oil scent, and 1 quart warm water. For a streak-free shine wipe dry with a sheet of crumpled newspaper or a coffee filter (cloth or paper towels will streak).

### Tile and Grout Paste

Mixing 1 cup water and 3 cups baking soda into a paste works great for cleaning tile and grout. Use a toothbrush to scrub the paste into grout.

### All Purpose Cleaner

Fill a spray bottle with 1:1 water and vinegar. Add 4 or 5 drops of lemon and eucalyptus essential oil. Lemon and eucalyptus essential oils are naturally antiviral, antibacterial, and anti-fungal. It leaves the walls, benches, floors and surfaces smelling great. And vinegar of course is great for zapping germs and bacteria.

### Natural Bleach

Mix 12 cups water, ¼ cup lemon juice, and 1 cup hydrogen peroxide. Add 2 cups per wash load or put in spray bottle and use as a household cleaner.

### Furniture Polish recipe

Mix together ½ cup olive oil to ¼ cup lemon juice. I like to add a couple of drops of lavender oil to this mix for a great smell. Rub in a small amount to the wood surface and then wipe clean with a soft dry cloth. Lovely shine with a hint of lavender.

### Clogged drains

Pour a ½ box of baking soda followed by 1 cup of vinegar then chase with a tea kettle full of boiling water. Take care to protect your eyes as the solution will bubble and foam and might spit.

### Silver polishing

Eliminate tarnish by rubbing a dab of toothpaste with a soft cloth on the silver object.

This works fabulously on silver jewelry as well.

## Garden Pharmacy: Essential Herbs to Grow at Home

It's wonderful to have a year-round herbal pharmacy for beauty, comfort, and health right at your fingertips. Planting in spring is the time to do it. If you don't consider yourself to have a green thumb, then consider that all of these can be grown in a flower box or in pots on the patio or balcony, with a minimum of effort. Good sun exposure, a little water, and you can begin harvesting the young leaves in a couple of months. I recommend making teas and infusions by soaking the leaves or flowers in a pot of hot water for a good ten minutes then straining into a cup to drink or apply topically right away. Most of the teas can be stored for up to five days in a tightly closed glass container in the fridge. Cut them fresh for adding to food recipes and dry them for long term storage and use. You'll never go back to store bought herbs again.

⌘ *Holy Basil (tulsi)* Tulsi (Sanskrit for "the incomparable one") has been a sacred plant and worshipped by Hindus for thousands of years. Water mixed with tulsi petals is given to the dying to raise their departing souls to heaven. The aroma emanating from tulsi is an intoxicating and refreshing fragrance. It is said to purify the blood from just inhaling the aroma first thing in the morning. Place the mature shrub near a doorway or window to get the full effect of its rich, spicy scent. Make an infusion of the leaves for a tea to drink, which produces high antioxidant protection against free radicals and helps bolster the immune system, purify the blood, and balance the digestive system. Chewing the leaves will support healthy gums and prevent mouth ulcers. Gargle the tea for sore throat relief and to break up mucus from post nasal drip.

⌘ **Lemon Verbena** leaves can be steeped and used as tea; it is extremely relaxing, lowers blood pressure, eases cramps and indigestion, and strengthens the nervous system. This rangy bush is the premier garden herb for tea drinking due to its superior and unique flavor. It has a tranquilizing effect on the nervous system and is good for an overtaxed and stressed out constitution. Mixed with lavender, the dried flowers and leaves make the most aromatic potpourri imaginable. The tenderest leaves can be chopped up in salad dressings, fruit salads, or left whole as a garnish for chilled drinks.

⌘ **Mint** (spearmint, pineapple mint, chocolate mint, peppermint)—a hot mint tea is good for colds, fever, indigestion, and stomach upset. Chilled tea made from dried leaves makes a great foot soak and face spray for a hot day. Fresh mint leaves can be mixed with fruit salad for a tasty twist. Add spearmint leaves to just about any kind of grain/legume salad (tabouli, couscous, or lentil); blend with cucumbers and yogurt for a classic *raita* dip.

⌘ **Thyme** is a member of the mint family with over one hundred varieties. Honey from bees that feed on thyme flower nectar is a gourmet delight. Yet interestingly enough, insects are repelled by thyme. Make a cup of thyme tea, put it in a plant mister, and spray around doorways and windows in summer to repel insects. Thyme strengthens the immune system, so when feeling a cold coming on, make a tea from the dried or fresh leaves. The fresh or dried leaves, as well as flower tops, work well to flavor soups, stews, baked or sautéed vegetables and are especially tasty when paired with olives.

⌘ **Rosemary**— the aroma from the growing plant increases brain alertness and counteracts depression and sadness. Its volatile oils are antimicrobial/antiseptic: put fresh sprigs in bath or foot soak for detoxification and to reduce swelling; make tea out of dried leaves for mouthwash to kill bad breath. Boil a handful of rosemary in two cups of water for ten minutes to yield an antiseptic solution for washing bathroom fixtures. Lay sprigs among linens. Scatter the stems on a barbecue to discourage insects. Add minced rosemary to breads and muffin dough; sprinkle on roasted potatoes or mix with butter for a tasty spread for roasted or steamed vegetables.

⌘ **Lavender** is a member of the mint family and is useful for easing stress and calming agitation; it is antimicrobial and antiseptic. Make a sachet of dried flowers to drop into the bath or to tie up in a mesh bag for a lingerie drawer sachet. Put the fresh or dried leaves into a mesh bag and place under your pillow for a calming and restful night's sleep. The weight of your head as it shifts during sleep will release the lavender's aroma. Mix the fresh flowers into honey and butter for lovely spreads to put on toast and scones. Mix into vanilla ice cream and cake batters.

⌘ **Sage** takes its name from the Latin *salvare* (to cure); there is no part of this plant that cannot be used. The leaves, flowers, and stems all have healing attributes. Use fresh sage for the most efficacy, and make into an infusion. Dab on insect bites, gargle for sore throats and mucus build up, or drink as a tea for respiratory congestion. Because sage has a powerful antiseptic effect, combine a tablespoon of strong sage tea with your toothpaste to help remove plaque and tone the gums. As a mainstay savory herb, add fresh or dried sage to bean and potato dishes, as well as gratins, casseroles, and pastas.

⌘ **German Chamomile** is a member of the sunflower family and has powerful flavonoids which affect the nervous system. Make a tea out of fresh or dried flowers for upset stomach, stress, or insomnia. Chamomile also has an effect on the immune system and helps fight off colds and infections. Cold chamomile tea is a great eyewash for tired and red eyes. A chamomile flower bath is great for relieving skin irritations. Wash your face with unsweetened chamomile tea to treat acne or bee stings.

⌘ ***Basil, oregano, lemon balm, garlic, and fennel*** are also easily grown and extremely beneficial herbs to have around for multiple uses (read through the food and nutrition sections for ideas).

## Drying and Storage of Herbs

Dried herbs are important to have on hand when you want them out of season and for cooking when using fresh herbs is a waste of their delicate flavoring properties.

An easy short-cut to drying herbs makes use of the oven as the genius tool at hand. Line a cookie sheet with parchment baking paper. (Do not use wax paper as the wax will melt and smoke and ruin the process). Spread out the herbs in a thin layer on the paper. Set the oven temperature to 110° F. Keep the oven door open a bit if your lowest temperature doesn't go down to 110° F. Don't use a fan (convection) oven. Delicate, leafy herbs will only take about an hour to dry, while sturdier ones a little longer. Check periodically and when they are easily crushed in your fingers, they are ready.

To retain the flavor and fragrance of dried herbs, store them in dark glass or pottery containers with tight fitting lids so the oils will not escape. Try to fill the jar all the way to the top so there is very little air remaining. If the jar is clear glass, then store in a dark cabinet away from light. Never store in a plastic container, as the plastics will leach into the herbs. Most herbs will have a shelf life of six months, when dried, but check them from time to time by smelling and observing their color to make sure they haven't gone bad.

## Media Fast

I love this quote from Paul Hawken:

> *Ralph Waldo Emerson once asked what we would do*
> *if the stars only came out once every thousand years.*
> *No one would sleep that night, of course.*
> *The world would become religious overnight.*
> *We would be ecstatic, delirious, made rapturous by the glory of God.*
> *Instead the stars come out every night, and we watch television.*

In our current era of on-demand media we seldom question the effect of its constant presence in our lives. Tablet computers, e-readers, television, and smartphones are all part of most people's everyday experiences. They enable us to stay informed while sometimes taking us on amazing journeys. But the content and experiences that these outlets offer also consume space in our minds that can have a profound effect on our emotional state and can impact our relationships, job performance, and creativity. Additionally, our ability to truly know ourselves from an authentic place must first traverse this barrier of information, noise, and chatter.

A media fast involves temporarily disconnecting from all personal computing devices, electronic toys and games, television, newspapers or magazines, e-mails, or even talking on the phone. Much like a food fast can help clear out and clean out a sluggish body, leaving it feeling refreshed and lighter, so can a media fast clear out our heads and hearts. As a seasonal spring ritual this is an excellent way to hit the personal reset button on your psyche and perhaps come to some very enlightening, if not profound insights. Done together with your whole family, it will be remarkable and could fundamentally change the way you communicate with one another

On the simplest level, undertaking this fast will free up thinking space. It will reconnect you to a different kind of cognitive awareness. Rumination and reflection have the effect of lowering blood pressure and heart rate. This physiological reaction may even introduce you to creative aspects of yourself that you didn't know existed, as you enjoy some quiet time and reconnect with other interests. Ideas will present themselves to you more readily and you will find yourself available to revel in the small joys of your own life. You also will be freer to live in the present moment, which is the foundation of a more authentic existence.

# Chapter 7

## Spring in Your Community and World

. . . . . . . . . . . . . . . . . . .

**M**uch of our discussion on this season has stemmed from ideas relating to inspired transformation (inside and out) so that we can determine with spirit how we want to live. Continuing our efforts to get out and about and really appreciate spring by interacting with it is best borne out by walking. An eye-opening way to interact with your immediate geography, as well as interact with members of your community, is to avail yourself of urban foraging workshops.

### Foraging as Community Building

I was recently led on a foraging expedition in my neighborhood about fifteen minutes from downtown Los Angeles. We collected lamb's quarters, wild radish, chickweed, and hedge mustard, which our class turned into a salad. We were shown how to mix the flower heads of wild buckwheat with wheat flour to make biscuits. Our teacher pointed out several carob trees which are very plentiful in the Southern California eco-system. She noted that it was the perfect survival food: rich in calcium and B vitamins, it tastes good, you don't have to cook it, and it lasts for years. Her overarching point is that wild foods are some of the most nutritious: dandelion has more beta carotene than carrots, purslane is the richest plant source of omega-3 fatty acids, curly dock has more vitamin A than most grocery store sources, and lamb's quarter, a spinach relative, is common in most urban areas and is nature's best mineral tablet.

Perhaps you won't ever need to use your food foraging skills to actually survive, but you will have met like-minded people who deeply appreciate what nature has to offer them in even the most urban of settings. And this can only lead to further appreciation of how to create habits that preserve our natural landscapes and wild places together, as a community. Springtime is the perfect place for beginning this journey.

### Earth Day Metrics

It's quite hard to believe, but since its founding in 1970, Earth Day (April 22) is now celebrated in over 175 countries and is the third-largest celebrated holiday in many of our nation's schools. The level of grassroots organizing for the last forty-five years around the day has been a major accomplishment. The official Earth Day website (www.earthday.org) is an unsurpassed resource for activities, art and culture projects, sporting events, contests, and more to promote and encourage any kind of participation from all quarters.

In anticipation, I'd like to point you to the Personal Footprint quiz devised to help you put into perspective just what your own, individual impact actually is on the Earth (http://www.earthday.org/footprint-calculator). Answering detailed questions about your lifestyle—the kinds of food you eat, how often you buy clothing, what your media consumption is, what modes of transportation you take—you will see how many planet Earths it would take to support your lifestyle if *everyone* on the planet shared your lifestyle. It's sobering.

In simple, visual calculations, the truth of our American way of life is illustrated. Its unsettling reality is mitigated by suggestions on how to lower your impact in immediate, short-term ways, alongside strategies for longer-term actions. It's no accident that Earth Day is situated in the spring. It offers the bounty of the season with the energy of starting anew. Our lives are illuminated and transformed by what we choose to do each day. Now is the time to start that process.

*But now I have spoken of that great sea,*
*the ocean of longing shifts through me,*
*the blessed inner star of navigation*
*moves in the dark sky above*
*and I am ready like the young salmon,*
*to leave his river, blessed with hunger,*
*for a great journey on the drawing tide.*

**David Whyte**

## Summer

**Element:** Water

**Human Aspect:** Emotion

**Key Words:** Quicken, Expand, Flourish

**Season of Life:** Children/Teenagers

**World/Kingdom:** Plant

**Energy:** Give

**Bodily Manifestation:** Laughter/Tears

**Time of Day:** Noon

**Heavenly Body:** Moon

**Earthly Manifestations:** Oceans, Lakes, Rivers

**Animal Totems:** Whale, Dolphin

**Human Manifestation:** Music, Singing, Poetry

**Self-expression:** Abundance, Joy, Generosity, Spontaneity, Imagination

# Chapter 8

## Themes of the Summer Season: Quicken, Expand, Flourish

. . . . . . . . . . . . . . . . . . .

The Medicine Wheel turns us to the summer solstice, June 21, the longest day and shortest night of the year. There is expansiveness in the world outside, as well as inside our psyches. Summer is about high fruitfulness—abundance, rapid growth, open-heartedness, peak energy, outdoor play, generosity, spontaneity, and emotional sensitivity. As summer unfolds, we luxuriate in the long days and are reminded of the abundance of nature in full bloom. The plant kingdom and all its magical, life giving, healing gifts is honored in the south on the Wheel. The plethora of gifts the plant world provides inspires the understanding of how to use the energy of giving, especially giving unconditionally, with our emotions. In summer, we see nature's accelerated growth and our own experiences are also ones of growth and high energy. The Wheel also counsels us to allow childlike wonder to come out and play. There is a natural summertime pull to spend time communing with water (lakes, oceans, and rivers); after all, water is the element of this direction and season. Water symbolizes the fluidity of emotional accessibility and of our ability to flow easily through emotional states of being. This season emphasizes our emotional life, music, and laughter and embracing the child within—all around us energy is moving.

## ⌘ Stories and Rituals to Turn the Wheel

### Yemaya: The Mother of the Waters

The Yoruba in West Africa call her Yemaya, the Mother of the Waters. She is the goddess of the living ocean, the moon, and the rivers whose healing powers are carried in the great waters to which she gave birth. New springs appeared when she turned over in her sleep and others gushed forth and turned into rivers wherever she walked. She is most often depicted as a mermaid or simply a beautiful woman standing amidst the waves.

As all life is thought to have begun in the sea, all life is held to have begun with Yemaya. She is motherly and strongly protective, and cares deeply for all her children, comforting them and cleansing them of sorrow. She is said to be able to cure infertility in women. To the Yoruban people, Yemaya was everything that sustained them, especially during the diaspora which brought them to the New World on the slave ships. As a consequence, Yemaya is now worshipped in many cultures besides her original Africa. In Brazil she is known as Yemanja or Imanje. She is the Sea Mother who brings fish to the fishermen and is honored as the ocean goddess at the time of the summer solstice.

### The Summer Solstice: Child's Play and Sunlight Forever

The summer solstice is when the Earth is tilted at its maximum toward the sun, which creates (in the Northern Hemisphere) our long days and short nights. Sol + stice derives from a combination of Latin words meaning "sun" + "to stand still. " As the days lengthen, the sun rises higher and higher until it seems to stand still in the sky. With the benediction of these endless summer days, we give ourselves over to the urge to baptize ourselves with a full immersion into cool, deep water. Our yearly migration to the seashore, the lakeshore, and to the running rivers begins.

We do love the summer release from school and work from the time we are small children. We associate the summers with vacations and camp experiences, road trips and family reunions, and long hours of lazy idle, usually involving some kind of body of water.

I was born in the summer in a seaside city in southern Texas; it's probably imprinted in my DNA that I station myself near water during summertime. Though our Gulf of Mexico water was always a bit lukewarm and a little on the muddy side, when compared with the cold, blue-green water of the West Coast that I now enjoy, it was still a big expanse stretching out mysteriously from the sandy white dunes. It evoked the urge to stand at the edge and stare out in wonder at the distance and depth of it, one of the main reasons for beach-going in my opinion.

Another feature of the geography of Texas is the watershed arrangement of long and meandering rivers that all flow south to empty out into this same gulf. These rivers have been dammed over the decades to manage the waters for flood control and provide drinking water and recreation and as such, Texas is populated with a lot of lakes. It makes it fairly easy to fulfill the common imperative in the blistering hot Texas summers to seek out a body of water in which to park oneself for the duration. One of the finest is to recline in the middle of a large inner tube and spend as much time as possible floating down a creek or river or bobbing on top of a placid lake. This is an excellent position to be in for ruminating on the meaning of life. In fact, I do not wonder at the origins of the full-body immersion baptisms of the Southern Christian born-again traditions. The blessings of God seem more apparent when standing outside in cool waist-high water than sitting inside a sweltering hot building.

The healing power of the water calls to all of us. It stands as a powerful metaphor that can cleanse, soothe, and slake the thirst from soul sickness. We still need to draw sustenance, beauty, and bounty from of our planet's waters, just as our ancestors did, so we must continue to honor the waters' beneficence. There is an imperative in learning how to negotiate the ebbs and flows of life with openheartedness, playfulness, and joy. Yemaya is truly the symbol of getting in and going with the flow.

### Twisted Crystals and the Piezo Effect

A fantastic advantage to living in Los Angeles is the ability to hop on a boat and partake in whale watching (one of the Wheel's summer animal totems) as the creatures make their yearly migrations to and from their summer feeding spots near Alaska and their winter breeding waters in Mexico. We get the best sightings from January to March. One trip I made with my extended family unfortunately resulted in a rare day of seeing no whales. After enduring a couple hours with endless commentary from the tour guides listing all the interesting facts about the whales we were not seeing, we took to staring into the middle distance of the ocean. We began excitedly pointing and exclaiming about an imaginary no-whale—a play on the narwhal, the whales with single tusks who live full time in the Arctic.

On our uneventful return ride, I told my daughter what I could remember of the Inuit myth about how the long, strange tusk on the narwhal, a cousin to the beluga, came to be. It seems a young girl hunting with a harpoon rope tied around her waist, was dragged into the ocean after the harpoon had struck a large narwhal. In the sea she was transformed into a narwhal herself and her hair, which was tied in a long, twisted knot, transformed into the horn. From then on, the narwhal tusks were bestowed with magical powers and became more valuable than gold.

The summer after our no-whale/narwhal expedition, I ran across a story about a project to uncover the mystery of the narwhal's tusk, which is actually a tooth growing out of its upper jaw. Its average size is nine *feet* long, making it the most extraordinary and unique tooth in nature, defying evolution and modern day explanation. The study concluded that the tooth is a sensor of some kind, used for detecting sound, temperature, or salinity of the water.

It was also speculated that there is a voltage potential across the tooth, since most bones and teeth (including those in humans) have what is known as a *piezo* effect: they contain crystals that generate a voltage when a mechanical force is applied to them. So when a twisted crystal like the narwhal's tooth is moving with a tremendous force through water, there's probably some kind of voltage across it. The narwhal would use this electrical charge to scan the water and detect its prey. This makes the tooth one of the most sensitive receivers in the animal kingdom.

### Emotional Clarity

Like a narwhal's tooth, or a crystal radio set, we too, have the ability to tune in to and increase our sensitivity to much more than we usually do on a regular basis. Understanding ourselves on an emotional level and gaining insight from that place, is the focus of the south and summer on the Medicine Wheel. Becoming sensitive might first begin with identifying our emotions and what we perceive as our emotional condition. We can use a variety of methods and tools to find these frequencies and gather the emotional wavelengths of ourselves for a clearer picture of our state of being. The most accessible is to simply sit in silence and meditate with an open mind, setting the intention for how we are really feeling to be revealed to us. This takes practice as often our true feelings are mixed up with other emotional clutter, imposed on us both from within ourselves as well as from outside forces.

Emotional sensitivity is a loaded concept to many people. It equates "overly emotional" with "unmoored or hysterical," especially if one is being sexist or misogynistic. In this regard, our culture has a message that relying too much on our emotions is a bad thing. Instead, rational thinking emanating from logic and reason is held out as the best way to operate, to understand ourselves and others. Emotions often get short shrift in this scenario, misplaced, stuffed down, ignored, or denied. Yet accepting your feelings is human and necessary and a way to deeply connect to Spirit.

What's important to discern is if hurt, anger, despair, and other negative emotions are generated by holding in or receiving with only the emotions (i.e. "holding onto anger" or taking in and receiving another's jealousy or fear). Assessing a situation with only the emotions *is* actually out of balance, as conveyed through the teachings of the Wheel. It should be done instead with Spirit (your Higher Self). Understanding the context of your emotions and receiving all pertinent information with an open mind before taking a course of action or solving a problem, is holistic balance. This will yield clearer, more precise outcomes because the emotion you are expressing is cleaner, more tuned in.

When you have tuned in sensitively, as with the narwhal's crystal tooth, then you can freely give with the best and most positive of your emotions. Unconditional expression of emotions, such as love, compassion, joy, generosity, and happiness means we don't expect anything in return. When this happens you will be creating the energy of unconditional love all around you. This is the purest expression of bliss and happiness there is. Imagine how this impacts your relationship to others, to those you love, those with whom you work, and even strangers on the street.

This imagining is the bedrock nature of a child and it is the true self-expression of trust and innocence. The place of the child on the Wheel is here in the summer. Although we can't be children again, we can still embrace the child within. We can embody the joy of being emotionally sensitive, with humans and non-humans alike, with all of nature, which teaches us how to give unconditionally and which this season symbolizes for us.

### Drinking in the Joy

One summer not long ago, I was in my backyard watering a row of sunflowers I had planted against a side fence. It was at the end of a hot day and I enjoyed the pleasure of getting slightly splashed at the same time; the cool water felt good against my dusty toes. I pushed my thumb against the hose opening to create an arcing spray that reached out in front of me by ten or fifteen feet. My mind drifted as I enjoyed playing with the water; the last rays of the sun caused it to sparkle if I angled it just so.

Slowly I became aware of a red-throated, male hummingbird swooping through the ends of the water spray. He'd fly through, disappear, and a few seconds later, reappear, and repeat the process. To the Native Americans the hummingbird is Joy, so I received my visitor as a welcome gift. Delighted, I held the stream as steady as I could, held my breath, and stood very still.

In a split second, at the same moment I vaguely remember thinking that he was getting a little too close to the water, it caught him just so and slammed him to the ground. I dropped the hose in a panic and ran to find him. He was lying soaked on the grass, with his eyes open, barely breathing, in a state of drowning. I hesitated for a moment, unsure about what to do. It seemed as though I had drowned my Joy.

Without thinking it through, I gently scooped the wee bird up in my hands and made a covered tent out of my palms. He was utterly still. I held him close to my mouth, whispered to him not to die, and began slowly exhaling hot breath on him. I don't know for how long I did this, maybe a minute, maybe two. I had never performed mouth to mouth resuscitation on a human before, much less simulated on a tiny bird. His little chest eventually fluttered and heaved and he blinked several times.

Hummingbird Joy then rolled over and seemed to be steadying himself on my open hand. After a few nerve-wracked moments, he flew away, but not before cocking his head and looking at me square in the eyes with his own small black buttons. I watched him fly up to the top of a nearby orange tree. He chittered for a bit and then buzzed off.

I picked up the still running hose and turned it off. My feet were soggy, my heart pounding in my chest. I was overjoyed at being able to rescue the hummingbird. I marveled at how such a precise flyer can mistake distance and space and be seduced by water to such ill effect. I bowed to the spirit of the bird that allowed him to surrender and let himself be saved (by a hot-breathed giant no less), and to his innate impulse to get up and fly again. Joy comes, joy falters, joy abides.

Joy contains the essence of possibility. Summer feels abundant with possibility.

# THE POSSIBILITIES RITUAL

Sunflowers are the quintessential plant of summertime. Sunflowers turn their heads to follow the path of the sun as it passes over them. When the sunflower nods, it will rain, according to an old gardener's adage. Cucumbers are sweeter when planted next to sunflowers. Bees enjoy the pollen and birds, especially crows and red-winged blackbirds, love the seeds.

Sunflowers have long been associated with creating a relaxed, comfortable happiness – the same sort you feel on a warm, sunny day. They combat depression or grief and protect from the negative. Following is a simple, yet profound ritual for illustrating the power of possibility that summer seems to radiate.

On your table or altar put a vase with several freshly-cut or picked sunflowers. Lay a small, fancy white cloth on the table. On top of the cloth, put a small decorative bowl and fourteen sunflower seeds. Light a yellow candle. Put seven of the seeds into the bowl and hold in your mind seven ideas for yourself that have to do with possibility and growth. (Seven is the traditional number for good fortune and high spiritual vibration.)

Put the second group of seven seeds into the bowl and hold in your mind seven ways you can begin today to implement those ideas for possibility and growth. (Write all of this down in a notebook to refer to for the future.)

While focusing on your candle flame, repeat this mantra seven times:

**Sanskrit:** Om Brm Brhaspataye Namah

**Pronunciation:** Om Berm Ber-has-pa-ta-yay Na-ma-ha

**Translation:** I honor the energy of generosity and connection

This is a mantra for expansion and possibility. Expansion comes as a result of feeling the generosity of the universe as well as from other people, of feeling connected to your community and to the world at large. As you begin to take in the sounds and energy from this mantra, a field of infinite possibilities will arise from within and expand exponentially, much like the ripple effect of a stone dropping on water. This mantra bestows the blessing of being able to see the highest truth and envision the highest outcome in all situations.

Make a bath immediately following and float the petals from one of your sunflowers in the water. Shake in seven drops of tarragon and seven drops of geranium essential oils. Both of these essential oils support expansion, emotional uplift, and open-hearted energy.

Within the next twenty-four hours, plant all fourteen of your sunflower seeds. (This can be anywhere outside, even if you don't have a yard yourself. A neighborhood park, a grassy median near your street, a friend's yard – literally anywhere outside will do.) In an area that gets strong sunlight for most of the day, push the seeds down about an inch into the dirt, making sure they are well covered with soil. Water lightly every other day and you should see the seeds beginning to sprout in about ten days. Keep well weeded and when the flowers reach about three-feet high, consider staking them.

# Chapter 9

## Essential Summer Health Practices

· · · · · · · · · · · · · · · · · · ·

I n summer, we can use two elements in abundance—plants and water—to assist our emotional renewal and accelerate our energy flow.

### Emotional Rescue with Bach Flower Remedies

Similar to a plant-based homeopathic distillation, the Bach Flower Remedies were developed in the 1930s by Dr. Edward Bach, a British bacteriologist, pathologist and homeopath. You may be most familiar with the best known formula, Rescue Remedy, an all-purpose solution for treating anxiety and stress. The idea of plant healing is not new or recent. What is striking about Dr. Bach's approach is his recognition of the spiritual energy between plants and humans as the key to unlocking emotional trauma.

I had the good fortune some years ago to meet Alexis Smart, a Bach Flower Remedies expert who uses the remedies to help people find their way toward a path of healing and health for everything from chronic illnesses to smoking cessation. She is a remarkable and intuitive healer and has shared her experience and wisdom in the context of a conversation we had for this book, as it involves the divine energy of plants, one of the guiding forces of this summer season.

**Question (Randi):** Because in herbal medicine, all parts of the plant are used—from the roots to stems, twigs and leaves, as well as flower—how did Bach arrive at the flower as the only part of the plant he was interested in using?

**Answer (Alexis):** He felt that the flowering part of the plant is the spiritual nature of the plant, it's where the life force of the plant is. A plant has to be at its peak in order for it to flower.

Although Bach was a practicing M.D., he was always connected to nature. And he believed in treating the whole person, not just the symptoms. He also wanted to find a system where people could heal themselves, since that is the ultimate goal in self-empowerment and the reason why so many people are ill; their mind-body connection has been lost.

**Q:** Can you explain how you think the remedies work?

**A:** The closest thing I can think of is in musical terms. When a note is played it has a measurable vibrational frequency that appears as a sound wave. In the same way, all living things give off a vibrational frequency. The remedies are also vibrational, they are operating on a frequency level—not like a crude substance that works on our physiology, our brain chemistry, or liver tissues. They are working on a spiritual level. So each plant has a different frequency. And every emotional state has a frequency.

**Q:** How do you convey the special nature of these remedies to anyone who's interested in working with them?

**A:** It's mostly about letting people discover that for themselves. Almost to a person, my clients will all tell me they feel a renewed connection to nature after being on the remedies. They report having been in communion with trees and plants. They suddenly feel the overwhelming benevolence of nature and this is coming from people who are the least likely to say things like that, believe me!

**Q:** Is it possible for someone to replicate this experience for themselves at home and work with the remedies on their own?

**A:** Dr. Bach made the remedies the way he did because he wanted people to have the means to heal themselves and their loved ones. They're really simple and easy to understand. All you need to do to figure out what you need is spend a quiet moment thinking about how you feel. Check in with yourself. I find writing longhand is a really good way to find out what you need help with. I tell people to write down three wishes and focus on them. Or write down predominant character traits about yourself; describe what kind of person you are. The way the human body manifests its symptoms is very telling of the personality behind it.

**Q:** Can anyone make a remedy at home by themselves?

**A:** Yes. You can go online and read about the thirty-eight remedies Bach created. Choose three remedies. Fill a 1 ounce dropper bottle 3/4 full with spring water, add four drops of each essence, and top it off with brandy or apple cider vinegar to preserve. Shake gently and then take four drops of this mixture four times a day.

**Q:** It strikes me that this is a very great way to come into a wonderful communion with yourself. A nice ritual to get quiet and check in and address any outstanding issues—even if you are not in crisis and don't particularly need a life raft, but simply are just looking for a good habit to practice as preventive wellness care.

**A:** Exactly. Dr. Bach felt that the first step on the path to good health and a large part of healing was self-awareness. We all think that to make something better about our lives,we need to change something that's outside of ourselves, but once your internal state changes, then your external conditions will reflect it. I think the flower remedies, instead of adding things in,and piling more things on, help a person remove all the obstacles to being who they are meant to be, what they're waiting to become.

**Q:** How do you address skeptics of this system?

**A:** I can only point to clinical evidence I've seen. If it's a placebo effect, then why does it work on babies, who don't have the ability to psychologically affect their health in the way that adults do? Or dogs? They respond to the remedies. I heal lots of pets, cats and dogs. This medicine is ahead of its time, in the way homeopathy is. It's in a class of medicine that relates to quantum energy. The usual methods of testing the veracity of the remedies are old-school, mechanistic, and not holistic. They test parts,and don't ever look at the whole. They see people as parts, and they are only looking to treat symptoms and not the cause of the symptoms. Holistic healing looks at everything.

### The Ritual Bath for Wellbeing and the Ephemeral Moment

Water is our continuing theme this season and there is no better expression of the water experience than the ritual of taking a bath. As the centerpiece of spa culture around the world for hundreds of years the healing bath has come to signify everything there is to know about the potential of curative waters. For eons before spa culture, the bath was inherent in every culture as the ritual for celebrating our human connection to water, the source of all creation.

And no one does the bathing ritual better than the Japanese. In their seminal book, *The Japanese Bath*, Bruce Smith and Yahiko Yamamoto explain that in the west, a bath is a place where one goes to cleanse the body; in Japan, it is where one goes to cleanse the soul, to be contemplative, and feel a part of nature's rhythms at the end of the day. This time and attention to the bath is equivalent to the time and care one takes with the preparation and cooking of a meal, something we Americans seem to slight in our speeded-up lives. The Japanese make bathing a ritual—a prescribed order of rinsing, washing, and soaking that is passed down from one generation to the next.

The advantage of saving your bath for the end of the day is that it acts as a transition between work and leisure, between public and private time. Typically, in Japanese family life, schoolchildren and working people come home and take their baths fairly soon and only then sit down to eat dinner. It's a wonderful chance for family members to relax together, spend time chatting about their days, and enjoy being close to one another.

This is the tradition of Japanese bathing—time spent soaking, sharing, cleansing, relaxing, separately or together—realizing, as with almost any kind of task, effort, or ritual we undertake with care and mindfulness that this is not just about bathing; it is about the very way we want to lead our lives.

*The Japanese Bath* illuminates the use and meaning of the phrase "ephemeral moment" throughout the book. It refers to the fragility of the moment, when one is aware of the passing of time in a brief instant. This usually occurs in a moment when one is happy and satisfied for no particular reason, except in gratitude of being alive and enjoying the beauty of the moment. To be fully alive is to recognize the value and rarity of the ephemeral moment; the ritual bath seeks to capture it within the context of its aesthetics.

The essential components of the ritual bath help cultivate the ephemeral moment:

⌘ *Sounds* perfectly express this as they come and go in an instant. Wind chimes, gurgling water, insects chirping (music made by insects) are essential components of the Japanese bathing ritual. Listening to crickets in small bamboo cages was traditionally an aesthetic activity in ancient Japan.

⌘ *A ground level garden*, seen from the height one experiences while in the bath, connects one to the aesthetic of nature. The bath is designed with some glass walls, large windows, or the ability to access an outside view in some way (i.e. sliding doors).

⌘ *Lighting* with soft lanterns in specific shapes and sizes is traditional. The garden is lighted so that the world is seen from the inside of the bath.

⌘ A natural mix of *textures* is common, such as bamboo, wood (particularly cedar for its aroma), and stone. These reflect the textures found in nature and serve to provoke a more sensory-based experience.

## A ROOM (ZEN SPA SANCTUARY) OF ONE'S OWN

Perhaps you have the means to create your own version of a precisely-styled Japanese bathing space. But even if you don't or if the Japanese aesthetic is just not for you, it's still important to develop a relationship to your own bathing ritual and to consciously create your spa sanctuary at home.

This effort, formed out of any kind of space, however humble, is to trigger "spa vibes" every time you engage with your bathing space. These vibes elicit a feeling of retreat from the world, that you are in a protected place of relief and relaxation when you can finally shut the door and have some alone time to recharge and regroup—nourishment for your body *and* soul. It's about how you *represent* a spa, how you make your bathroom *feel*. Large sums of money don't have to be involved, just some considered thought.

**Conscious color**: Consider blues, greens, lilacs (cool colors promote calmness and serenity) and avoid hot colors (bright yellow, orange, red); however, if you love these colors, then temper them with their cool opposite on the color wheel. Color affects mood. It's no coincidence that spas around the world are enveloped in white, the essence of Zen cool. The white color palette need not be boring—it has a huge range of undertones, from blue to yellow to pink—which give interest and depth.

**Lighting**: Natural light (from skylights and windows) is best, but for privacy purposes use white or natural color fabric coverings on the windows. Choose lighting fixtures that are simple and throw direct light with soft CFL bulbs.

**Textures**: Use organic cottons and bamboos (include a variety of textures that you can see and touch) for mats, shower curtains, wall hangings, and window shades. Avoid anything artificial (polyester or plastic). Natural grasses and other fibers (linen, hemp, and wood) evoke a sublime spa feel.

**Linens:** (towels, robes, slippers): I like white because of its association with freshness, and again, the spa vibe, but it is notoriously hard to keep as time passes (especially with kids). My solution: put out everyday towels in darker colors. Save the nice whites for your private spa time. Try to buy the highest quality you can afford (organic cotton or bamboo fiber mixture if possible). Choose non-toxic laundry products with no artificial fragrances. Avoid dryer sheets, which are highly toxic.

**Bath soaking area**: Make it luxe. Replace broken or cracked tiles around the tub. Re-grout to have nice clean grout. Change the feel of your bath/shower area with small hits of decorative tile materials (if re-tiling). Install a shower-head filter. Just as you wouldn't drink unfiltered water, nor should you expose yourself to unfiltered water in the shower.

**Keep it clean**: Use all natural cleaning products to scour, get rid of soap scum, disinfect and clear drains. Avoid toxic cleaning chemicals at all costs.

**Clutter**: Put all the stuff you normally leave out on the counter in the medicine cabinet, a drawer, a nearby closet or collect some creative and interesting containers with lids to put it in. Let your eye and brain register counters with empty spaces when you enter the room. Room spaciousness has the effect of eliciting internal expansion in addition to just being very relaxing.

**Aromatherapy**: Set the mood. Cedar essential oil will replicate the traditional scent of Japanese baths, as cedar wood is prized for *ofuros* (soaking tubs). Avoid artificial fragrance and use only pure essential-oil candles (vegetable wax is preferable to soy which has high pesticide residues; avoid paraffin as it is a petroleum by-product). Make your own potpourri out of dried flowers and herbs to set around your bathroom in pretty ceramic bowls.

### Thallasotherapy and Seaweed Soaks

From the Greek word *thalassa* meaning *ocean*, true thalassotherapy incorporates all of the healthy marine elements by way of water exercise, ingestion of salty air, and absorbing sea minerals through the pores. Benefits touted as a result of thalassotherapy include deep relaxation, improvement with circulation and respiration, boosted immunity, sleep improvement, a reduction of inflammation, and psychological wellbeing.

Rene Quinton (1866 - 1925), also referred to as the "French Darwin," was a naturalist, physiologist and biologist. In 1904, he was the first to discern that human blood and seawater contained identical nutrient ratios. His scientific experiments obtained results that were dramatically unexpected: several people who were expected to die, did not, and recovered fully. His introduction of this theory gave birth to this form of sea-based therapy, now found all over the world in all kinds of spas and health centers.

Trace elements of the mineral composition found in sea water (magnesium, potassium, calcium and sodium) are ingested into the lungs and pores in a thalassotherapy session through mud baths, hydrotherapy (bathtub soaks), massage and body wraps. Seaweed, algae, and sea-salt are also main ingredients in the treatments, all rich in minerals and vitamins, and full of health and beauty renewing qualities.

You can create homemade versions of thalassotherapy by adding seaweed (dulse and kelp are the best for this purpose) to your bath. Put a cup or two of dried seaweed in a muslin drawstring bag and steep for five to ten minutes in a pot of boiling water. Pour the seaweed tea (along with the muslin bag) into your hot bath. Add a handful of Dead Sea salts and soak away.

As you soak, a slight gel or film from the seaweed will softly coat your body. Once it dissolves and you don't feel it on your skin any more, you know your bath is done and you've absorbed the seaweed's benefits (boosts thyroid functioning, soothes adrenal glands, balances hormones).

Caution: Those with high blood pressure or other health problems should consult their doctors before having a hot seaweed bath. The seaweed has a very high iodine content (⅓ cup contains more than two thousand times the RDA).

### Dead Sea Salt Healing

Cleopatra knew a good thing when she saw it. This queen of ancient beauty was legendary for her magically youthful looks throughout her life. The real secret to the beauty of her silky skin was the anti-aging effect of bath salts, mud, and cosmetics made with Dead Sea salt. It was gathered for her at the factories she had built on the shores of the nearby sea. Today, people from all over the world travel to the Dead Sea for relief from their skin ailments such as psoriasis and eczema.

Nothing like regular salt, Dead Sea salts are comprised of a wide variety of minerals which are present in a high concentration. Whereas regular sea salt is made up of over 90% sodium, salt from the Dead Sea is only about 10% sodium and the rest is made of minerals which are essential for the proper function and health of skin. The minerals present in the salt (mostly magnesium, potassium, bromine, and calcium), are also naturally present within skin cells, but commonly get depleted and can cause severe dryness, wrinkle development, and dull-looking skin.

Dead Sea salts are easily available at most health food stores and online (make sure the label mentions that they are imported from Israel). I always recommend buying the plain salts and creating your own mix of add-ins.

## HEALING WITH DEAD SEA SALTS AND ESSENTIAL OILS

**Detox:** Juniper and Cypress

**Energize:** Grapefruit and Ginger

**Calm and soothe:** Lavender and Roman chamomile

**Immune booster:** Eucalyptus and Bergamot

For every eight ounces of Dead Sea salts, mix in seven to ten drops of each essential oil to start. When you are ready to have your soak in the bathtub, throw in a palmful or two of your mixture, and keep the water just comfortably warm. Water that is extremely hot will cause your body to start sweating and purging in reaction to the heat, and while this is a good thing under other circumstances, in the case of working with the salts, you want the body to do the reverse and absorb, rather than release. Give yourself a good twenty minutes at least, longer if possible, to allow your body to fully absorb the salts and the essential oils.

A quickie version of a whole body bath, is to just soak your feet. The feet are wide open portals for the action of the salts and oils to enter into your circulatory system. After a long, stressful day, nothing is more relaxing than a good foot soak in a pretty bowl. Make sure the water level is at least up to your ankle bone. Drop a few flower petals or fresh herbs such as rosemary or spearmint into the bowl for an extra connection to nature's beauty and healing.

## ⌘ Yoga, Meditation, and Breath Exercises for Summer

Summer, with its key word—quicken, gives us the ability to regard our bodies as we would if we were growing children: full of boundless energy, gaining muscle strength and stamina for the long days of outdoor play and activity. Core strengthening is done as a prelude to support the skill sets needed for all poses this season. The poses that follow are a Warrior pose (great for toning legs that gain additional exposure in summer), hip openers (a class of poses which cultivate emotional accessibility) and back bends which open up the heart (our emotional center) while releasing fear. All are key efforts in our season of accelerating possibility, joy, and enthusiasm.

### Core Strengthening of the Solar Plexus and Manipura

Your core space holds the solar plexus, the seat of the third chakra, which is developed during late childhood and puberty. *Manipura*, or lustrous gem as this chakra is called, represents our ego and the outward manifestation of personality, self-esteem, and personal power. How you express yourself to the outside world comes through this chakra. Becoming aware of and strengthening your core connects you directly to all the warmth and charismatic happiness which we are nurturing during this summer season.

The core is vital in creating protection and support for the low back to avoid injury, but it also provides the fulcrum point with which your body can balance itself and perform better in any kind of activity from swinging a golf club to doing the Lindy hop in swing dance class. Knowing where your center is and how to activate it provides for better understanding of your basic physiology. It allows you to grasp the psychological impact of where your body is in relation to space and gravity. This is especially critical for exploring balancing poses, as well as inversions.

The actual, physical place of the core area is at your natural waistline and encircles your body like an energetic cummerbund or corset. Core muscles also support strong breath energy for speaking and singing.

Tips for core strengthening:

⌘ Good old fashioned sit-ups are excellent. Make sure you put your feet flat on the floor and bend your knees to avoid back strain. Clasp your hands behind your head and avoid jerking the neck up. Make a "V" shape with your elbows out to side of your ears as you widen the space between the shoulder blades. Let your head rest easily in the basket of your hands. Feel your core muscles doing all the lifting instead of your head and neck.

⌘ These poses (p. 106) are both versions of *Navasana* ("boat pose"). Keep your spine lifted and straight. Pull the chest up and out as you relax the shoulders. Keep your breathing strong and steady through the nose. Hold for as long as you can then start setting timed goals as you progress.

### Warrior Pose (Virabhadrasana II) for Strength and Stamina

This *asana* employs the words *Vira* (hero) and *Bhadra* (friend) to invoke the concept of a spiritual warrior who bravely does battle with the universal enemy of self-ignorance. Strength, courage, and stamina are needed in any battle, so considering the meaning of the word *warrior* and finding your own version within yourself are important when performing a Warrior pose.

Every style of fitness and dance employs lunges as a way to strengthen and tone the legs and buttocks. Yoga is no different; only you get the added bonus of back and arm work in this mix. Lunges also require skillful balancing to hold the proper distribution of weight throughout the body.

Additionally, while the legs and buttocks are blazing full of energy and hardcore muscle tightening, the upper back, shoulders, and arms need to stay relatively relaxed in their uplifted or outstretched positions. Core awareness also helps the body to become centered, grounded, and thus, more in balance.

Tips for Practice:

⌘ Rotate the hips strongly away from one another. Press one hand against the hip attached to the back leg, to help feel how it can open and pull away from the front hip.

- ⌘ Push your back shoulder out over the back hip and knee as you pull your front shoulder and shoulder blade in toward the spine. Also pull your front waist in toward the spine. These adjustments will more properly line up your torso over your hips.

- ⌘ Strive to hold a 90 degree angle in the front knee. Visually line up the knee over the ankle.

- ⌘ Drop the shoulders and relax the space between the blades as you let energy travel lightly out toward the fingertips.

- ⌘ Lift your head and ears away from the shoulders to help lengthen the neck.

- ⌘ Feel your feet holding and grounding into the floor as the crown of the head floats up.

### King Pigeon (Eka Pada Rajakapotasana): Surrender and Bloom

Recall when you've seen time-lapse photography of flowers blooming. The opening is tentative at first, then the surge of energy coursing through the bud causes it to burst forth, the petals unfurling one after the other in critical mass until the very center of the flower is exposed and pushing up toward the light. To me, this is the journey of the body, mind, and spirit in pigeon pose.

Pigeon is one of the best yoga postures in which to explore the spiritual metaphor of supplication and surrender, since everything in your known universe is rebelling at this point. To fight is the default and normal reaction; to push back against the resistance of the localized muscles, the body as a whole, and your thought processes, means action is being taken on behalf of results. Action means strength, right? Not necessarily. Surrender in this pose is the pathway to victory when we abandon fighting for peace, when we gain flexibility in the midst of rigidity, when

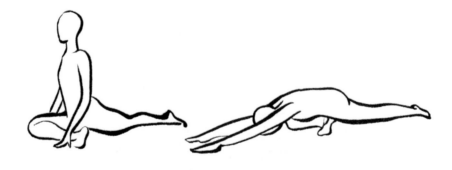

intransigence yields to suppleness. These realizations overflow in this pose and offer up a state of grace, a sublimation of ego that often leads to a great welling up of emotions. Feeling humble in the presence of something larger than oneself is always a refreshing palate cleanser.

Tips for practice:

⌘ Fold your front foot up under your opposite hip, almost as if you were going to sit on it, if you are new to this pose. Once you get used to this position then you can start moving the foot away from your body.

⌘ Slide your back foot as far away from your body as possible, but keep your leg straight and the back of the knee pointed toward the ceiling.

⌘ Try to keep your torso evenly situated with the weight distributed equally between right and left pelvis. It's common to roll onto and sit on the hip attached to the front bent leg. Avoid that by rolling the front of the thigh on the back, outstretched leg, down toward your mat.

⌘ Rest first on your elbows, which should be on the floor in front of your forward-facing shin. Traction out your spine and lengthen it away from the tailbone. Take the measure of your breath for a few cycles and then gradually drop your forehead down to the mat and stretch out your arms and hands in front of you.

⌘ Emphasize the exhales, making them long, slow, and deliberate.

⌘ Stay at least five minutes before moving to the other side.

⌘ If your back is feeling open and your hips relaxed, you can try sitting up into a straight, upright position, opening the chest and tilting your head back to gaze upward. This will put a strong arch in the low back, so proceed with caution.

### Camel Backbend (Ustrasanana): Turning Fear Into Joy

This pose is about turning fear into joy. We hold fear in our backs. We open to joy through our hearts. This pose asks you to lean backward into the support of your back so your chest can open and radiate heart-chakra energy. Because you have to let go and trust as you drop backward into a place of empty space, you are staking a huge amount of faith in your body to hold you up. The spine is achieving maximum compression in this pose, which greatly stimulates the nervous system. Because you make your heart so open (and vulnerable) in camel, this often leads to dramatic emotional displays from giggling to sobbing while in the pose.

The good news is that the work of holding your body up comes not from the back, but from the two strong legs beneath your back that are very used to holding your entire body up and getting it around all the time. The quads get a nice conditioning workout here, which also tones and lifts the buttocks. Because you have confidence in your leg strength, your mind relaxes and allows your back to relax as well, consequently opening and softening into a gentle curve reminiscent of a camel's hump—the vessel that holds all the nourishment (water) the beast will need on his long journey to the next oasis.

Tips for Practice:

⌘ If your knee caps are sensitive, practice on a rug or carpet, or roll your mat up double for padding.

⌘ Rest on your knees with your toes tucked under, heels lifted up. As you increase your skill level, let the tops of the feet rest on the floor.

⌘ Line your shoulders up over your hips, your hips over your knees. Head should be floating level on top of a long, lifted neck.

⌘ Tuck your tailbone down toward the back of your knees and suck your lower belly inward so you feel your lower spine lengthen.

⌘ Put your palms on your thighs and practice lowering your torso backward, stopping when you feel yourself starting to lose any part of your straight torso alignment. You should feel your quads (thighs) start to engage. Go back and forth a few times to get the feel of the pose's action.

⌘ Now put your palms, fingers facing up, on your low back. See if you can lift your spine up as you lower your thighs backward.

⌘ If you feel like progressing further, drop your hands back and reach fingertips toward heels. Otherwise, keep your hands in your low back and keep thrusting your chest upward. Breathe here for a count of ten.

⌘ Push the chest up and out and lift the energy of the hips and spine upward toward the shoulders as you drop them back. Keep hips over knees. Keep your chin pointed toward your chest.

⌘ Going further (if appropriate for your back), untuck toes and hold the heels with the hands. Drop the head back and let it hang loosely while the chest and upper back lift. Keep hips over knees.

### Breath Work

*Shitali Pranayama,* the Cooling Breath

Much like animals instinctively pant to cool themselves off, humans have the same ability through the *Shitali Pranayama* (Cooling Breath) exercise to achieve the same thing. Try this on a hot, humid, frustrating day when your last good nerve is worked. As with most timed-breathing exercises, part of their uncanniness at achieving results is because they divert the mind from the agitations it's holding so that it can concentrate on the counting and rhythm of the exercise in front of it. Overheated emotions are soon calmed and restored to a workable balance.

⌘ Roll the tongue into a tube (as best as you can) and stick the tip of the tongue out of the mouth.

⌘ Inhale through the tongue and hold the breath in to a slow count of five, with the chin pressed against the chest.

⌘ Exhale all air forcibly through the nose.

⌘ Repeat five to ten times.

### Sound Meditation for Chakra Healing

Music, singing, and therefore, sound is positioned in the south and summer on the Medicine Wheel, existing within the emotional body in the human aspect. Sound chanting is extremely important in the spiritual teachings of classical yoga, with its roots in both Hinduism and Buddhism, both of which have rich traditions of chanting as part of their sacred liturgies. Making sound with the human voice is emotional, elemental, and a conduit to deep joy and happiness.

There are particular sounds that are used in meditation to energize, balance, and align each of the *chakras* (energy wheels) so that they may be at their most elevated level of functioning. We already know music affects mood and emotion very profoundly. So in the same way, these sounds are considered powerful agents of transformation, as is music or any other sound which can directly or indirectly affect the *chakras.*

Sound consists of electromagnetic waves which contain energy. Recall the *piezo* effect in the narwhal whale's twisted crystal horn/tooth. Piezoelectricity is the power of pressure. For this reason, bone, tendons, enamel (the material of the narwhal's tooth and human teeth), dentin, DNA, and proteins make the human body a virtual powerhouse of piezoelectric current. Technology is already being applied to replace batteries with human electricity to power everything from smartphones to pacemakers, using motion (walking, running), *piezo* pressure, and the body's own innate rhythms.

All fifty sounds of the Sanskrit language exist within the *chakras* of the human body. There are a certain number of petals activated by sound around each chakra. Each chakra is represented by a *bija* or essential seed sound. The chakras may be metaphorically described as buds of flowers. As they open, various experiences and new awareness takes place. The path of spiritual alchemy can be accurately described as the progressive opening of the chakras, using sound to affect change on a mind/body level.

Here is the list of *chakras, bija* sounds, their locations and colors associated with each. Seeing the *chakra* color will also help you to envision a particular energy along with the sound:

**Lam** *muladhara* (earth) chakra located in the perineum area. (red)

**Vam** *swadhistana* (water) chakra located in the prostate/ovaries area. (orange)

**Ram** *manipura* (fire) chakra located above the navel. (yellow)

**Yam** *anahata* (air) chakra located around the heart. (green)

**Ham** *vishudda* (ether) chakra located in the throat. (blue)

**Om** *ajna* (third eye) chakra located in the center of the forehead between the eyes. (purple)

**Om** *Sahasrara* (beyond elements) chakra located on the crown of the head. (white)

The first five seed syllables are said with a nasal *hngh* sound ending more than a *mmm* type ending as in langh, vangh, rangh, yangh, and hangh. Om is pronounced *aum*, drawing out the "au" almost as a diphthong, or two-syllable vowel sound.

Tips for Practice:

⌘ Situate yourself in a comfortable, seated position on the floor. A meditation cushion or chair cushion or thick rug makes the best surface area under the bum.

⌘ Find the sound pitch that feels good for your range. You may opt to start at a lower one for the root *chakra* and move it up in range to the highest pitch for the crown *chakra*. You might want to keep the pitch the same for all of them. Again, it's whatever speaks most authentically to you in this moment.

⌘ Remember to go slowly and deliberately, using all the power of your breath and voice, making as large and full a sound as you possibly can. After all, you are making electricity to power up your internal grid of healthiness, happiness, and wholeness.

## ⌘ Healing Bodywork for Summer

Water as a conduit to mind-body healing and healing emotions through mind-body triggers are the focus of this season's bodywork.

### Watsu: Going with the Flow

Watsu combines the benefits of both water therapy and shiatsu massage. The therapy, which involves a focus on deep breathing while the recipient's body is moved weightlessly through warm water by the therapist, is often called *water breath dance*. Watsu was developed by Harold Dull in 1980 during his residency at Harbin Hot Springs Retreat Center in Northern California.

Watsu is administered in accordance with the same meridian map that is so vital to shiatsu massage and acupressure; however, Watsu therapy also incorporates gentle stretching in order to loosen and relax the muscles. Watsu sessions are performed in a therapeutic pool (never below 96° F) so that the therapist can support and maneuver the client into the various stretches without disrupting the relaxing and peaceful setting. The water allows the therapist to move the patient gracefully through the stretches and to apply acupressure massage to the upper body, then the lower body, while continually supporting the spine. The body experiences the anti-gravitational characteristic of water—a deeply healing and relaxing state. The warm water encourages the muscles to stay relaxed while improving circulation.

Here's how Harold Dull describes it, "Watsu interweaves movement and stillness. It has a beginning and an end. And it is endless. Its lesson in letting go into the flow whatever comes up (and a lot does come up) can be carried into your everyday life. "

When I was newly pregnant with my daughter, I led a yoga retreat to a center in Hawaii on the Big Island that offered Watsu as part of its therapeutic body care experiences. It quite unexpectedly ended up becoming one of the peak moments in my life.

For a while in my session, I was just enjoying the back and forth energy of the bodywork, of staying conscious of my breath, and the feeling of the warm water swirling around me. Those things alone would have created a magical experience. What eventually transpired for me was an intense communion with my unborn baby in a way I hadn't yet experienced. This feeling expanded outward to form a deeply emotional sense of peace and overwhelming love for not only my baby, but a feeling of "at oneness" with everyone and everything. It was both heart-opening and heart-breaking because I wanted it to last forever and ever, and yet I knew it couldn't. It was one of those ephemeral moments.

Most of the ephemeral or peak moments of our lives are born out of feelings like the ones I experienced: glorious, heart-wrenching stabs of emotional overwhelm, breathtaking understanding of connection and oneness to every living thing, and tidal waves of love and gratitude.

Peak moments can come unbidden, most cannot be willed into existence. The best we can do is to lay the groundwork for them. This includes learning how to be present as often as possible throughout daily life, releasing expectations about how something ought to be or how someone ought to behave, and staying open to possibility, grace, or Spirit. A good example of how to cultivate these moments is to observe small children. Their play *is* their work and they approach it with complete attention, happy to get lost in the experience as it unfolds, open to the wonder and awe that can arise from any situation.

### Jin Shin Do:  Awakening Emotional Meridians

This unique and fascinating mind-body therapy was developed by psychotherapist Iona Marsaa Teeguarden in 1975 in California, based on her study of healing bodywork in Japan. Recognized as a major form of Asian Bodywork Therapy, Jin Shin Do (meaning *the way of the compassionate spirit*) combines gentle, yet deep, finger pressure on acu-points with simple body focusing techniques to release physical and emotional tension. This treatment, performed on the fully-clothed client, is a synthesis of a traditional Japanese acupressure technique, classic Chinese acupuncture theory, Taoist yogic philosophy, and breathing methods.

A main distinction between Jin Shin Do and other acupressure techniques is that it relates specific emotions to specific meridian points in the body. In the basic tenants of acupuncture, the meridians are the intersections on the energy grid of the body where the needles are placed. These points correlate to organs, glands, nerves and other components of the body. When the needles interact with them, they unblock and enliven blood flow to the area, thus triggering change (healing) in those places.

Jin Shin Do is referred to as a two-hands technique, with both hands usually holding different points, one of which touches the area of the patient's pain or tension. The therapist guides the client to become aware of any feelings, emotions, or images that may arise. Specific verbal techniques facilitate the process of listening to the inner self and tapping into the unconscious mind, getting at the real cause of emotional pain and trauma that is trapped in the body and is expressed outwardly as physical pain.

As in yoga, Taoist philosophy observes that life consists of polarities (opposites). This is commonly illustrated by the yin-yang symbol. It follows, then, that our feelings are also polar in nature. As Teeguarden explains, "At its extreme, an emotion will turn into its opposite, just like night turns into day and winter into summer. Fear (related to the kidney) can be transformed into resolution and willpower or can instead become chronic and lead to a general timidity. In that case, there will also be an opposite tendency to direct the fear outward, in the form of suspicion and mistrust."

## ⌘ Plant Healing for Summer: Aromatherapy, Herbs, Teas, and Tonics

### Aromatherapy

Looking inward, enjoying emotional renewal and expansion, we also begin to fundamentally alter the *experience* of our own inner world. We heal towards the things we deeply desire (as the sunflower follows the sun passing overhead), creating a movement away from any fears and concerns we harbor which might be holding us back or repressing us. Our efforts with aromatherapy parallel those in yoga and bodywork: emotional expansion, joy, possibility, and cultivating a strong emotional heart center. There are also essential oil recommendations for soothing overwrought emotions, as well as for stimulating energy—a necessity for stamina during summer's myriad activities.

⌘ **Lavender** (*Lavandula angustifolia*) is my summertime go-to for about a thousand reasons. It is the steady hand of reason reigning in emotions when they have galloped away. It is the essence of tranquility. It is the one great all around defender, champion and tonic for all reasons and for all seasons, always bright, always helpful, always uncompromisingly proactive, practical, and helpful.

⌘ **Lemongrass** (*Cymbopogon citratus*) has a fresh, earthy, citrus scent and has an intense, radiant energy inspiring expansion on all levels. It is excellent for cleansing, banishing, inviting new things into one's life, and for creating new energy and ideas. Lemongrass lifts the spirits and helps one to move past limitation or restrictions. Most importantly, it enables the mind to shift towards fascination about what is possible; it encourages discovery, dreaming, imagining, and achievement.

⌘ **Geranium** (*Pelargonium graveolens*) is irresistible, compelling, bright, and cleansing; geranium blows your fearful thoughts away and banishes tentativeness in all forms and occurrences. It is perfect for instances when you need to be swept up and away, when you need to clear out old thinking and habits, or for when the tendency is to brood or get too negative. Geranium takes a stand for joy.

⌘ **Tarragon** (*Artemesia dracunculis*) is delightful and refreshing with its fresh, spicy scent and undertones of anise. It is excellent for repairing holes and filling voids in the psyche's energy system; not just for healing purposes, but with a view to future expansion and growth. It is very positive, very life affirming, and an excellent boost for people who don't just want to be healthy, but who are working to make their mark on the world.

By unwinding emotional blockages, tarragon helps us to draw in the energy of life that is all around us. It fosters more than just the desire for health or the will to live; it inspires us to seek and to find energy enough (and some to spare) for us to accomplish all that we desire. Note: Avoid this during pregnancy because of the thujone (a plant keytone) content.

---

## MIDSUMMER

---

In ancient Celtic mythology, Airmid was the Goddess of Herbs and Healing. She resided in the mountains of Ireland where she healed elves, faeries, and humans with her gifted insight into plant properties and herbal potions. She used practical knowledge and magic to bring health and happiness to those she touched. Midsummer, thought to be a highly charged time of magic, was Airmid's season.

# ⌘ Herbs, Teas, and Tonics

Solutions for the seasonal emphasis on strength and energy are highlighted now. Skin that takes a hit from outdoor activities, fatigue and sore muscles, and overexcitement are three common side effects of summertime on the go. The following herbs address these issues. Adding the dried version of certain herbs is a quick and easy way to travel with them.

⌘ **Licorice Root** *(Glycyrrhiza glabra)* Licorice is a perennial plant which produces pretty blue flowers. Grown mainly in Europe, it is now cultivated in many parts of the world and is used in many treatments and home remedies. Besides tasting delicious, licorice is an excellent source of iron. The roots of the plant are crushed and boiled to extract the juice. Hundreds of potentially healing substances have been identified in licorice as well, including compounds called flavonoids and various plant estrogens (phytoestrogens). The herb's key therapeutic compound, glycyrrhizin (which is fifty times sweeter than sugar), exerts numerous beneficial effects on the body, making licorice a valuable herb for treating a host of ailments.

Glycyrrhizin seems to prevent the breakdown of adrenal hormones such as cortisol (the body's primary stress-fighting adrenal hormone), making these hormones more available to the body, which is good for fatigue and adrenal exhaustion. Possibly by its action on the adrenal glands, licorice has the ability to improve resistance to stress. It should be considered for use during times of both physical and emotional stress, or when feeling tired and run down. It has an aspirin-like action and is helpful in relieving fevers and soothing pain, such as headaches.

The best method for ingesting this essential herb for summertime activity, exhaustion, and overexcitement is through teas (loose leaf or bagged) or as a liquid tincture mixed into a cup of hot or cold water.

⌘ **Witch Hazel** *(Haemamelis virginiana)* is also known as Spotted Alder or Winterbloom. There is hardly an inflamed condition internally or externally that will not respond to this herb, making it an excellent addition to a summer wellness kit on the go. In liquid astringent form it is good for all kinds of skin conditions from soothing the itch of sunburn, bug bites, and poison ivy, to wound care (scrapes, scratches, burns) and bruises. Taken as a tea or tincture mixed with water, it is good for traveler's diarrhea, dysentery, and menstrual cramps.

Native Americans have been using witch hazel water as a medical astringent for centuries, since it is actually a flowering shrub common all over North America. The leaves, bark, and twigs of witch hazel are high in tannins. Tannins are found in any natural astringent because of their ability to tighten, dry, and harden tissues that have been cut, scraped, or otherwise distressed.

⌘ **Sweet Tea Vine** (Jiaogulan) (*Gynostemma pentaphyllum*): belongs to the same plant family that includes cucumbers, gourds, and melons. Its other names are *poor man's ginseng*, *miracle grass*, *fairy herb*, and *gospel herb*. Sweet Tea Vine is known as an adaptogen, which is an herb reputed to help the body to maintain optimal homeostasis  (metabolic balance). Adaptogenic effects include regulating blood pressure and the immune system, and improving stamina and endurance. Sweet Tea Vine is also believed to be useful in combination with Bellflower (Codonopsis) for jet lag and altitude sickness, both found in many summer trips to high mountainous regions. The very tasty blue-green leaves may be eaten fresh (as in a salad) or in a tea made from the dried leaves.

# Chapter 10

## Healing Beauty Rituals for Summer

. . . . . . . . . . . . . . . . . . .

When I think of summer beauty, I am picturing that loveliest of human visages—the gently sun-kissed, no-makeup, fresh-from-being-outdoors look that money can't buy. Sun, sand, and salt water are reflected in that certain glow of carefree summer living.

If this sounds like a distant memory, or one that you only observe in children, then you are past due for something to bring these facets of summer life into your own. I would recommend giving yourself permission to take a day trip to the beach or a lake and upon your return lock the door to the bathroom and spa it up. Or head to the backyard. As you sit in the shade and drink a tall glass of iced tea, spritz, rub, and massage your homemade recipes on, crack open your "beach read," and let the abundance of this season's ingredients do their magic.

Abundance is not only the feeling of being sated and filled up; it can also be the feeling that you are *already* overflowing with everything you could possibly imagine you *might* want. Summer gives you the opportunity to feel the absolute, overflowing luxury of nature's bounty at your fingertips. Your relationship to your ingredients and the ritualistic care with which you engage them, is the heart of conscious beauty.

### Summer Sun Care:  A Vitamin D Prescription

No matter where you live, it's important to stay on top of the latest information being released about sun exposure, sunscreen, and skin cancer. As one of the most important health and beauty issues to me, here are the basic tips that I feel are easiest to implement for enjoying your time in the sun:

- ⌘ Adults and children should remain indoors (at work and school or play) during the hottest part of the day and when they venture out they should be sure to cover themselves properly. Schedule gardening, errands, or play for early morning or evening hours.

- ⌘ My recommendation for natural sun protection: loose-fitting clothing, shady trees, and big floppy hats.

- ⌘ Better to choose sunscreens with a small percentage of zinc oxide as the main ingredient, with no nano particles of titanium dioxide in them, no Benzophenone-3, and those with a plethora of organic, plant-based ingredients (aloe, green tea, grapeseed oil) included in the mix. My favorites are Soleo Organics and Badger brands.

- ⌘ Take endorsements and seals of approval on packaging with a grain of salt. The Skin Cancer Foundation gives a "seal of recommendation" to sunscreens, but only if their manufacturer has donated $10,000 to become a member of the organization.

### Homemade Sunscreen

¼ cup of zinc powder (available online)

1 cup of your favorite unscented organic body lotion

Tinted non-toxic, mineral-based* liquid makeup (amount will vary depending on each product)

1. Combine all the ingredients thoroughly, mashing lumps to create a smooth texture.

2. Apply often while in the sun.

Note: You will want to get a liquid makeup in a shade that is closest to, or slightly darker than, your own skin tone. This will help the sunscreen to blend better onto your skin when it's applied. *Use non-nanoparticle makeup, usually found at natural food grocers or online. My favorite brands are Jane Iredale and Dermablend.

# WHAT'S THE TRUTH ABOUT SUNSCREEN CHEMICALS?

With each passing year, more information seems to be added to the debate about sunscreen, which ingredients to use, and their true efficacy. On the one hand, small amounts of sun are healthy. We need the absorption of vitamin D to help strong bone growth and to help our bodies process calcium. On the other hand, we need to protect ourselves from the harmful effects of the sun shining through depleted ozone layers.

There is no question most skin cancers are related to sun exposure, yet even with sunscreen sales approaching $1 billion a year, skin cancer rates continue to climb. According to the Centers for Disease Control, melanoma diagnoses have risen nearly two percent a year since 2000 and are increasing even more among young white women. The chief culprit is thought to be an overuse of tanning beds among teenagers and even pre-teens.

There is a substantial body of evidence that shows that there could be an increase in cancer even when sunscreen products are used. Both chemical sunscreens (avobenzone, methoxycinnamate, padimate-o, oxybenzone) and physical sunblocks containing the minerals titanium dioxide and zinc oxide (though less so than the chemical sunscreens) have been found to generate free radicals when exposed to sunlight, which can then attack the nuclei of your skin cells and cause mutations. Furthermore, sunscreen chemicals have been found to pass through the skin and mimic the effects of estrogen, which may disrupt the delicate balance of the body´s natural hormones.

Other studies show that cytotoxicity (danger to the cell) was dependent on the particle size of titanium dioxide. *The smaller the particle size, the more toxic it is.* This conclusion is relevant to us as consumers, because of our insistence on (and subsequently, the cosmetics industry's response to), the use of micronized pigments or nanoparticles in sunscreens and color cosmetics. Nanoparticles of titanium dioxide are used in sunscreens because they are colorless at that size (no big schmear of white goop on your face) and still absorb ultraviolet light.

Last, an unintended consequence of the campaign to get people using sunscreen: over five metric tons of sunscreen are washed off swimmers into the world's oceans every year. The highly toxic nature of one of the main ingredients in sunscreen, oxybenzone (benzophenone-3), has been shown to prime the growth of a deadly virus in coral reefs. The dangers are greatest, of course, where the most swimmers are drawn to the beauty of the reefs. The question then becomes, if it's killing the reefs, what is it doing to you when you slather it all over yourself year in and year out? Oxybenzone in humans is a hormone disruptor, allergen, and interferes with certain functioning of the immune system.

### Green Tea Health and Beauty Remedies

Green tea is one of my all-time favorite components of a cool and beautiful summer. The healing properties of green tea are myriad, especially in its benefits for the skin, and they work their magic in many ways as a key beauty ingredient. Use unflavored, unscented plain green tea of the highest quality you can afford. Organic does make a difference.

1. Bring one quart of filtered water to a boil, then add one cup of green tea leaves. Turn off burner and let tea steep, covered, in the pot, for 15–20 minutes.

2. Strain into a clean, sterilized glass bottle. (To sterilize, run all components of the bottle through the hottest cycle on your dishwasher.)

Use your tea recipe:

⌘ As a cooling face wash, splash, or spritz on your face, blotting gently to dry. Do not rinse

⌘ To refresh strained or tired eyes. Soak a cotton ball, squeeze out the excess, and lay it gently on the eyelids, letting them rest on the lids for about 10 minutes. Repeat if necessary

⌘ To apply slices of zucchini soaked in the tea to the eyes, which will help reduce puffiness.

⌘ To treat blemishes, spritz on face, or dot on a blemish with a cotton ball. Do not rinse

⌘ As an anti-fungal foot soak in a quart of the tea; do not rinse

⌘ As a mouthwash to treat bad breath and gingivitis; gargle with a mouthful

*Great uses for leftover leaves after brewing:*

- ⌘ Allow spent tea leaves to dry thoroughly, then crush them and blend with coconut oil for an anti-aging facial mask

- ⌘ Sprinkle the dried and crushed tea leaves in shoes that have lingering foot odors (especially sneakers). Let the leaves sit in the shoes between wearings for a fresher smell

## Cooling Aloe Vera Sunburn Treatment

The aloe vera plant is a superstar succulent, used by people all over the world for centuries to heal and treat burns and other skin conditions. My family uses it liberally all over our bodies after every day at the beach. In this recipe, the yogurt and cucumber, together with the aloe vera, leaves the skin cooled, moisturized and soothed.

4 tablespoons of aloe vera gel

2 tablespoons of plain organic yogurt (regular or vegan)

6 tablespoons of freshly juiced cucumber

1. Mix all ingredients well and gently apply to any areas of the face and body suffering sun overexposure.
2. Let mixture set for 15 or 20 minutes. Rinse gently with lukewarm water.

## Sunflower Seed Nourish and Glow Mask

Hydrate, smooth, brighten and balance all skin types with this essential summertime beauty recipe. Sunflower seeds are packed with nutrients including vitamins A, B6, D, and E, as well as iron and magnesium for feeding and nourishing skin. The wheat germ and flax are also nutrient dense, so this is one powerful cereal/serial beauty mix. If you want to go bonkers and worship at the altar of the mighty sunflower in all ways, you can include this beauty ritual with the Possibilities Ritual, page 95.

1 teaspoon raw, hulled sunflower seeds

1 teaspoon wheat germ

1 teaspoon flax seed

1 tablespoon sunflower seed oil (cold pressed if possible)

1. Grind seeds and wheat germ to a fine powder in a coffee bean grinder or blender.

2. In a small mixing bowl, gradually add the oil, a little dribble at a time, and mash with a spoon to make the consistency of paste you desire. It should be spreadable, somewhat like peanut butter.

3. Apply mask liberally to a clean, dry face. Let mask dry and harden up a bit, at least 15–20 minutes.

4. Wash off with lukewarm water. Splash with cold water to close pores. Pat dry.

### Honeydew Mask and Bodyscrub

Because of its high water content, honeydew, like all melons, is cooling, soothing, and hydrating to ingest as well as use for beautifying skin treatments, making it a prized summer fruit. It is a good source of vitamin C, the highest vitamin C content of all the melon varieties, except for cantaloupe. Vitamin C plays a vital role in encouraging tissue repair and regeneration. Honeydew is also high in potassium, minerals, lipids, and mucilage. Its bioflavonoids and carotenoids improve the elasticity of the skin and leave it silky smooth.

### Mask

¼ peeled and seeded honeydew melon

2 tablespoons oats

4 or 5 finely minced mint leaves

2–3 drops tea tree essential oil (optional)

1. Mash the melon with a fork and set aside.

2. Grind oats to a fine powder in coffee bean grinder or blender.

3. Blend the oats and mint with the honeydew until it is a sticky paste. (Make it an anti-acne treatment by adding 2 or 3 drops of tea tree essential oil.)

4. Spread on face and leave on for 20 minutes or so. Rinse with cool water and pat dry.

### Bodyscrub

1. Substitute course sugar for the oats and eliminate the tea tree oil. Consistency should be that of wet sand.

2. Massage over body and shower off with warm water.

## Lavender Bath Cookies for Summer Skin Healing

Lavender is one of nature's most versatile plants and summer is one of the most useful times for it, as it is a cure-all for many skin issues that the season brings. In general, you can use cotton balls soaked with a little lavender oil for relieving the itch of bug bites, for treating accidental cookout burns, for dabbing on acne breakouts, and for treating heat rashes, sunburn, and mild cases of poison ivy. Lavender is one of the few essential oils that can be put directly on the skin with no reactions or side effects (others should first be diluted with carrier oils, such as almond or avocado).

Although lavender has excellent antiseptic properties, it is also very gentle on the skin. These bath cookies are the quintessential use of lavender: when dropped in a cool bath at the end of a long hot summer day, "exquisite relief" comes to mind.

5 tablespoons ground flax seeds

6 tablespoons water

2 cups Dead Sea salt (finely ground)

½ cup baking soda

½ cup cornstarch

2 tablespoons virgin coconut oil

3 capsules vitamin E oil (break open and add to mixture)

5 drops lavender essential oil

1. Preheat oven to 350 degrees.

2. In a large bowl mix the ground flax seeds with water and soak for 5 or 10 minutes for the seeds to become gelatinous. Stir well.

3.  Add the rest of the ingredients to the flax mixture and combine to create dough.

4.  Shape dough into teaspoon size balls and place them on a baking sheet. Bake for 10 minutes or until golden. Do not overbake. Cookies will harden as they cool.

5.  Store in a tightly sealed, dry container until used.

6.  Drop two cookies in the tub and let dissolve. Makes 24 cookies.

---

## SWEET GREEN PITS:  NATURAL BO PREVENTION

Sometimes it's more than hot muggy summer days that cause unrelenting sweating. Stress, hormonal fluctuations, and spicy foods are the other culprits we blame. Most of us also assume that excessive perspiration is the root cause of body odor. However, perspiration by itself is basically odorless; it is the bacteria and odors coming from other sources that are the real culprits. Anaerobic bacteria, which flourish when your body doesn't have enough oxygen, may well be the cause. As the body's metabolism goes to work, it gives off odors which are the body's way of ridding itself of waste products. Any imbalances in metabolism will result in stronger odors.

Deodorants help destroy bacteria and disguise odors. Antiperspirants work by clogging, closing, or blocking the pores with aluminum salts in order to prevent the release of sweat, effectively changing the function of the body. Antiperspirants are considered to be drugs because they affect the physiology of the body, and as such, are regulated by the Food and Drug Administration.  Consider products with tea tree oil, known for its antibacterial and antifungal properties. Or use a deodorant stone, made from mineral salts. Antiperspirants reduce bacteria-feeding moisture—but they block sweat glands from doing their thing—that is, cooling down and detoxing the body through fluid (perspiration) release. For this reason, they are not recommended by natural health experts.

In addition to your deodorant, try using a mild solution of hydrogen peroxide (3%) that can be picked up at the pharmacy. Put a teaspoonful in a glass of water and wash the underarm. Increase the amount of peroxide if you still have recurring odor. Make it a point to use pH-balanced soaps and skincare products to maintain the protective acid mantle of your skin. Excessive sweating may have underlying causes, so it is wise to be diagnosed to see if you have a medical problem.

### Hair Guacamole: Flaxen Locks Again

Summer brings out the water baby in all of us, so your hair will most likely be overexposed to lots of saltwater, chlorine, and sun. If you've noticed how your bathing suit's colors are fading and the material is becoming dried out, the same damage is happening to your hair. Here is my favorite hair care remedy which will revitalize and bring back a luscious shine to your active summer locks.

The vitamin E, and fatty protein of the avocado are terrific for nourishing sun-fried and chemically-fried hair.

1 avocado

1 tablespoon plain yogurt, regular or vegan

1 teaspoon olive, coconut, or hemp oil

3 drops lime essential oil

1. Mix ingredients. Massage into hair and leave on for 10–15 minutes.

2. Rinse off thoroughly with warm water.

# Chapter 11

## Summer Kitchen Rituals: Food, Nutrition, Recipes

. . . . . . . . . . . . . . . . . . .

Honoring the full glory of the plant kingdom is made all the easier now with the overwhelming abundance of beautiful fruits and vegetables making their way to your table. Preparation methods should be simple to showcase the thrill of those sun-kissed tastes and textures, just picked, juicy and ripe.

Stone fruits and berries are in abundance right now and appear in many of the recipes. It's also a given that the pull to be outdoors is high on your list of priorities most days during the summer, so many of the recipes feature a make-ahead aspect; you can pull a chilled dish out of the fridge and be on your way to a picnic or outdoor supper under the stars.

Nutritionally there is a focus on food that feeds our summer energy levels to peak performance and sustains us when we are a little too action-packed for our own good. Certain foods cool and calm our internal systems, while others are simply a comforting reminder of childhood summers, but with a modern, adult twist. Outdoor living and eating go hand in hand and summer is the time and place to indulge.

### *Peach Cobbler Breakfast Smoothie*

The flavors in this recipe call to mind those of a peach cobbler — one of my favorite summer treats. This version is cool, creamy, and certainly more portable. It has all you could want for nutrition on the go. Peaches and nectarines are high in vitamins C and A, beta carotene, and potassium. They are also a great source of antioxidants which can help protect the skin from damaging UV rays by counteracting free radical activity.

Peach herbalism has long and ancient roots both in American/European and Traditional Chinese Medicine practices. Peach is considered cooling, slightly moistening, relaxing, and deeply restorative for overextended psyches and tempers. It's used for hair-trigger immune systems reacting to the slightest provocation and is therefore tremendously effective for many allergic reactions and in the treatment of venomous insects. It's nice for burns and wounds, too, and especially for severe nausea in pregnancy. Herbalists use all parts of the peach plant (flesh, leaves, twigs, and especially the pits) for teas, and tinctures cured in brandy.

½ pound fresh, ripe peaches, peeled and cut up (about 5–6)

1¾ cups vanilla flavored rice, almond, soy or coconut milk beverage, chilled

½ cup oats

1 tablespoon maple syrup

Dash of ground ginger powder

Dash of ground cinnamon

3–4 cubes of ice

2 tablespoons chia seeds (optional)

1. Puree all ingredients in a blender. Blend until mixture is thick and smooth.

2. Garnish with a slice of peach. Makes 2–3 servings.

### Coconut Green Smoothie Cup

This is a make-ahead way to have a fresh, nutritious smoothie when you have no time to fuss.

2 cups coconut water

¼ cup almond butter

2 cups greens of choice (kale, spinach, chard)

1 celery stalk, chopped

½ small cucumber, peeled and seeded

¼ cup fresh mint

½ orange, juice and pulp

1–2 tablespoons (or to taste) of sweetener of choice (agave, honey, or brown rice syrup)

1 inch section of peeled, fresh ginger

2 cups frozen mango cubes

1. Blend all ingredients until smooth.

2. Divide mixture among 12 muffin cups and freeze until solid.

3. When ready for a refreshing drink, place 1 cup coconut water or regular water in a blender followed by two of the frozen green cups and blend until smooth. (Cut smoothie cups into pieces if your blender is not very powerful.)

## CUCKOO FOR COCONUT HEALTH BENEFITS

Westerners have suddenly discovered the astounding array of benefits offered by the mighty coconut that our tropical brethern have known about for centuries.

**Coconut Water** is the clear liquid from young (green) coconuts.

⌘ It's a natural isotonic beverage, with the same level of electrolytic balance as we have in our blood

⌘ Coconut water is low fat and contains important electrolytes such as potassium, magnesium, calcium, sodium, and phosphorous. In fact, the potassium content in coconut water is close to twice the amount in a banana

⌘ As a sports beverage or quick energy booster, choose a beverage that is 100% coconut water with nothing else added

**Coconut Milk** is a creamy, rich liquid made from the meat of mature coconuts.

⌘ Vitamins C, E, and many B vitamins are abundant in coconut milk

- ⌘ It's rich in antioxidants and in lauric acid, a medium-chain fatty acid that is abundant in mother's milk. Lauric acid has many germ-fighting, anti-fungal, and anti-viral properties that are very effective at ridding the body of viruses, bacteria, and other illness-causing invaders. Medium chain fatty acids are burned up more quickly by the body than other fats, making these fats heart healthy

- ⌘ Low-fat and regular coconut milk can be substituted for cow's milk in most recipes, for a delicious and creamy vegan alternative

- ⌘ It is also excellent and nutritious as a non-dairy beverage and yogurt. This is the form called for in smoothie recipes, as it has been thinned with water and is more drinkable

**Coconut Oil** is extracted from the kernel or the meat of mature coconuts.

- ⌘ For cooking, use coconut oil as a substitute for butter or margarine. It can be used in stir-frying, sautéing, baking, making non-dairy ice-cream, and in candy making

- ⌘ It's an anti-inflammatory and is a great digestive aid. It helps in controlling blood sugar and improves the secretion of insulin, so it can help reduce cravings for sugared foods. It provides a natural source of energy that has no bad side effects (like carbs and refined sugars)

- ⌘ Its medicinal uses include: treating upset stomachs, prevention of tooth decay, treating fungi and yeast that cause candidiasis, ringworm, athlete's foot, thrush, and diaper rash. It speeds up the healing process for bruises when applied directly on them

- ⌘ For any kind of topically-applied beauty treatment it imparts immense skin, hair, and nail softening properties to restore and revitalize dry and damaged cellular structure

- ⌘ Look for extra virgin, 100% organic coconut oil to insure the level of purity that is important to consuming it on a regular basis. Otherwise, it can be polluted with pesticides and other chemical residues, as well as being cut with other oils

## Lemonade Slushies with Mint and Lemon Verbena

This is a beautiful tonic to dip into for an afternoon when you get to be lazy and feel guilt-free about it. The verbena has a very mild sedative effect, good for soothing frazzled nerves and an upset stomach, too.

1¼ cups water

⅓ cup plus 2 teaspoons raw cane sugar

⅓ cup fresh or dried lemon verbena leaves (found in most specialty tea shops or online)

Zest of 2 lemons, cut into 3-inch-long strips, plus ¾ cup fresh lemon juice

½ cup fresh mint leaves

2 cups ice

1. In a small saucepan, combine the water with the sugar and bring to a simmer over low heat, stirring to dissolve the sugar. Add the lemon verbena leaves and the strips of lemon zest and simmer for 10 minutes.

2. Remove the saucepan from the heat. Stir in the lemon juice and mint and let stand at room temperature until cool. Refrigerate until thoroughly chilled, about 20 minutes.

3. Strain the lemon mixture into a blender along with the ice. Blend on high speed until smooth and frothy. Pour into tall glasses and serve right away.

Make Ahead: The strained lemon mixture can be refrigerated for up to 3 days.

## Blackberry Cardamom Chia Seed Jam

One of my favorite childhood summer memories was of sleeping late in the mornings and waking up to my mother's scratch biscuits and blackberry jam. Blackberries ripened in early summer at the U-Pick fields near our Texas home before it got scorching hot. What made it back to the house was occasionally made into a jam the old-fashioned way by my mother; I guess that's why it felt so prized and special to me.

This version is quick, simple and involves no fuss at all since the chia seeds, miracle things that they are, do all the jelling and setting up for you. No pectin, sterilizing of jars or any other time-consuming business. Yet the full-throttle flavor of blackberries still explodes on the tongue. I've added a hint of cardamom for an exotic perfume that could give you your own summer breakfast memory if you'd like.

3 cups fresh blackberries*

3 tablespoons pure maple syrup, to taste (or other liquid sweetener such as honey or agave)

2 tablespoons chia seeds

½ teaspoon pure vanilla extract

Pinch of cardamom

1. In a medium-sized non-stick pot, bring the blackberries and the maple syrup to a low boil. Stir frequently, and reduce heat to low-medium to simmer for about 5 minutes. Lightly mash the berries with a fork, leaving some for texture.

2. Stir in the chia seeds until thoroughly combined and cook the mixture down until it thickens, about 15 minutes. Stir frequently so it doesn't stick to the pot.

3. Once the jam is thick, remove from heat and stir in the vanilla and cardamom.

Store in an air-tight glass container for up to one week.

Makes 1 cup of jam.

*Feel free to substitute any kind of summer berry you'd like, as well as experiment with your added flavors and spices. Blueberries and lemon, strawberries and cinnamon, cherries and vanilla: the combos are endless.

# CH-CH-CH-CHIA IS A SUPERFOOD

That funny hairy little ceramic donkey from the TV commercials was the harbinger of the new chia craze. It was given a kick start a few years ago with the bestselling book *Born To Run*, when it was revealed that chia was the secret, in part, to some ultra-marathoners' stamina-producing diets.

This could be why:

⌘ Chia has the highest concentration of omega-3s of any other botanical source. Chia is also very high in dietary fiber and antioxidants

⌘ Chia seed offers about five times the amount of calcium found in a cup of whole milk

⌘ Chia is hydrophilic—it will absorb many times its own weight in water. This property prolongs hydration which helps the body regulate its absorbtion of nutrients more efficiently and will leave you feeling full much longer

A couple of tablespoons a day is the recommended dietary supplement, but there is really no limit to the amount you can eat. It has a very mild flavor, similar to raw sesame or poppy seeds. Stirred into water or juice, it will absorb the liquid and get gelatinous after five or ten minutes, resembling tiny versions of the tapioca in a boba drink. The seeds absorb the liquid content of the batter from any recipe it's used in and becomes an invisible and tasteless ingredient in the final form. I use it as an egg substitute in vegan baking when a binder is needed.

Tips for chia in your daily diet:

⌘ Stir into juice or a smoothie

⌘ Sprinkle dry on a salad as you would poppy seeds for crunch and texture

⌘ Add to pancake or waffle batter

⌘ Add to cookie, quick-bread, or brownie batter

⌘ Make "pudding" by stirring 3 tablespoons chia with 2 cups coconut milk beverage and 1 cup sliced fruit. Refrigerate for 30 minutes, stir, and refrigerate another hour. Stir well again before eating. Top with nuts, cacao nibs, shredded coconut or cinnamon.

## Zeke's Cherry Salsa

Being a Texan by birth and a Los Angeleno by choice, I practically bleed salsa when I cut my finger. I'm always on the lookout for any kind of variation on the theme; this one turned up at a beach potluck I attended a couple years ago and I instantly went crazy for it. I don't know who Zeke is, but I love his clever use of cherries as the unexpected ingredient; so perfect for a summer backyard party.

At its most basic, salsa is really just a quick pickling of a fruit or vegetable with an acid such as vinegar or citrus juice. The play of sweet, tart, and spicy that it evolves into with its companion ingredients is what elevates it to the sublime. Cherries are very heart-healthy and loaded with vitamin C.

4 or 5 medium-size tomatoes (ripe but firm)

1 pint firm cherries*

½ bunch cilantro

1 small red onion

1 large clove garlic

1 teaspoon fresh jalapeño

1 tablespoon apple cider vinegar or fresh squeezed lime juice

1. Chop tomatoes into bite-size bits. Finely chop garlic, cilantro, onion, and jalapeño.

2. Pit and slice cherries into quarters if they are big, halves if they run small.

3. Mix all chopped ingredients together with vinegar or lime juice in a large bowl.

*Can be replaced with an equivalent amount of other summer fruit, such as: peach, mango, nectarine or papaya.

### Chilled Avocado Mint Cucumber Soup

In my humble opinion, this is the trifecta of summer produce, right here. As a refreshing tonic to soothe the fiery beast of summer and for when wild summertime adventures have caught up with you and left you depleted, this is the antidote.

Nutritionally avocados (called the "alphabet fruit" because they contain all the vitamins, from A to Zinc), are full of beneficial fats and provide all 18 essential amino acids necessary for the body to form a complete protein. They are the fruit with the highest protein content which is readily absorbed by the body because of their high fiber content. Cucumbers have a cooling, astringent action and remove accumulated waste and toxins from the body, making them ideal for cleansing and restoring balance to the body. Mint is well known for its ability to soothe the digestive tract and ease stomach aches and headaches.

4 ripe avocados, pitted and peeled

6 tablespoons fresh lemon juice (about a whole large lemon)

Juice of 3 large cucumbers

1 cucumber, chopped, reserving 6 whole, very thin slices

3 cups of plain organic yogurt (regular or vegan)

2 cups of vegetable stock

¼ leek, finely chopped (all the white and just a smidge of green)

⅓ cup fresh spearmint leaves, chopped + 6 whole leaves

Generous pinch of sea salt

1. Coarsely chop the avocado and toss with the lemon juice.

2. Peel and juice 3 cucumbers, peel and chop one cucumber.

3. Add the cucumber juice and meat (except for the 6 slices), along with the yogurt, stock, leek, and the chopped spearmint leaves to the avocado and stir well.

4. Transfer the mixture to a food processor, add the salt, and process until fairly smooth, scraping down the sides of the bowl, if necessary. Do not puree entirely; a bit of texture should remain.

5. Transfer soup back to original mixing bowl, cover and refrigerate for at least 2–3 hours.

6. To serve, garnish each bowl with a whole mint leaf and a whole cucumber slice.

Makes 6 portions.

### Garden Gazpacho

Summer without gazpacho is, well, not summer in my thinking. Other than being ridiculously easy, cold, and refreshing it is the LBD (little black dress) of the summer kitchen: a basic, indispensable staple that can be dressed up or down, depending on the occasion, your mood, and energy level. This version includes the culinary equivalent of a single strand of pearls in the form of cute, white beans with which to accessorize. It makes for a more nutritionally complete dish and what's more chic than that?

4 pounds of very ripe and soft tomatoes (about 5–6 large)

2 large cucumbers, peeled and loosely chopped

1 large red bell pepper, seeded and loosely chopped

1 medium onion, peeled and loosely chopped

1 small fresh jalapeno pepper, seeded and finely diced

½–⅓ cup red white vinegar (to taste)

⅓ cup fresh cilantro, loosely chopped

Salt and pepper to taste

One can of cooked, small white beans (navy or cannellini are best), drained and rinsed well

1 cup tomato juice

1 lime, cut into slices

Toasted pepitas (optional)

1. Put everything except the beans and tomato juice into a blender or food processor, putting tomatoes first, so they provide the necessary liquid for blending.

2. Blend to a course puree, stopping before mixture is completely smooth. Taste and add salt, pepper, or vinegar if desired.

3. Transfer mixture to large bowl and stir in beans and tomato soup, mixing well.

4. Cover and refrigerate for at least 2–3 hours.

5. Garnish by squeezing lime slice over each bowl and sprinkling with pepitas.

Makes 4–5 portions.

## Spicy Mock Tuna Rollups

Just like with veggie burger recipes at the start of summer grilling season for non-meat eaters, the internet becomes awash in ideas for seafood substitutes when new reports are released with ever more alarming news about the state of the oceans and the dwindling fish supply. After trying and tweaking many iterations of this recipe, I believe this one hits the bullseye for texture and snap; it's never failed to elicit interest from vegans and non-vegans alike when I serve it. For many of us, there is an abiding love of the taste and smell of seaweed that this dish replicates, so that we can still revel in "sushi-like" sensations. For others, the hope is that you'll simply enjoy the inventiveness and healthfulness of a recipe that is full of creativity and fun. After all, "rolling your own" is always better.

1½ cup cooked or 1 can of garbanzo beans (chickpeas), drained and rinsed with water

1 rib of celery, finely chopped

¼ cup of sweet onion, finely chopped

3 tablespoons of vegan mayo (or to taste)

1 teaspoon of dijon mustard

2 tablespoons of sweet relish

2–3 tablespoons dulse flakes (or other dried seaweed/sea vegetable of choice)

½ teaspoon lemon juice

½ teaspoon red pepper flakes or wasabi

Salt to taste

Sesame seeds

Sheets of *nori* seaweed sushi wrappers

1.  Drain chickpeas and mash thoroughly with fork .

2.  Stir in chopped onion and celery.

3.  Add mayo, mustard, relish, dulse and red pepper flakes.

4.  Season it with a little bit of salt and lemon juice, mix well.

5.  Taste it, add more lemon and salt, if needed.

6.  Place a couple tablespoons of "tuna" mixture on a *nori* wrapper and roll up.

7.  Cut into bite sized sushi-like pieces, sprinkle cut ends with sesame seeds.

8.  Makes appetizer-sized portions for 4 people.

Or, use the mixture as you would tuna-fish salad, and spread on crackers or bread.

Makes enough for 4 complete sandwiches.

## SEA VEGETABLES, SEA JEWELS

Sea vegetables, often called seaweed, are some of the ocean's most beautiful jewels, adorning the waters with life and providing us with a food that can enhance our diets, from both a culinary and nutritional perspective. There are thousands of types of sea vegetables that are classified into categories by color, known either as brown, red, or green sea vegetables. Each is unique, having a distinct shape, taste and texture. Some of the most popular types are: *nori* (famous for its role in making sushi rolls), *kelp* (oftentimes available in flake form), *hijiki* (looks like small strands of black wiry pasta with a strong flavor), *kombu* (generally sold in strips or sheets, oftentimes used as a flavoring for soups), *wakame* (similar to kombu, most commonly used to make Japanese miso soup), *arame* (sweeter and milder in taste than many others), and *dulse* (soft, chewy texture).

Presently, Japan is the largest producer and exporter of sea vegetables. This may explain why many of these precious foods are often called by their Japanese names.

Sea vegetables are an excellent source of iodine, vitamin K, folate, magnesium, the B-vitamins riboflavin and pantothenic acid, iron, and calcium.

Look for sea vegetables that are sold in tightly sealed packages. Avoid any that have evidence of excessive moisture. Store them in tightly sealed containers at room temperature where they can stay fresh for at least several months.

Some easy ways to incorporate sea vegetables into your diet:

⌘ Make vegetable sushi hand rolls by wrapping sticky rice and vegetables (carrots, cucumber, zucchini, avocado) in sheets of nori

⌘ Slice nori into small strips and sprinkle on top of salads

⌘ Keep a container of kelp flakes on the dinner table and use instead of table salt for seasoning foods

⌘ Combine soaked hijiki with shredded carrots and ginger. Mix with a little olive oil and tamari

⌘ When cooking beans, put kombu in the cooking water. It will not only expedite the cooking process but will improve beans' digestibility by reducing the chemicals that can cause flatulence

### Cold Noodles and Tofu with Creamy, Spicy Peanut Sauce

During the years I was leading yoga retreats, one of my favorite places was the Zen Mountain Center near Idyllwild, a small mountain community a couple hours from Los Angeles. This recipe is a variation on one of the standbys from the kitchen when Tom Pappas was a chef there. Offering a double whammy of protein, this dish is super fuel for your summer activities.

You can make it with any kind of noodle that suits your fancy, but my favorites are udon and soba (buckwheat). The peanut sauce makes an excellent all around condiment. I use it in spring rolls, as a dipping sauce for crudités and kebobs, and a spread on crackers and flat bread. If there's nothing to dip in it or spread it on, I've been known to eat it off a spoon, it's that tasty. It keeps for a couple weeks in the fridge.

1 pound of noodles

1 pound tofu, drained and pressed

1 thumb-sized piece of fresh ginger, peeled

4 cloves of garlic, peeled

1–2 fresh jalapeño peppers, seeded

4 scallions, cleaned and roughly chopped

½ cup chopped fresh cilantro

1 cup smooth peanut butter (unsalted)

¼ cup rice vinegar

2 tablespoons shoyu or tamari sauce

½ lime, juiced

2–3 tablespoons brown rice syrup (or to taste)

2 tablespoons toasted sesame oil

1. Cook the noodles according to the package directions, drain, and set aside.

2. Place the tofu between two flat plates, set a heavy book on top, and tilt so that the excess tofu water drips out into the sink.

3. Lightly puree ginger, garlic, peppers, scallions, and cilantro in food processor with a few pulses.

4. Add the rest of the ingredients, except for the tofu, and blend until very smooth. Add water if it's too thick or more peanut butter if it's too thin. You want it to have the consistency of thick, but pourable, ketchup.

5. Cut the tofu into small one-inch cubes.

6. Toss the peanut sauce with the noodles and tofu, then chill in the fridge for 1 hour.

Makes 4 servings.

### Summer Fruit Crumble

There is nothing that says "summer" more than a rustic fruit crumble, made from the freshest farmer's market fruit that you can find. You can stick with just one kind of fruit or get creative and mix it up. The basic spices of cinnamon, ginger, and nutmeg enhance any fruit as long as you don't go overboard and use too much.

This version takes very little preparation and uses a fairly low temperature on the oven to bake, so it doesn't overheat your kitchen too badly. Serve with whipped cream, ice cream, or naked in all its glory. This will always impress others at any dinner party you attend, making it seem like you labored for hours in the kitchen.

*Filling*

6–7 cups of sliced, pitted fruit (peaches, nectarines, plums, apricots, cherries, or berries of any kind; use more berries than the other fruit as they cook down more)

Generous pinch of cinnamon, nutmeg and/or ginger

2 tablespoons honey

1 teaspoon lemon juice

1 tablespoon arrowroot flour

*Crumble Crust*

1½ cups rolled oats

⅓ cup oat flour (grind whole oats in food processor, blender or coffee grinder to a fine powder that looks like whole wheat flour)

2 tablespoons vegan butter

3 tablespoons maple syrup

3 tablespoons unsweetened applesauce

½ teaspoon cinnamon

½ teaspoon vanilla

Pinch of salt

1. Mix filling together, spread out evenly in a shallow 6" x 9" baking dish.
2. Mix crust together well. (Butter may make it a little lumpy; it will melt into the other ingredients in the oven.)
3. Sprinkle crust onto fruit, making sure to reach the outer edges and so very little fruit shows through.
4. Bake at 350° F for 40 minutes, then bake at 375° F for 10–20 extra minutes or until crust is somewhat golden. Place a pan under the baking dish to catch juices if they boil over.

Makes 4–5 portions.

# Chapter 12

## Summer in Your Home and Family

. . . . . . . . . . . . . . . . . . .

Ⅰn order to construct a conscious lifestyle, you must be able to implement your plan on a practical, daily basis in your home. This is never more apparent than when we need to take care of a blistered finger or upset stomach and we open the family medicine cabinet. Summer activities seem to bring on a rash of incidents that we need to address. By using the natural healing properties of plants at home we are connecting to the symbiosis we have had with plants for millennia. It imbues critical moments of pain and upset with soothing ritual. The beginning of summer is a great time to replenish your medicine cabinet and have a treatment plan for summer mishaps.

*Note: This guide is intended for minor first-aid treatment only. Call 911 for serious and life-threatening emergencies. Contact your health-care provider with any symptoms that you are unfamiliar with or that are prolonged (more than a day or two).*

## ⌘ Natural Medicine Cabinet and First Aid Kit

| Problem | Remedy | Treatment |
|---------|--------|-----------|
| Burns | lavender essential oil | Swab affected area liberally with a cotton ball soaked in oil. |
| Bruises, sore muscles | arnica cream or gel | Rub prepared ointment into affected area. |
| Cuts, abrasions | manuka propolis honey (anti-bacterial | Swab on affected area. |
| Cuts, scrapes | witch hazel (anti-bacterial) or hydrogen peroxide | Soak on a cotton ball, swab affected area generously. |
| Dry, itchy skin, chapped lips, diaper rash, bruises, athlete's foot, ringworm, thrush | coconut oil (anti-fungal) | In solid form (keep in fridge) rub on affected area. As liquid, gargle for mouth issues. |
| Digestive bloating and gassy stomach | fennel seeds, dried | Drink tea made from 1 teaspoon of seeds steeped in 1 cup of boiling water. |
| Food poisoning | apple cider vinegar | Drink a mixture of 2 tablespoons in ½ cup of water. |
| Headache | peppermint and rosemary essential oils | Dab a little oil on temples and inhale from bottle or dabbed on a tissue. |
| Insomnia, anxiety, nervousness | chamomile, lemon verbena, or valerian root | Drink tea made from dried plant parts. |
| Sore muscles, cramps, splinters | epsom salts | Sprinkle 2 cups into hot bath. Soak finger in mixture of 1 tablespoon and ½ cup water to remove splinter. |
| Sore throat | raw, unfiltered honey | Eat 1 teaspoon and do not drink or eat anything for 30 minutes after. |
| Sore throat, post nasal drip cough | sea salt | Gargle 2 tablespoon mixed in cup of warm water. |
| Sore throats and laryngitis | slippery elm | Drink tea made with dried leaves, gargle and drink. |

| Problem | Remedy | Treatment |
| --- | --- | --- |
| Sunburn | black tea | Soak in bath infusion by steeping several family sized bags in lukewarm water. |
| Sunburn | aloe vera gel | Massage liberally into all affected areas immediately after sun exposure and for several days after. |
| Upset stomach, nausea, digestive issues, car sickness; Sore muscles | ginger | Peel a section of fresh root and chew until juice is gone, eat dried, or candy chews; soak in hot bath with large piece of fresh root grated into water. |
| Upset stomach | peppermint or spearmint leaves | Drink tea made from dried leaves and also chew fresh leaves. |
| UTI (urinary tract infection) | baking soda | Drink it (1 teaspoon in a cup of water 3 times per day) and sit in sitz bath with half a box sprinkled in the water. |

Fresh herbs need to be used as soon as possible (hopefully your supply is also stocking your kitchen for double duty); essential oils and dried teas/herbs keep for up to six months, liquids need to be checked every six months. Store everything in airtight containers in a cool, dark cabinet. Herbs and oils should be stored in dark glass bottles or jars.

# Chapter 13

## Summer in Your Community and World

· · · · · · · · · · · · · · · · · ·

We circle back to where we started by looking at the life-giving qualities of water and the bounty of those waters, particularly the oceans. As we now profoundly understand, we are bound to consider the global impact of our actions, needs, and desires on the rest of the planet; it greatly affects our own health and wellness. The bad news is: it's all connected. The good news is: it's all connected.

### It's a Fishy Issue:  Conscious Seafood Consumption

Nothing is healthier than eating fish, right? Over and over again we are told we should supplement with fish oil and eat deep water fish weekly for its health and beauty benefits. Not to mention sushi! Who doesn't love their sushi? Manna from heaven. But there is another side to the story.

By 2048 the UN predicts that the entire planet's oceans will be commercially fished out.

For every pound of seafood that is caught, five pounds are thrown overboard and wasted due to accidentally caught fish that aren't wanted. Of the 125–155 million *tons* of seafood caught every year, 25–40% goes bad due to improper storage. A 2012 report by the Species Survival Commission found that forty species of fish that live in the Mediterranean could disappear in just a few years due to overfishing, pollution, and habitat deterioration. Some of the most popular fish are in danger, including blue fin tuna, dusky grouper, sea bass and hake. Many seafood aficionados consider blue fin tuna to be the best tasting tuna and it is often used in sushi (distinguished as *maguro* or *toro*). Almost half the species of Mediterranean sharks and rays are endangered.

Nearly all fish and shellfish that we consume now contain traces of mercury, which can cause major harm to the human nervous system, especially in pregnant women, nursing mothers, and young children. Mercury is released into the air through industrial pollution, which then falls from the air and is absorbed into streams and oceans where fish live.

Though salmon is not on the endangered list, some species of wild salmon are also expected to go extinct in less than ten years. Salmon is commonly raised in factory farms, where they are fed antibiotics (more than any other form of livestock) and GMO food pellets made from other fish which gives them seven times the level of PCBs than wild-caught salmon. Because of their close confinement, farm raised salmon have thirty times the lice problem of wild fish. This ends up contaminating and killing wild fish living in nearby rivers and streams. Chemical dyes are added to these salmon to make their flesh look fresh and pink.

So what habits can you embrace to make a difference? Stop eating fish. If this sounds difficult or you're worried about where you'll get the same health benefits, here are some ideas:

⌘ Find mock, plant-based seafood, which is available in many frozen varieties in natural markets and some big grocery chains—the new iterations are delicious and amazingly just like the real thing in taste and texture.

⌘ You can get omega fatty acids from walnuts, avocados, flax, pumpkin, chia, and hemp seeds; and from grapeseed, walnut, and olive oils.

⌘ Try the fishier tasting kelps and seaweeds in foods. It's the minerals in the sea that make fish and sea plants taste what to us is fishy. So get those sea minerals and you just might kill that craving you had.

⌘ There are DHA supplements made from sea vegetables. The nutrients come from what the fish is eating, not the fish.

If you do not want to give up fish entirely (at least not yet) and want to eat seafood responsibly, Greenpeace suggests that you refrain from eating Red List species (see the Monterrey Bay Aquarium's website) and support responsible seafood merchants by shopping with them.

### More Precious Than Gold: Water Conservation

The paradox of where I live now is that I dwell on the edge of the continent, next to a vast ocean, a monolith of water that permeates everything we do here in Los Angeles. At the same time, much of the West is experiencing persistent, record-breaking drought. Coast to coast in America, underground freshwater aquifers are being pumped at alarmingly faster rates than they are being filled, so that many parts of the country can no longer rely on groundwater to supply their future needs.

Meanwhile, the Texas-sized plastic island floating in the Pacific Ocean is growing larger, its main component the single use plastic water bottle. Americans spend over fifteen billion dollars on bottled water, using and disposing of fifty billion single use plastic bottles every year, of which eighty-six percent (forty-three billion) never get recycled and become landfill or litter.

These undeniable facts point to a desperate need for new water-use habits. Every country in the world must develop them, since a mounting global crisis over chronic shortages is already underway in many parts of the world. The onus of creating a new relationship to water is particularly on America, since we gobble up a disproportionate amount of the world's resources in our water footprint for our consumables through their reliance on water for their creation and manufacture.

Water usage educators feel it is imperative to cultivate a water ethic among Americans and move ideas about water usage into the same categories of social consciousness as buying hybrid autos and recycling trash.

## SOME NEW WATER-USE HABITS

- ⌘ Use community recycling efforts to do your part to keep pollutants out of landfills, which leach into ground water supplies. Check with your community sanitation department to find out where to take your old electronics, paint and painting supplies, batteries, old furniture and other sources of pollutants

- ⌘ Buy organic fruits and vegetables. The herbicide atrazine is one of the most widely used agricultural pesticides in the world and also one of the most commonly found pollutants in water. In one study, it was found in 80 percent of drinking water samples taken in 153 public water systems

⌘ Check the ratings for your municipal water supply and if yours is not acceptable to drink, put filters on your taps. Read consumer reports online about the best in whichever cost bracket you can afford. Most good ones cost around $100. Replaceable filters last for one year serving the daily drinking and cooking water needs for a family of four

⌘ Break the habit of buying domestic bottled water. It is not safer than your filtered tap water; it *is* just tap water—filtered and put in a plastic bottle. Imported water from faraway places such as Fiji or the fjords of Norway should be rejected on ecological footprint values alone

⌘ Cut your shower time by two minutes—a family of three could save forty-six thousand gallons of water a year

⌘ Use drip irrigation systems for home gardens; they are better than traditional sprinkler systems, and use 30% less water

All life depends on water. The quality of your life, all your health, your beauty, your wellbeing, and that of your children and their children is dependent on how we think of ourselves in relation to water. Everything is connected. When someone asks us what we are grateful for, the answer could be "water."

*Yesterday I was clever*
*so I wanted to change the world*
*and today I am wise*
*so I am changing myself.*
**Rumi**

# Autumn

**Element:** Earth

**Human Aspect:** Body

**Key Words:** Mature, Realize, Fulfill

**Season of Life**: Adult Male and Female

**World/Kingdom:** Minerals/Rocks

**Energy:** Hold

**Bodily Manifestation:** Bones, Sexuality

**Time of Day:** Twilight

**Heavenly Body:** Earth

**Earthly Manifestations:** Mountains, Caves, Rocks, and Crystals

**Animal Totems:** Snake, Horse, Deer

**Human Manifestation:** Magic, Duality

**Self-Expression:** Intuition, Assessing, Gathering, Balancing, Changing, Gratitude

# Chapter 14

## Themes of the Autumn Season: Mature, Realize, Fulfill

. . . . . . . . . . . . . . . . . .

This season turns the Medicine Wheel to the place of the adult male and female with an emphasis on finding balance and equanimity within this dynamic. Change is in the air as summer's energy abundance of heat and light is waning and cooling. Autumn and the west hold the human aspect of the physical, the manifestation of the mature physical body, and the teachings it gives us. In the Wheel's alchemy of energy, the body holds; it becomes a container for a certain kind of mature knowledge. This maturation of knowledge is symbolized in the body through our sexuality and in the actual framework of humans—our bones. We "know what we know" deep down in our bones. We can rely on our intuition more, cultivate our personal magic to navigate and manage the vagaries of life's changes, as well as the physical changes inherent in maturing. The west/autumn is the position on the Wheel for the mineral kingdom, the place that holds the energy of minerals, rocks (the bones of the Earth), caves, and a resultant grounding energy and earthiness. Autumn is the time of reaping what we've sown in spring and summer. Gathering in the results of actions, behaviors, and projects automatically requires an honest assessment of their success or failure, and most important, of expressing gratitude for everything we've experienced.

## ⌘ Stories and Rituals to Turn the Wheel

### The Autumnal Equinox: Coming Into Maturity and Balance

The equinox on September 22 is an opportune moment to take a step back and take stock of where we are on the Wheel of Life. It marks the astronomical movement of the sun, one of two times a year when the sun crosses the equator, and when the day and night are of approximately equal length.

At this moment of perfect balance at the equinox the earth in the Northern Hemisphere is tipping out of the long days of summer (*yang* or outward, male energy) into the approaching longer nights of winter (*yin* or inward, female energy). Although we relish the shift in the weather patterns that comes now, from the hot languid days of late summer to that first blast of cool autumn air, we perhaps feel a little melancholy about what is being left behind. Everything new and exciting about summer is beginning to fade. While there is anticipation about the coming season, there is sadness about endings and the things that are subsiding. Summer brought out the playful inner child in all of us, and like Peter Pan, there is reluctance about growing up and a fear of the changes underfoot.

Autumn on the Wheel is very much about being a grown up, about wearing the mantle of adulthood with grace, honor, and poise. While most adults consider themselves grown-up in the literal sense of the word (jobs, mortgages) there is also a streak of widespread arrested development running through American culture which has a lot of us kicking and screaming all the way through adulthood and what we think it means. This could be because we are ill informed about what it can truly signify for us. The rallying cry seems to be "never let them see you age!" If fifty is the new thirty and forty is the new twenty, then who are the seasoned adults in charge? Our culture is obviously obsessed with youth and getting older is considered a fate worse than death. However, something important is being lost in the quest to be mistaken for a college kid while walking down the street, when we are long past that era in our lives.

It is true that the crucible of figuring out adult happiness is sometimes painful and difficult, but it cannot be avoided nor should it. The most successful and happy adults I know have quietly and diligently applied themselves to finding their larger purposes in life and much of that includes finding a way to be of service. There is a richness to life that is revealed when we turn our efforts away from being selfishly all about ourselves as we were when we were young and unformed, and toward thoughts of others.

However, the end of childhood doesn't mean that fun and excitement about life also have to come to an end. It takes an adult who's been around the block to truly appreciate some of the more remarkable and unexpectedly wonderful experiences that come from living a certain amount of time. Time passes, everything changes, and if this elicits regret, longing, or disappointment then how fortunate that we have an entire season at hand naturally created to help us grapple with these feelings of transition.

The equinox is a powerful doorway through which to walk and take advantage of the opportunity to restore balance and harmony to key life goals, projects, and relationships. The sun appears to be standing still in the sky as it transitions across the equator, straddling the line between what has passed and what is to come. All life can be perceived as a duality and here the two opposites exist visibly—with the equinoxes as the transition points. This is the perfect moment to look at cultivating balance in your life and to turn and face the strange changes that are happening in and around you. By letting this natural flow of energy and movement guide you, you can bring your big picture into focus or recalibrate it if need be. Instead of just thinking about what you need and want, now you can count your blessings and express gratitude for what you already have; there is much to be grateful for.

## PRAYER OF AUTUMN  (EVERYTHING CHANGES)

**(Adapted from Sun Bear)**

*We pray to Mother Earth for carrying us on her back and providing for us and our needs.*
*We seek the guidance of the powers of the West as we aspire to maturity.*
*We pray for strength, adaptability, responsibility, teachings, leadership, and power.*
*We ask for help in discerning our purpose in life and then pray for help to fulfill that purpose.*
*We ask for help in going beyond ourselves to work for the welfare of others.*
*We ask help in using our abilities for the good of the people.*
*It is at this time we pray for the ability to serve others with strength, courage, and kindness.*
*We give thanks for unknown blessings already on the way.*
*In this, we accept the idea of change with grace and humility,*
*for everything changes.*

## Magic Hour

Photographers and cinematographers refer to the magic hour of twilight as the time of day between when the sun has set and when it is dark. It's a natural light that is beautiful and soft and makes everyone and everything look extraordinary. The paradox of magic hour, though, is that it only lasts for a very short while. You must be all set up and ready to shoot in advance of when it hits or you'll never have enough time to get what you want. It's both magical and stressful at the same time.

This season, where twilight lingers, is when we are all being held in the magic-hour light. We're surrounded by this quietly seductive, very brief slice of the day, of the year, and yet feel a certain intensity about the transitions that are underway. We perceive these transitions on all levels of our being, in our psyches, in our physical bodies. We are registering and reacting to autumn's magic hour marking the passageway between the heat and high energies of summer and the colder, darker days of winter. In this space is the special mystery of whispered secrets; it calls for an understanding that goes beyond words and moves into areas of intuition and visionary insight.

## Awakening Intuition with Snake, Horse, and Deer

The three animal totems—Snake, Horse, and Deer—found in the west on the Medicine Wheel all have a connection to awakening the powers of intuition and to trusting our interior mysteries. Learning how to be comfortable in the parts of our lives that defy easy explanation is something that Carolyn Myss, the noted medical intuitive and author, encourages: "Don't wish away your mysteries. These are the things that get us out of bed in the morning and charge us up, the things we still have left to do ahead of us on the path."

Snake symbolizes a sharpening of intuition, and is the guardian of transitions, new opportunities, and changes. Snake reminds us that there is energy and healing in life's transmutations. (Think of how snakes constantly shed their skins to make way for the new as they grow older). Snake is also representative of the energy of wholeness, the knowledge that all things are equal, and the notion that there is value in persisting through adversity.

Horse has long been honored as a helper, a messenger, and a harbinger of Spirit knowledge to the Native Americans. Their dependence on their horses for everyday survival was intense and can't be overstated, so their spiritual connection to these creatures ran very deep. Horse leads us toward the higher callings of our spiritual selves. (Interestingly, Carl Jung quite independently observed the horse in dreams to represent the intuitive aspect of human nature.)

Many indigenous cultures living around deer, including Native Americans, observed them to be very savvy when it came to finding the best herbs in their shared foraging areas. The people learned to follow the deer to prime herb patches—many of which proved to be highly beneficial for their medicinal powers. Because deer have an uncanny sense of where to find the green freshness the earth provides, the Wheel counsels us in meditation to ask Deer for help in seeking out our inner treasures, to lead us into deeper communion with our souls and the limitless treasures within.

### Nutting Season and Hazelnut Divination Ritual

Around the middle of September, the nut season starts as the ripe bounty of nut-bearing trees begins to fall to earth. This was especially important in Western Europe where ancient traditions placed a huge significance on trees and their symbolism in folklore and legends. Nutting Day is September 14 and is still commemorated going on five hundred years now in England. In the hedgerows and the woods the hazelnuts begin to ripen and break open and this date is supposedly when they are perfectly ripe and ready to gather. Hazel is associated with the Celtic tree month of Coll which translates as "the life force inside you." Hazelnuts are connected to wisdom and protection and are often found near sacred wells and magical springs. The branches have long been considered to make the most powerful wands and divining rods.

## AUTUMN HAZELNUT DIVINATION RITUAL

Working with any divination tool is an exercise in developing trust in the powers of intuition and sensitivity to information that doesn't always present itself as obvious. This kind of knowingness can't always be articulated, but it can prove to be a smart, savvy approach to problem solving or getting new perspective while navigating through a difficult transitional time.

A few years ago when I was shown the symbols from a Celtic nutting day ritual, I was immediately attracted to their minimalist aesthetic similar to the Runes. However, the best part of working with them is the aspect of having to draw them yourself on a handful of hazelnuts. This becomes a perfect organic delivery system and a great beginning to this particular kind of meditative thought process. Drawing activates the intuitive right brain.

⌘ Light a candle in one of the colors of autumn: red, gold, orange, brown

⌘ Obtain ten fresh hazelnuts in the shell. In indelible marker, draw the symbols listed below. Put them in a special drawstring bag and shake with your left hand. Draw the hazelnuts out with your right hand

⌘ Have your journal on hand to record the date, your question/dilemma, the symbols you chose, and any reflections you might have about the experience. Use your journal entry to track the unfolding of your guidance and any breakthroughs you have as a result. It's always informative to check back and compare previous experiences each time you sit down with the hazelnuts to do a reading

There are three ways to do a reading:

1. Think of a question or dilemma about which you need guidance. Draw one hazelnut out of the bag. This is your guiding answer

2. Draw three nuts out of the bag for a past, present, and future reading. Place them on the table in front of you left to right

3. Use all the nuts for a reading by shaking them out of the bag onto the table

The nuts closest to you and in the middle range of the table are energies and concepts that are coming into being now or very soon. Those nuts furthest away from you on the table are ideas, goals, or concepts that will show up in the future. This is the reading that is helped most by picking a specific time frame (a month, three months, six months) into the future to chart the movement of your reading.

**THE SYMBOLS:**

| Choices (Diverging Roads) | Love (Broach of Tara) | Abundance/ Growth (Cornucopia) | Solutions (Rake or Comb) | Travel/Spirit Moving (Road or River) |
|---|---|---|---|---|
| | | | | |
| Strength/Patience (Stag Antlers/ Helmet) | Protection/Proceed With Caution (Shield) | Loss/Letting Go/ Transition (Broken Arrow) | Self Awareness (Mirror) | Knowledge (Fish) |
| | | | | |

## Record Keepers: Bones of the Earth

I began the seasonal section of stories and rituals in the spring chapter by discussing sweat lodges as the perfect ritual for springtime transformation. An important component for the sweat lodge experience is the rocks upon which the water is poured to make the hot steam possible. The Rock People sing and hiss during sweats and are the sacred representatives of the earth element in the ritual. Rocks are also the precise symbol of how to alchemize the energy of the west and autumn and how to hold those energies with steadiness and strength in the physical body.

On the Medicine Wheel, the west/autumn is the place of the mineral kingdom. This includes all rocks, crystals, and caves which are the literal embodiment of Earth. Just as the west holds our human equivalent of the physical—or corporeal selves—our flesh and bones, rocks are the bones of the planet and hold its geologic record. The Native Americans called them the Record Keepers for they hold all the stories of the ages, of Earth's evolution through eons of history. The quartz, mica, feldspar, iron, and other minerals were born out of magma that cooled then were tumbled and tossed as the earth and its continents were being formed. Every single rock has a vibrational energy holding its incredible journey that started so long ago.

### Turning Over Every Stone and a Record Keeper Meditation

Working with rocks and stones during this season is an easy, fun, and creative way to hold the energy of the Earth, its history, and its mysteries in your hand. You don't have to limit yourself to just one; there are as many colors, shapes, and weights as there are stars in the sky and fortunately they are everywhere. It's also interesting to find out the healing properties of the stones that are traded and sold for such purposes.

Any stone or rock—and I emphasize *any*—that you choose to work with is perfect. Your stone can be one you've picked up at the end of your driveway because it glinted at you in the sunlight this morning or one you've been carrying around from a beach trip as a kid. What's important is that your stone holds a special attraction for you and when you hold it in the palm of your hand there is a palpable sense of warmth, pleasure, good energy, or, if you will, good vibrations.

There are three stones I think alchemize pretty impeccably the qualities of the west and autumn. They are inexpensive, and can easily be found through rock and gemstone retailers online, or at your local metaphysical *objects d'art* store.

⌘ **Botswana agate** is a striated stone containing milky greens, rusts, purple-y browns, and white layers that has the look of ripples in motion on a pond. It is sometimes called the *change stone* because of its property of helping handle change in a positive way. For transitions of any kind, it gently shows that change is not as difficult or painful as it could be without it; it is a comforting stone. It helps focus on solutions instead of problems and thereby increases creativity. It elevates the power of one's intuition.

⌘ **Angelite,** a milky blue stone, can bring serenity, inner peace, and a sense of calm. It's excellent to use in moments of stress and overwhelm. Angelite dispels fear, anger, and encourages forgiveness. Psychically, angelite is used to connect with spirit guides, the higher self, guardian angels, and spirit journeys. Angelite is also excellent for creating a shield of psychic protection and for creating balance between ethereal and physical energies.

⌘ **Charoite** is a beautiful, marbled purple stone which assists in recognizing one's path-of-service and how it can be manifested on an everyday basis. It clears negativity, assists with energetic boundaries, and facilitates the release of unconscious fears, allowing healing balance to take their place. It gives the ability to see old patterns with new possibilities. Charoite opens heart, inspiration, service, seeing clearly (mentally, physically, psychically), and facilitates faster healing.

---

## RECORD KEEPER MEDITATION

With your stone in hand, sit in a quiet place. Feel your stone warm to your body heat as you take in the stone's energy through your skin. Invite it to:

**Help** you during this transitional time of changes, to steady and balance your physical health and stress levels

**Bring** an easy, relaxed state of knowing-ness and intuition about all your decision-making

**Protect** all the powerful, mysterious parts of yourself that you are still uncovering so that you may walk in your highest truth, grounded and connected to the beauty of Earth below your feet

---

### The Body Electric:  Challenging Physical Limitations

Spiritual insights that come through the information channels of the physical experience that the body holds can be mighty. Autumn on the Medicine Wheel is devoted to emphasizing the body's ability to contain this very special form of perception and knowledge.

For eons, humans have also used the physical body to push the limits of pain and pleasure to new heights in order to experience spiritual ecstasy. Native Americans do it with their sun dance rituals. It is seen in the whirling dervishes of Sufi dancing, in making long and arduous walks and pilgrimages such as walking to Mecca or hiking the Camino de Santiago trail in Spain. It's not for nothing that there are whole industries in our modern secular world now devoted to providing peak physical experiences. Some require years of preparation and training and cost thousands of dollars. Fire-walking on hot coals, fundraising marathons and bike races, mountain climbing, transcontinental hikes: there is no shortage of ways to bust out the adrenaline and find out who you really are when the rubber hits the road.

It is a basic human need (in some more than others) to find the moments large and small which test our physical limits. It's important to feel a sense of accomplishment within the body, since it can be profound and life changing. It doesn't have to put you in danger, though, or empty out the savings account. The important thing is to regard such an opportunity as a chance to discover something new about yourself that has been buried underneath your everyday, work-a-day world. The benefits are innumerable. Now is the season to embrace this goal.

### Flying Dakinis and In-Between Spaces

There are Tibetan historical and tantric texts which refer to the famous Land of the Dakinis, a matriarchal place west of Tibet, where the spiritual leaders were women. The place was called *Odiyana* or *Uddiyana*, which translates as "vehicle of flying." Dakinis represent those essence principles within the self which are capable of transformation to a higher octave. Dakinis are *sky dancers*, heavenly angels devoted to the truth. They serve as instigators, inspirers, messengers, even tricksters, pushing the aspirant across barriers toward enlightenment.

Several years ago, right after I learned about Dakinis, I came across a newspaper article about a circus arts school located in a Hollywood warehouse. It had just started a series of drop-in classes to the public with no prior training or skills. Anyone who wanted could sign up and learn how to fly on a trapeze, so I immediately committed my women's circle of six to a Saturday afternoon. This seemed to me to be the absolute, perfect expression of Dakini energy. We ranged in age from our late thirties to mid-forties, average women (some of us moms chasing little kids around) fitting our fitness haphazardly into our hectic lives.

The instructors at the circus arts school never let on about the full extent of what we were going to end up doing, clever people that they were. Instead, they slowly worked us up onto the full sized, thirty-foot-high trapeze rig skill by skill. After two hours we were able to perform a two minute sequence that culminated with a flip out over our bar to clasp the outstretched hands of an instructor flying toward us on his bar—something I wouldn't have believed that I could do if I had been shown it in the beginning.

What I remember most is the extreme body sensations that I felt between white-knuckle terror and breathtaking exhilaration, and the next day every muscle in my body was sore in a new way. But the cool thing was, incredibly, at the end of our time on the rig, we all managed to achieve a ballet of precision, timing, and enough muscular control, that we actually became The Flying Dakinis, trapeze troupe extraordinaire. It was a beautiful thing to behold—six regular women flying through the air. Learning trapeze parallels learning how to navigate transition. The same way you must trust you'll be caught by the person on the other trapeze bar when you let go of yours, you trust you'll make it successfully over to the next phase of your life when the time is ready. It helps to know that this transition moment is unavoidable, but doesn't have to be a bad place. In fact, it can be liberating.

For the truth is, all of life is marked by transitions, both big and small. Some we can see coming and prepare for, others are thrust upon us without warning. One day you are someone with a job, the next day you are not. One day you are in a relationship, the next you aren't. One day you are not a parent, the next you are, and the next you are an empty-nester. One day you have a mother and a father and the next day you are without them. How each of us manages these transitions is a life skill that can be learned, taught to us by parents, friends, loved ones, and others we look to for guidance. Some is just intuitive knowing, and some we learn by trial and error, by letting go of the bar and just flying through it.

My feeling is that the more we are able to identify these states of transition for what they are, to recognize they are impermanent, the more we can keep our wits about us and know that what awaits us on the other side is growth, insight, deeper awareness. Sometimes white-knuckling it as we hang on for dear life is all we can do. But there is more to be gained than just trying to survive. There is a special elevation of the soul that transpires the more we can be a fearless and willing participant.

# Chapter 15

## Essential Autumn Health Practices

. . . . . . . . . . . . . . . . . . .

A s we grow older, it's clear we can no longer take our health for granted. Every day that we are alive and healthy is cause for gratitude and celebration. No longer can we burn the candle at both ends and not expect consequences to our health. It's also important to establish tried and true health routines that nurture your spirit, give you energy, strength, vitality, and which provide calm and focus during times of stress or change. Autumn's focus is living in balance. This means giving equal attention to your own time outs from the myriad demands we all face each day from work, family, children, schedules—the stuff of life that can deplete your inner resources if you aren't careful. Now is the right moment to let yourself examine what may need changing in terms of your daily schedule; reassess your priorities and adjust accordingly. By making small changes, we develop the skills to look at the bigger, more important ones without flinching so much. We fear change less because we know it will bring new experiences and insights.

### *Gratitude for Good Health*

Ancient cultures structured ceremony around the meaning of the harvest, of the need to express gratitude for the blessings of its substance as well as a reward for the hard work of the prior growing season. It was elemental to be grateful for the food that would help the family or village survive through the winter. The American Thanksgiving holiday in November is a direct offshoot of these rituals, of course.

Others saw in autumn transitions a "thinning of the veils," or the time when the veil between the living and the dead was at its thinnest. It was a time of honor and gratitude for ancestors, for all those who came before and who made the descendants' lives possible (All Hallows Eve and Day of the Dead, October 31 and November 1 respectively). The Jewish religion contains in its high holy days of autumn two of my favorite spiritual concepts: the idea of infinite possibilities where each one of us becomes a vessel for bringing into being that for which we most yearn (Rosh Hashanah) and atonement (Yom Kippur), for reviewing and making amends for regretful actions and behavior. A key component in forgiveness of self and others is gratitude for the opportunity to embrace regret as a wellspring for learning and a blessing in disguise.

What all of these traditions, celebrations, and holidays have in common, is the concept of gratitude as a cornerstone of a life well lived. Gratitude is the mature well-earned response for more than just being able to live another day; it is a key factor in living authentically, humanely. Recent science on the subject says it is also a major factor in enjoying good health. Scientists at the University of California, Berkeley in collaboration with UC/Davis, have begun to chart a course of research aimed at understanding gratitude and the circumstances in which it flourishes or diminishes. They're finding that people who practice gratitude consistently report a host of benefits:

⌘ Stronger immune systems and lower blood pressure

⌘ Higher levels of positive emotions

⌘ More joy, optimism, and happiness

⌘ Acting with more generosity and compassion

⌘ Feeling less lonely and isolated

One of the goals of the initiative is to expand the scientific database of gratitude, particularly in the key areas of human health, personal and relational wellbeing, and developmental science. Perhaps you are familiar with the saying, "it's not that happy people are thankful, it's the thankful people who are happy." The Berkeley study found that people who kept gratitude journals (writing down three things for which they are grateful every day), were measurably less prone to illness and depression than those who did not write down their blessings. So there is a real physical, body-related outcome to gratitude. It can affect everything we do and everything we are concerned about with good health.

You, too, can begin to incorporate gratitude as a pillar of your wellness routine. Some ideas include keeping your own gratitude journal, beginning each day with a quick meditation or prayer by giving thanks for the good fortune to have the new day in front of you, and by taking turns around the dinner table giving each family member an opportunity to express something for which they are grateful from their day just concluded. Like all the health and wellness habits this book has explored, developing the habit of gratitude practice is one that has no downside.

### The Lifestyle of Healthy Sleep

So many of us are now leading such over scheduled, hyper vigilant lives that an astonishing eighty percent of women report insomnia at some time in their lives. The use of prescription sleep aids among women peaks from ages forty to fifty-nine, when most are at the apex of their working lives and have school-aged children under their care. In 2013, over eight million American women got a prescription for helping them sleep, nearly twice that of men.

Insomnia, as debilitating as it can be, is really just the canary in the coal mine. *Everyone* when sleep deprived, not just women, is at increased risk of immune system crashes which lead to more colds and flus. But consistent lack of sleep which turns into insomnia, leads to much higher risk of serious chronic disorders, including cancer, depression, heart attack, and diabetes.

Maintaining healthy sleep is a lifestyle choice and is not, unfortunately, achieved through a quick fix for lasting results. We don't go to the gym once and expect immediate fitness or drink green juices for one day and expect weight loss. Healthy sleep, like a healthy diet and regular exercise, represent a prioritization that comes before other ways you choose to spend your time. Your best, rested self is a holy act of self-care. It is an affirmation of self-love and self-regard.

## RECLAIMING HEALTHY SLEEP

⌘ Treat your routine of preparing for sleep as you would any other devotional ritual for your wellbeing. The brain needs oxygen rich blood and calming thoughts to prepare it for sleeping and dreaming. *Do not engage with electronics or television right before going to sleep.* In fact, remove them entirely from your bedroom. Practice deep breathing and meditation techniques for relaxation outlined elsewhere in this chapter

⌘ Make your bedroom a sanctuary to blessed sleep. Make the room as dark as possible. Blue lights from TVs, digital clocks and computers suppress the secretion of melatonin, the sleep promoting hormone, another reason to remove them from your bedroom

⌘ Body temperature plays an important part in combatting insomnia. Take a very hot bath right before bedtime. This will cause your body temperature to fall after it has been increased through the hot water immersion. Wearing socks to bed keeps the blood vessels in the feet dilated and draws blood away from your core. This has the effect of cooling you down which initiates sleep. And finally, keeping your body temperature cool during sleep slows down all of your metabolic processes, including the processes of the brain. Keep your bedroom at sixty-five degrees or colder (the worse your insomnia, the colder it should be)

⌘ Avoid heavy meals right before sleeping, reduce or eliminate caffeine intake (including chocolate) in the last half of your day, and avoid using alcohol to fall asleep (twenty percent of people who use this method report interrupted and fitful sleep as the alcohol wears off). See the herbal teas section of this chapter for a list of sleep inducing and calming herbs

⌘ Practice routines of sleeping and waking that are consistent from day to day. The body (and mind) functions best with predictable routines. Only stay in the bed if you are actually sleeping. Rather than tossing and turning, get up and do a light breathing routine or quick mindfulness meditation

## Bone Health and the Minister of Power

Our two most basic health concerns as modern women, coincidentally, are reflected in the wisdom of the Medicine Wheel in the autumn: bone health and reproductive/sexual health. The Wheel is aligned most clearly here, with the point in life when we are fully mature adults.

Just as rocks are the record keepers of Earth, our bones are the record keepers of our physical bodies, providing the framework for how we live and age and grow older. It's interesting how so many aphorisms and folk wisdoms have to do with how we perceive our reality, feel and know things, through our bones ("feel it in your bones," or "down to the bone," or "bare bones," or "make no bones about it"). They are the tuning forks of the psyche urging us to delve deeper and stay alert to our intuition. They are also the part that remains long past when the rest of the body is turned to dust and ether. They are your future fossil record.

Bones can be thought of as bank accounts with a limit, according to the National Osteoporosis Foundation. The bone bank account gets its deposits as bone is built from birth to about age thirty for women. During childhood and adolescence, more bone is deposited than withdrawn, so the skeleton grows. By age thirty bones have reached peak bone mass, the strongest and densest they will ever be. After that, bones slowly start to weaken, in both men and women. During menopause there can be rapid bone loss for several years, which is why osteoporosis is of greater concern for women than men. Approximately one in two women over age fifty will break a bone because of osteoporosis. Asking your doctor for a bone density test once you reach fifty is a good way to determine what your needs are to optimize your future bone health.

For those younger than thirty, know that this is an important time to invest in your bone bank account. After age thirty, it's still not too late. No matter how much bone density there is in the account, making sure the withdrawals are limited will lengthen the amount of time that the bone is healthy. Smoking, drinking alcohol, consuming sodas rather than calcium-rich beverages, and lack of exercise deplete the bone bank account, while weight-bearing exercise (power walking, running, dancing, yoga) and loading up on calcium-rich foods is money in the bone bank.

In Traditional Chinese Medicine (TCM) it is the kidneys that rule the bones and joints. The kidneys are key to regulating levels of phosphate and calcium in the body, two minerals needed for strong bone health. The kidneys also help activate vitamin D to absorb calcium from food.

When TCM principles were created thousands of years ago, this likely was not known, yet it has been proven to be right on the money through modern scientific methodology.

Like phosphorus, magnesium is largely found in the bones. Magnesium and phosphorus collaborate with calcium to mineralize bones and teeth. Magnesium might also work with potassium to prevent blood from becoming too acidic, which can leach calcium from bones. Chemical reactions in the body, including bone and mineral metabolism, rely on magnesium.

Nurturing kidneys includes the following:

⌘ Drink a minimum of ten to twelve cups of water daily to keep kidney function highest

⌘ Consume foods that support the kidneys and contain high levels of calcium and magnesium: legumes such as kidney beans, black beans, lentils, and garbanzo beans; sea vegetables (dulse, kombu, nori), buckwheat, black rice, barley, walnuts, and chia

⌘ Eat fruits and vegetables daily which are rich in calcium and magnesium: artichoke, kale, cooked Swiss chard and bok choy, cooked spinach, sweet potatoes, turnip greens, broccoli, berries, cranberries, and watermelon

⌘ Daily cardio exercise is important to increase blood and oxygen to the kidneys. Additionally, forward bend and backward bend-type exercises activate the muscles in the low back and strengthen the blood flow to the tissues in the kidney area

### Natural Reproductive Cycles

The defining traits of being in a female body are expressed in our reproductive systems. From dealing with PMS to menopause, the miracle of the body that prepares itself monthly for the ability to grow a baby and then in time discontinues that phenomenal effort is almost beyond comprehension. Our breasts, used to feed an infant or not, are marvels of construction and purpose. Yet no matter your sexual orientation and history or reproductive plans, we all have to figure out our approach to breast cancer prevention, our sexual preferences and dislikes, STD prevention, contraception, and if we opt for it, fertility capability and pregnancy. It's a long and winding path we travel in these bodies of ours.

The most important part of the journey for each of us is that we are equipped with as much knowledge as possible to care for and nurture our health so that our experiences with our bodies are vibrant and meaningful.

In addition to playing a major role in bone health, TCM considers the kidneys (known as *The Minister of Power*) to be the organ system of growth, maturation, sexuality, fertility, and aging. Like a seed which holds the potential of an entire plant, your kidneys hold the genetic blueprint of who you are and how healthy and strong you will be.

The kidneys are the most deep-seated of all your internal organs and for good reason. It's the root of all substances in your body and is responsible for providing the tools you require to fulfill your deepest needs—survival and reproduction. The kidneys act a bit like the Energizer Bunny as the home of your deep reserves, but as such it's also the organ system most damaged by stress.

Sexuality and creativity are emotional components of the kidney system. It is responsible for libido and sexual attraction, so issues with fertility, libido, or the menstrual cycle generally are kidney problems. The kidneys are also the source of artistic creation. In addition, the emotions associated with this deepest organ are fear and anxiety driven by fear. Fear has the ability to shake you to your core, and if chronic, creates unrelenting stress, which is extremely damaging to the kidneys. Stress hormones are pumped out of the adrenal glands located right next to kidneys. Managing stress on a daily basis and addressing fears and anxieties as they come up are vital acts of nourishing the kidney, and thus, the reproductive system.

Stress, fear, anxiety, depression (in addition to bad diet and sleep deprivation) can all play a part in throwing our reproductive system off balance and into a state of disorder. According to TCM, a healthy menstruation will be synchronized (more or less) with the new moon and ovulation with the full moon (or one cycle every 28 days). Just as the moon's phases affect the ocean's tides, they also affect bodily fluids. Three to five days of menstrual flow should occur each month, and should be a vibrant, red color, without any abnormality in color or flow. The rest of the month, including the days leading up to menstruation, should pass without pain, digestive issues or other symptoms. In other words, PMS should be rare or nonexistent in a well-balanced and healthy body.

By supporting healthy periods through diet and nutrition, stress reduction habits, aromatherapy, sleep, and exercise you will know a few days in advance when you will start your period and begin proactively treating your body with efforts that will help to mitigate symptoms, rather than waiting until they are upon you full force. Chronic and debilitating PMS symptoms should be addressed with your health care provider, but consider that they are the body's way of communicating imbalance.

Additionally, a healthy woman with high kidney system function, experiences a gentle, brief transition through menopause with minimal symptoms. This would not include extreme hot flashes, emotional fluctuations, or sleeping disturbances. Exposure to mental stressors, physical trauma, and various chemicals (including hormones in food, tap water, and birth control medications) tend to decrease reproductive system function, potentially leading to the severe symptoms that many women experience during menopause.

## HOW TO MAKE A BABY THE AYURVEDIC WAY

Ayurveda, the traditional Indian system of health and wellbeing, has a wonderful perspective on male and female fertility. In Ayurveda, fertility is regarded as the sum total of all optimally-digested foods and experiences. This logic is based on the principles of Ayurvedic anatomy and physiology, which considers that eggs and sperm are the result of the deepest level of nutritional transformation. All that we eat and drink is continually refined until it is transformed into the most vital essence, the potential of life, known as *shukra* in Sanskrit. This is the seed of life.

Optimum fertility involves the quality of the digestive fire, the quality of the reproductive organs, healthy nutritive tissues and freely-flowing circulation. When these are all functioning properly then the reproductive tissues can be nourished and fertility can take its course.

I've also been told by Ayurvedic practitioners that feeling loved is also one of the best tonics for fertility, that love feeds immunity, fertility, and vitality as the sun warms the earth. By tuning into the great cosmic spirit that sparkles through us at every moment, this energy is then transmitted to the cells that will eventually come together and become a baby enlightened in every way: physically, mentally, emotionally, and spiritually.

## Best Breast Health

All our reproductive health is important to pay attention to, but none more so than our breasts. One in eight American women will be diagnosed this year with invasive breast cancer. While there are many factors that play a part in this startling statistic, increasingly, lifestyle factors are assuming a larger role in the discussion.

Cultivating diligent habits within this sample of four areas of daily life offer clear results.

⌘ **Exercise:** New research from the University of Minnesota shows how exercise plays a vital part in reducing breast cancer. It seems to change the way the body handles estrogen, which often fuels breast cancer. Nearly thirty studies have shown that women who exercise at a moderate to vigorous level—anything from brisk walking to running—for three to four hours per week, reduce their risk of breast cancer by *thirty to forty percent*. That's *about the same* benefit that one gets from tamoxifen—one of the drugs considered to be among the best at breast cancer prevention.

⌘ **Diet:** Micronutrients found in fruits and vegetables, lower the risk of certain types of breast cancers, while blueberries have been shown in animal studies to reduce ER positive breast tumors—the type that affects 70% of breast cancer sufferers. Researchers recommend one cup of blueberries a day (fresh or frozen).

⌘ **Personal Care Products**: Synthetic chemicals in everyday products like deodorants, makeup, shampoos, shaving cream and even toothpaste, include parabens (preservatives), lead, triclosan (classified as a pesticide), and pthlatates (known endocrine disrupters); they may get into the bloodstream or accumulate in breast tissue. There they enhance or emulate the effects of estrogen, which stimulates the growth of cancerous breast cells. Avoid these ingredients by reading labels and making the switch to all-natural, chemical-free, organic, and plant-based products.

⌘ **Clothing:** PBDEs or polybrominated diphenyl ethers used as flame retardants are known to cause increased risk of cancer. Adipose breast tissue and breast milk have been found to contain the largest deposits of these flame retardants in the body. Bras are one of many products that contain PBDEs because of their spandex and foam padding construction (two of the fabrics containing the highest concentration of PBDEs). The longer you wear a bra the longer your skin is exposed to PBDE flame retardant used in a bra fabric. The PBDEs in padded and spandex bras are absorbed through your skin, and can accumulate in breast tissue and milk. Switching to organic cotton bras and undershirts, ditching any extra bra padding, and reducing your bra-wearing time, will decrease your breasts' exposure to these harmful chemicals.

## ⌘ Yoga, Meditation, and Breath Work for Autumn

Stress doesn't just make a person feel older. In a very real sense, it can speed up aging. A recent study published in the *Proceedings of the National Academy of Sciences* found that stress can add years to the age of individual immune system cells. The study focused on telomeres, caps on the end of chromosomes. Whenever a cell divides, the telomeres in that cell get a little shorter and a little more time runs off the clock. When the telomere becomes too short, time runs out: The cell can no longer divide or replenish itself. This is a key process of aging and it's one of the reasons humans can't live forever. In one study, researchers checked both the telomeres and the stress levels of healthy premenopausal women. The stunning result: On average, the immune system cells of highly-stressed women had aged by an extra *ten* years. The strong causal link is that stress hormones shorten telomeres and cut the life span of cells.

One of my yoga teachers, Gurmukh Khalsa, talks about how yoga helps alleviate the effects of pain, broken hearts, anger, disappointment—all the things that we go through on our human journey that contribute to our stress levels and prematurely age us. The following exercises are inspired by Gurmukh's ageless wisdom. They work to build and repair the nervous system and restore vitality and radiance.

Other yoga exercise for this season demonstrates how to hold balance in the body, a useful larger metaphor that reflects the work of autumn in general. Inversions (any pose where the feet are higher than the head and heart) help us achieve a change in perspective as stress constricts our ability to have perspective.

## A Kundalini Arm Set for Tonifying the Nervous System

Specific Kundalini yoga exercises rejuvenate the nervous system and mitigate the effects of stress on it. They work off the idea that advancing motor control in the body helps build new neural pathways in the brain and nervous system. Here are three that strengthen and tone the arms while creating motor movements all the way through to the hands and fingers. Breathe slowly and deeply through the nose for all parts of this set. Start at two minutes for each exercise then work your way up to eleven minutes each when you are fully conditioned.

It is common practice with Kundalini yoga to "tune-in" with an opening mantra: "Ong Namo Guru Dev Namo," known as the Adi Mantra, connects the practitioner to all teachers, gurus, and sages who have come before and those yet to come. At the conclusion of a practice, the mantra "Sat Nam," meaning "truth is my identity," is chanted.

### Circling Arm Extensions

Sit on the floor or yoga mat in easy pose, legs crossed in the way that is most comfortable for you. Extend your arms, elbows locked, up into a high V shape. Fingers are pressed tightly together and pointing straight out. Hands should be above shoulder height slightly. Make small, tight circles rotating the arms backward.

### Criss-Crossed Arm Extensions

Perform this exercise seated in easy pose or standing with feet hip distance apart. Arms are straight overhead, elbows locked, hands open, fingers straight. Cross arms rapidly back and forth in front of your face, alternating which arm goes in front.

### Hand Flapping

Stand with feet hip distance apart, knees very slightly bent (not locked). Raise arms overhead with elbows locked. Begin shaking the hands back and forth as if shaking water off to dry them. Flap hands rapidly and strongly back and forth, making sure to keep elbows very straight. Arms are positioned close to the head. The only movement is in the hands which flap at the wrists.

### Tree Pose (Vrksasana): Dynamic Balance

Perhaps you've heard of the definition of enlightenment as being the ability to hold two opposing ideas or viewpoints in the mind at once. Balancing poses serve as a practical way to give us strength in our legs and feet and are weight bearing exercises which strengthen bone mass (important in preventing osteoporosis) and help us grasp this concept.

Through attempting to maintain balance in the body, we begin to understand that it is the opposite of a thing that defines it, that makes it necessary to better understand it: day needs night, full needs empty, up needs down, love needs loss, female needs male. All would be diminished without the presence of the opposing force to help define them and give them counterbalance. Room must be made for both to exist together so wholeness is achieved. Balance is a state of pushing, as well as pulling, holding as much as releasing.

Tips for practice:

⌘ Place one foot on the inside of the ankle, calf, or upper inner thigh of the opposite leg.

- ⌘ Keep your standing knee a little bit loose; don't lock it fully.
- ⌘ Press the entire sole of the raised foot into the leg that is holding it up, at the same time press that leg's energy back into the foot.  At some point, begin to play with relaxing into this dynamic internally, adjusting the relationship between energy versus relaxation to keep your balance. Imagine your standing foot sending roots down into the earth, while the crown of your head lifts to the sky.  Feel the two opposing energies ground and elongate your body in space.
- ⌘ Hold your hands in prayer pose at your heart, or when you feel steadier, lift them overhead.
- ⌘ Keep the shoulders relaxed and the belly energy pulled in and up.  Keep the low back long; tailbone dropping.
- ⌘ Stay in the pose for at least a minute, longer if you are able, breathing deeply the entire time. Then switch legs.

### Shoulder Stand (Salamba Sarvasgasana):  Inversion for a New Perspective

Inversions provide a liberating feeling by allowing us to escape the normal forces of gravity that have us always walking upright, and to see the world from a new perspective. They are extremely beneficial to the body's physiological systems (lots of blood flow to the brain, stimulation of all organs and glands), but more importantly they afford us the opportunity to shake up our rigid view of a situation, see it from another angle. This is especially valuable when we find ourselves wound tight from layers of stress and worry. Under these conditions it's almost impossible to find a clear way of thinking, responding, or problem solving.

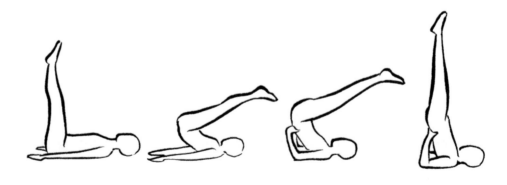

There are many inversions to work your way up to (headstands, handstands, and so forth), but one of these versions of shoulder stand should be accessible to most everyone.

Tips for Practice:

⌘ Lay flat on your back and using your core strength, lift your feet up toward the ceiling. Try to straighten the knees. This is a great stretch for the hamstrings in the backs of the legs.

⌘ Begin pulling the feet toward your head so that the hips begin to lift up off the floor.

⌘ Press your arms into the mat firmly and use your core energy and strength to hold your legs in the air.

⌘ Keep facing forward with a long, relaxed neck. Do not turn your head from side to side.

⌘ If you are able to safely take the pose further, put your hands under your sacrum area and prop your hips up with the support of your elbows. The elbows should form a triangle with your head.

⌘ If you are able, work to straighten the legs up so the feet are lined up over the hips, the hips over the shoulders. Slide your hands up your back toward the mid-spine area for better support and assistance lifting and holding the hips. At this point the bottom tips of the shoulder blades should be off the floor.

⌘ Your chin should be pointed toward the chest. Your body weight should be resting in the shoulders, not in the neck. Come out of the pose if the neck is not feeling comfortable.

⌘ Stay as long as you are able in any of the positions then roll slowly back down to the floor, using this release as an opportunity to again utilize your core abdominal muscles.

## A Forward Bend to Neutralize Stress

Any standing forward bend in yoga is considered a stress-relieving, mind-calming pose. This is because the brain is situated lower than the heart, allowing it to fill with blood and oxygen. This can immediately dampen down a panic attack and suppress nervous anxiety as a default response to life's upsets. Think of the folk wisdom that advises anyone suffering from nausea or who is hyperventilating to sit in a chair, lean over and hang their head between their knees. These yoga poses serve the same purpose with additional benefits—your leg muscle flexibility and toning will also be increased.

Tips for practice:

⌘ Stand with your feet wide apart. Feet should be firmly pressed into the mat. Start with your knees slightly bent, not locked.

⌘ Slowly drop over at the waist and dangle your head and torso toward the floor.

⌘ Let your fingertips reach toward the floor right under you.

⌘ As your flexibility allows, gradually begin to press your knees straighter, getting a nice deep stretch in the inner thighs and hamstrings in the back of the legs.

⌘ If you are able, press your palms into the mat and bend your elbows back toward your body. Draw your head back to line it up under your hips. Shake it gently to keep neck loose.

⌘ Stay as long as you'd like in the pose, letting your deep breaths continue to relax and release tight leg muscles.

⌘ Roll up slowly and carefully to return to a standing position.

### Breath Work

*Alternate Nostril Breathing For a Calm and Balanced Mind*

*Nadi Shodhana*, or *the sweet breath*, is a simple form of yogic alternate nostril breathing which balances left and right brain hemispheres. *Nadi* (channel) refers to the energy pathways through which *prana*, or life force, (*chi*) flows. *Shodhana* (cleansing)—so *channel cleaning. Nadi Shodhana* calms the mind, soothes anxiety and stress, and promotes clear thinking.

⌘ Hold your right hand up and curl your first two fingers toward your palm. Place your thumb on your right nostril and your ring finger by your left. Close the left nostril by pressing gently against it with your thumb and inhale through the right nostril. The breath should be slow, steady, and full as you fill up the lungs completely.

⌘ Now close the right nostril by pressing gently against it with your thumb and open your left nostril by relaxing your ring finger. Slowly exhale all the air in your lungs.

⌘ Close off the right nostril, inhale through the left nostril, close it, and then exhale through the right nostril.

That's one complete round of *Nadi Shodhana*. Begin with five to ten rounds and add more as you feel ready. Remember to keep your breathing slow and steady.

## Chant for Bringing about Balance

Here is a yogic mantra chant which utilizes deep breath, and sound from the breath. It is useful for days that run you ragged, where obligations and responsibilities make your head spin and curling up in a tiny ball in the middle of the floor would at least give you a chance to get off your feet. This chant is said to bring about an integrated and balanced development of body, mind, and emotions in harmony with the divine or inner self. If you tape it to the top of your computer screen, car dashboard, and bathroom mirror you have it there already when you may need it.

Take the very deepest breath you have, then start making the syllable sounds of the chant (I've given you the pronunciation) in a resonant, rich tone that makes your chest area vibrate. Emphasizing the "m" part of each syllable by drawing it out—mmmmm—will make more of a vibration. Think of the bones in your chest as being like a tuning fork. Keep the sound and breath going until you've said all five syllables once through and until you have no breath remaining. Hopefully they will end together. Then refill very deeply and make the chant again, as long as you possibly can, until the very last bit of breath seeps out. Repeat ten times:

### OM HRIM KRIM HUM SHRIM

Definition of chant syllables:

**OM** *(aum):* gives strength, protection, and grace. It connects us with the guidance power of the inner Guru.

**HRIM** *(hreem):* increases our aspiration and receptivity to Divine light, wisdom, and truth. It opens the lotus of the heart to the Inner Sun of consciousness.

**KRIM** *(kreem):* gives energy and transformation. It helps awaken and purify the subtle body.

**HUM** *(hoong):* It is used to destroy negativity and creates great passion and vitality. It represents the soul hidden in the body, the Divine immanent in the world.

**SHRIM** *(shreem):* It opens the heart and gives faith and steadiness to our emotional nature. It gives love, joy, bliss, beauty, and delight.


## ⌘ Healing Bodywork for Autumn

### Hot Stone Massage

This method of bodywork connects the season's themes of grounding and developing a relationship to the mineral kingdom. Stone therapy has been used for over two thousand years. Native American women used to place a warmed stone on their belly during menses. Pilgrims would put a hot stone at the end of their bed to warm their feet. Fasting Japanese priests would wear a sash around their bellies in which three warm stones were placed to help to slow down their digestive process. Hot stone therapy was brought into modern day usage by Arizona massage therapist Mary Nelson, in the mid-1990s.

Basalt is the preferred stone for hot stone massage because of its unique ability to retain heat for longer periods than any other type of stone; natural basalt has a very high iron and magnesium content. Basalt rocks were formed when hot lava spilled out of a volcano as it erupted. Exposed to the elements for millions of years, the minerals were compressed into a concentrated mass of minerals and crystals. Basalt helps to dissipate anger.

The rocks of choice for therapists are those that are perfectly smooth, round or oblong, and flat. The heat from the specially-warmed basalt stones deeply penetrates muscular structures, soothing and releasing tension and toxins, warming and sedating the body's systems.

Warm and hot stones are placed in a formation directly on the body. The localized placement of heat on a particular area increases circulation of fluids and can assist in alleviating organ congestion and may even dissolve masses. This therapeutic bodywork is excellent for PMS and menopausal symptoms. The stones are also used as a massage tool to release knots and soreness deep in the tissues.

## Somatic Movement Education and Therapy

In autumn we seek understanding of our physical bodies and the energy we require; somatic therapy may be a helpful modality. *Somatics* is the term for techniques and approaches that focus on the individual developing and deepening a sense of the self within the body. In the 1960s and 70s people were looking for unconventional cures for their pain and illness and diving deeply into practices based on the mind-body connection. Somatic bodywork aims to free the body from habitual patterns (outward manifestations of the deeper mental and emotional aspects of a person), which cause imbalance, pain, and illness or which have been caused by trauma from injury or disease.

In a state of health, the *soma* moves with grace, ease, and coordination. Conversely, stress, trauma, inner conflicts, and unresolved psychological issues manifest in chronic holding patterns or what is referred to as *muscular armor*.

Regardless of whether pain is physical or emotional, skeletal muscles reflexively contract around pain creating this armor. Chronic contracting creates muscular imbalances that restrict motion, leads to postural problems and if not effectively treated, ultimately causes more pain. A somatic approach will consider these muscular holding patterns as a gateway to unraveling deeper body-mind connections.

Another precept the somatic modalities share is that body awareness is the primary tool for change. The practitioner's gentle touch helps a client become more aware of his or her body—a first step to change. The patient is led through everyday movements (walking, sitting, bending, reaching) to become aware of the body while it is in motion.

The patient is then educated about his or her patterns. He or she becomes an active participant in body explorations that reveal old patterns as well as new, healthier ones, which leads the neuromuscular system toward greater stability and wellness.

All somatic therapy is very noninvasive and gentle with no wear and tear on the body, benefiting anyone from injured dancers and athletes to people suffering back pain from a car accident to someone with a chronic stiff neck. Three of the more well-known examples of somatic movement-based bodywork are the Trager Approach, Alexander Technique, and Feldenkrais Method. Be sure and check the training and accreditation for your practitioner by locating them through their respective institute directory.

## ⌘ Plant Healing for Autumn: Aromatherapy, Herbs, Teas, and Tonics

### Aromatherapy

In many cultures, and especially in the East, the root of a plant is an emblem of its vitality. This is in contrast to the preference we show in the West for all things green, fresh and fragrant. We have no problem admiring the fresh, bracing tang of pine, lavender, or lemon oil, the leafy brightness of violet or geranium, the heady floral top notes of jasmine and ylang-ylang. Not so when it comes to the odors from the earth. Rooty, earthy, musky kinds of smells we can only take in small or diluted quantities.

Yet the root is where plants concentrate their vitality and a vigor that endures and sustains. It is for this reason that in Ayurvedic and Traditional Chinese Medicine there are more remedies derived from roots than from other plant parts.

Roots ground, center, and focus. They impart perseverance, tenacity, and steadfastness. Roots are fundamental components in bringing our attention and awareness into the physical realm of the body for autumn. They are the precise symbol for the down-to-Earth efforts we need to hold when dealing with adult concerns such as stress, insomnia, and reproductive health.

⌘ **Vetiver** (*Vetiveria zizanoides*): this holy herb has its name etched in the oldest sacred book of Hindus—the Bhagavad Gita, where Lord Krishna says, "I am the fragrance of the soil." In its heavy and obscure aroma we can sense the depth and power of roots and the earth in which they thrive; it is redolent with the earthiness of the tropical jungle where it is found. The effects of vetiver are grounding, cooling, strengthening, and desensitizing, helping one to come down from the head and into the body, enhancing all that is sensual, concrete, realistic, and practical in life.

With the use of vetiver, abstract mental gymnastics and neurotic overthinking behavior that thrive on stress and tension are mellowed out and slowed down. For these reasons, it is ideal for work addictions resulting in physical and emotional burnout personified by existential exhaustion. As a natural tranquilizer it assists with sleep and insomnia concerns. Three to four drops of vetiver oil in a warm-water bath before sleep will relax your muscles and help you sleep tight.

It is very helpful for PMS symptoms of depression and crankiness. It seems to exert a regulating action on the hormonal secretions of estrogen and progesterone, which also makes vetiver an appropriate choice during menopause when both these hormones need supplementing, helping to ameliorate hot flashes. Adding a few drops of vetiver oil to carrier oils like coconut or almond oil and massaging your belly, lower abdomen, and pulse points (wrists, neck, behind ears) provides great relief from all these conditions.

⌘ **Angelica Root** (*Angelica archangelica*)

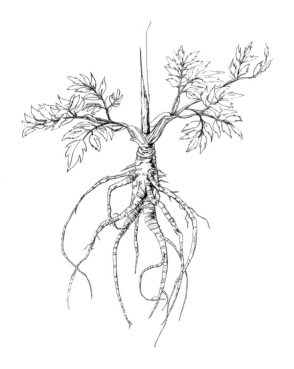

Also known as the Holy Ghost or Holy Spirit Root, Archangel Root and Oil of Angels. Energetically, this essential oil assists the user to be open to the angelic realm, source energy, and higher self. It is a large, aromatic plant related to parsley and carrots. The essential oil is steam distilled from the rhizome with a rich, peppery-sweet, musk-like aroma, reminiscent of the essence and stillness of ancient forests.

Angelica's pleasant yet strange aroma enhances introspection. It is helpful when one is feeling blocked or cut off from their higher self, guides, or higher information. Angelica Root essential oil is very effective when working with the root chakra, since as a root, or underground part of the plant, it is grounding, centering, and stabilizing. It is a wonderful essential oil for times of high anxiety, fear, depression, and instability. A drop or two on the soles of the feet before bedtime can be a wonderful sleep aid and also call in beautiful dreams.

⌘ **Clary Sage** (*Salvia sclarea*) Salvia comes from a Latin word *salvere* meaning "to heal or save" and Clary comes from a Latin word *clarus* meaning "clear," used long ago by the ancient Romans. Its mellow, warm, hay-like, bittersweet and woody aroma is the kind of peculiar, mysterious scent that wafts up when you brush against its host plant in a garden. Its effects on the nervous system are both euphoric and sedative and it is rich in omega 3 antioxidants. Clary Sage soothes the stressed nerves and emotions provoked by hormonal spikes.

One of the many components of Clary Sage is sclareol, which is a natural phytoestrogen, so it can be beneficial to the female reproductive system with hormone balancing effects. This may be useful for amenorrhea, cramps, and menstrual pain. For perimenopause hot flashes, a sponge bath with a few drops of Clary Sage in cool water can help. Its antidepressant characteristics are especially helpful in the treatment of menopausal or PMS emotional rollercoasters. It is likewise effective for feelings of paranoia, panic, or hysteria. Avoid during pregnancy until labor begins.

Many describe Clary Sage's euphoric properties as opening a doorway to the authentic self, feminine knowledge, and inner vision. It seems to augment perception of oneself and clarity of thought, making it useful in meditation and for enhancing true sight.

⌘ **Atlas Cedarwood** (*Cedrus atlantica*) oil is calming, centering and strengthening, helping to resolve insecurities, worries, and emotional upheavals. Rather than elevate and stimulate one's energies like the other fresh-herbaceous conifers (pine, fir, cypress), cedarwood instead descends and calms them. The oil is helpful for mental or emotional burnout and promotes perseverance and will power. Inhaling the oil of cedarwood increases the ability to think clearly and enhances the awareness needed for effective prayer and meditation. This is because of all the essential oils of the world, cedarwood contains the highest concentration of sesquiterpenes (organic scent compounds), which have the ability to pass through the blood-brain barrier and oxygenate the brain directly upon inhalation by way of the nasal passages and the olfactory nerves.

Atlas cedarwood stimulates the limbic region of the brain (the center of emotions) and the pineal gland, which releases melatonin, a hormone important in regulating sleep and to the circadian cycles of the endocrine system. Taken in a bath before bed, cedarwood calms and relaxes and prepares the body for a deep sleep.

## Herbs, Teas, and Tonics

During times of stress, people often feel as though they have nothing solid to stand upon; as if the bottom has given out; the ground beneath their feet feels shaky. The herbs for autumn can be used to help you feel like you are standing on more solid ground. Roots support and firmly ground a person during stressful times. The best delivery system is in dried powder form combined with water for a tea to drink. Brewing up a soothing cup of tea is a calming, peace-inducing ritual in and of itself.

The herbs listed here are referred to in herbal medicine as *nervines* (nerve tonics) and *adaptogens* (any herb that decreases cellular sensitivity to stress). These are herbs that strengthen, tonify and restore balance and harmony to the nervous system. They often contain minerals such as calcium and magnesium, and B vitamins.

⌘ **Astragalus Root,** from the pea family, is one of the fifty elemental herbs that are at the heart of TCM. It helps reduce the effects of stress and tension in the body, which can range from a lowered immune system, heart weakness, high blood pressure, poor digestion, and general malaise. Astragalus is a key herb in traditional Chinese *FuZhen* therapy which concentrates on the body's own ability to rejuvenate. High in antioxidants, iron, and zinc, astragalus is excellent for boosting low energy and lethargy.

⌘ **Ashwaganda** has been used for thousands of years in Ayurvedic medicine. Like Asian ginseng, *ashwagandha* is used to help increase vitality, energy, promote longevity, and strengthen the immune system. It is used to treat high blood pressure, insomnia, chronic fatigue syndrome. It enhances endocrine function, especially the thyroid and adrenals, which absorb and can be overwhelmed by chronic stress. Ayurvedic healers have long prescribed *ashwaganda* to treat exhaustion brought on by both physical and mental strain. (*Caution*: Avoid during pregnancy, if you are taking sedatives, or if you have severe gastric irritation or ulcers. People sensitive to the nightshade group of plants should also exercise caution.)

# Chapter 16

## Healing Beauty Rituals for Autumn

. . . . . . . . . . . . . . . . . . .

*The great thing about getting older is that you don't lose all the other ages you've been.*
*~ Madeleine L'Engle*

In autumn we seek to create a more conscious passage through adulthood's ups and downs, and so, our beauty-care attention is on the aging process and its particular challenges. No matter where you are numerically, chances are you've formed your own opinions (or defenses) about it.

What is your response to looking in the mirror and seeing little lines around the mouth, crow's feet at the eyes, and graying hair? Do you deny it, fight it, or accept it? Maybe it's a blend of all three as we each find our way. Most days I try and figure out how to be and feel inwardly as healthy and vibrant as I possibly can, in the hopes that my outer mien will surely reflect those efforts.

Treating your body as precious cargo, day in and day out, is the best defense against premature aging that there is. Eating nutrient dense foods, avoiding the sun at its most damaging times, avoiding chemical exposure in your beauty products, as well as your physical environments, and exercising regularly for fun and enjoyment, all play a part in how you look as you age. Working on your spiritual development, staying happy and optimistic about the future, as well as appreciating the here and now, being loved, loving others, and managing stress effectively will show up on your face as well. No big secret there.

We're all still gonna get old—if we're lucky. What matters is how you go about it and what you discover about yourself in the process. And if you can set aside a few of the hours you spend beautifying yourself to beautify your neighborhood or some of the money you spend chasing youth to help an actual youth in need, then all the better. A beauty ritual can look like anything and can be anything.

Autumn's roots, gourds, and berries are nature's secret weapons. Their abundance is what we give thanks for at the dinner table, yet miraculously they also possess all the anti-aging components that beauty-product companies are spending millions to market to you. Take in these colorful gifts in all their glory undiluted.

### Carrot Anti-Aging Mask and Blemish Treatment: Collagen Powerhouse

Is there anything more annoying than having to deal with mid-life blemishes while dealing with mid-life wrinkles? The forties get it all: pregnancy hormones still rage for some while others are in full blown perimenopause just a few short years later. Both can wreak havoc on the complexion if not carefully managed. Here's a treatment that addresses each concern with one amazing vegetable.

Carrots are a massive delivery systems for beta carotene which is converted to vitamin A in the body. Vitamin A helps stimulate the production of collagen, encouraging skin cells to behave more like youthful skin cells, diminishing fine lines and wrinkles. Carrots also tone and clarify the skin, since they are naturally antiseptic, as is coconut oil. This makes both of them a reliable treatment for blemishes and breakouts.

4 medium-sized carrots, peeled

4 teaspoons virgin coconut oil

1. Cook (steam or boil), cool, and mash 2 of the carrots and mix with enough of the coconut oil to form a paste.

2. Spread on clean skin and let it set for up to 20 minutes.

3. Rinse with lukewarm water and pat dry. (This mixture can also be used as a hair rejuvenating treatment. Apply after shampooing as you would any deep conditioner. Leave on for up to 10 minutes. Rinse well with warm water.)

4. Juice the other 2 carrots.

5. Whisk the juice with the remaining coconut oil.

6. Spot dab particular stubborn blemishes with a cotton ball dipped in the carrot mixture. Store mixture in a glass jar in the fridge for up to 3 days. Use 3 times a day for best results.

## Brown Rice and Sesame Facial Wash: Ayurvedic Beauty Secret

The rice sloughs off dead skin cells, the fatty acids in the coconut oil make the formula creamy, and the green tea is loaded with antioxidants to unclog pores and fight wrinkles. Sesame seeds are high in vitamins and minerals and a key component in Ayurvedic beauty routines. Use sesame oil to massage rough patches of skin to soften and smooth, as well as to deep condition hair.

1 tablespoon long grain brown rice, uncooked

1 green tea bag, cut open and the tea removed

1 teaspoon sesame seed oil (pure, untoasted)

1. Grind rice and tea in a coffee grinder or blender until smooth.

2. Place in a bowl and stir in oil.

Wet face, and apply with your hands in a circular motion. Rinse with lukewarm water.

## Cranberry Antioxidant Face Scrub: Wrinkles Be Gone

Rich in antioxidants and vitamin C, cranberries are not only a great addition to our diets to help prevent diseases, but also great when applied topically to our skin to help ward off wrinkles, reduce redness, and prevent any signs of skin damage. Vitamin C can regenerate oxidized vitamin E, making this antioxidant combination work synergistically on your skin. Together, they can increase antioxidant power up to seventy times greater than when used individually.

½ cup of whole fresh cranberries

2 tablespoons whole, rolled oats

Liquid from 2 vitamin E capsules

½ teaspoon cane sugar

2 drops of orange essential oil

1 teaspoon Coconut oil

1. Blend cranberries and oats in a blender to small particles.

2. Transfer to a bowl and add the other ingredients. Adjust sugar or add a little bit of coconut oil to make mixture more spreadable.

3. Massage slowly into face in circular motion.

4. Leave on for up to 20 minutes, then rinse off with lukewarm water.

## *Pumpkin Pie for the Piggies: Revitalizing Enzymes*

Pumpkins are just as much fun to work with as a beauty ingredient as they are for eating and Halloween. Pumpkin is comprised of fruit enzymes that break up protein in skin cells when applied topically, making it ideal for sloughing off rough skin. Pumpkin treatments leave skin moisturized, feeling soft and revitalized.

½ cup pureed pumpkin

4 tablespoons organic cane sugar

4 tablespoons sesame or coconut oil (more if needed)

1 generous pinch cinnamon

½ teaspoon natural vanilla extract

1. Blend ingredients thoroughly in a small bowl.

2. Sit on the edge of the bathtub, feet in the tub.

3. Massage mixture into feet (and if desired, hands and body), focusing on rough areas and cuticles.

   Allow mixture to remain on skin for 10 - 20 minutes and then rinse off with warm water.

## Apple/Oatmeal Exfoliating Mask for Toning and Tightening

This dual-action scrub is wonderful because it exfoliates and tones at the same time. The oats and cornmeal work to rid the skin of dead cells and the apple juice tightens and tones. Oats have long been used for enhancing the quality of skin—they are chock full of phytonutrients and antioxidants that feed the tissues of the skin and help to keep it glowing and youthful. Honey has natural anti-microbial properties and works with the oatmeal to calm inflamed skin.

2 tablespoons rolled oats

1½ teaspoons cornmeal

1 tablespoon honey (vegans substitute any kind of sticky syrup—agave, maple, etc., to act as binding agent)

½ apple, peeled and cut into chunks

1.  Mash oats, cornmeal, and honey into a thick paste with a fork.

2.  Combine with the apple pieces in a food processor or blender until smooth.

3.  Apply in a circular motion on face and then let sit for 20 minutes.

Rinse with lukewarm water.


## Oatmeal and Milk Skin-Smoothing Bath

This is a great treatment for cultivating youthful skin quality, as well as soothing dry, itchy or irritated skin. The lipids (fats) in the milk help rejuvenate skin cells and brighten skin tone. The lavender induces deep relaxation in the brain, and helps irritated skin calm down.

1 cup powdered whole milk (organic if possible)

2 cups oats, ground into a fine powder (use food processor or coffee bean grinder for this)

3–5 drops lavender essential oil

1.  While running lukewarm water into the bathtub, sprinkle the milk and oats into the water under the faucet so they can get churned and blended into the bathwater.

2.  Add the lavender last. Shake the drops out evenly over the whole tub full of water.

3.  Soak as long as desired.

# Chapter 17

## Autumn Kitchen Rituals:
## Food, Nutrition, Recipes

. . . . . . . . . . . . . . . . . . .

The food and rituals of food for the autumn are, of course, centered on the harvest and giving thanks for it. The foods of autumn reflect the colors of the changing trees— red (apples, pears, pomegranates, beets), gold (yams, carrots, persimmons, parsnips, pumpkins and squash), and brown/purple (figs, rutabagas, nuts, and seeds); their shapes big and symbolic of mature abundance, their outer shells and skins firm, durable, substantial. We think of the delicate, fragile fruits and vegetables of spring and summer and our desire to eat them raw or lightly cooked to showcase their natural, just-picked taste and beauty. More of autumn's hardy foods require cooking, to provide internal warmth and comfort as we head into cooler days and nights.

The stars of this season don't just fall off a tree or bush and into our outstretched hands, but have to be dug up from their hiding places underground. Just as we've been using roots through aromatherapy and medicinal purposes this season for their ability to convey support, steadfastness, and sturdiness we turn to roots for the same kind of decisive, resolute energy and nutrition they can give us at the table. All root vegetables contain healthful fiber and slow-digesting carbohydrates for sustained energy. Because they feed off their nutrition from the soil in which they're nestled, they contain copious amount of minerals, beta carotenes, and antioxidants. Eaten regularly, their soluble fiber encourages a full feeling and discourages overeating or between-meal snacking, habits necessary for healthy weight maintenance.

Because autumn is the place of the adult on the Medicine Wheel, this season addresses concerns particular to adult eating and nutrition, including stress and how we cope with it through food. Tips are given on how to identify and subvert stress eating. The positive outcome is that when healthful eating habits are practiced, the true glory and sensuality of our food is never more apparent.

Mostly the foods of autumn trigger a feeling of home, friends, and family; deep sense memories of feasts around a communal table celebrating all that is good and glorious about cooking and eating inside by the hearth, while the weather changes around us outside. For this we give many thanks.

## MEAL BLESSINGS AS AN EXPRESSION OF GRATITUDE

In seeking to create a vivid, nourishing relationship with the cosmos, one of the best and most immediate opportunities to do so is through meal blessings. Every day, day in and day out, we have the opportunity to give thanks for the gifts of our food. It's not so much the words themselves, but the state of mind evoked by the expressions of gratitude that is potent. Allowing humbleness to wash over us for an instant, temporarily crowds out self-importance. The larger purpose of our lives often gets lost in the hectic pace of day to day existence. Pausing to bless our meals brings us into the present like nothing else, a simple time-out for peace amid the chaos.

You can create your own expression of gratitude, or employ a family prayer you grew up with. Here is a favorite that has inspired me over the years:

### Unitarian Prayer

*The food which we are about to eat*
*Is Earth, Water, and Sun, compounded through the alchemy of many plants.*
*Therefore Earth, Water and Sun will become part of us.*

> *This food is also the fruit of the labor of many beings and creatures.*
>
> *We are grateful for it.*
>
> *May it give us strength, health, joy.*
>
> *And may it increase our love.*

### Keep the Doctor Away Smoothie

Though most people think the flesh of the apple is the most delicious part, the skin is definitely the most nutritious. The apple skin contains quercetin, an antioxidant compound preventing oxygen molecules from damaging individual cells. This can prevent cell changes that can lead to cancer. Asian pears are customarily given as a pricey and precious gift in China, Japan and Korea. They are high in Vitamin C and potassium. Together the pear and apple give a sweet-tart element to lift this smoothie from the ordinary to the sublime, especially with the neon green hue from the all-important greens.

1 green apple, sliced with peel on

1 Asian pear, sliced with peel on

1 cup fresh kale, spinach, or chard, torn into small pieces

1 inch piece of fresh ginger, peeled

½ cup organic, unfiltered apple juice

Purified water

1. Blend all ingredients until smooth.

Add water to reach desired consistency.

### Autumn Super Granola

The original California hippy food, granola (itself a riff on European muesli), now occupies a vaunted place in our American health-food psyches. With a history stretching back to 1894, there are as many versions of granola now as there are grains of sand. The basic holy trinity of oats, nuts, and fruit has never changed, though. And like almost anything homemade, the end result is just that much more tasty than store-bought. DIY granola is super easy, super quick, and super-efficient as a make-ahead breakfast or portable healthy snack.

This recipe is adapted from Real Food Daily, a Los Angeles institution and mini-chain of vegan restaurants founded and run by Ann Gentry. One of her signature items brings all the latest and greatest high-value foods we are all talking about now into one super-nutritious and delicious combo. I've added applesauce for an even crispy-crunchier texture. A super way to start your day.

3 cups rolled oats

1 cup raw, shelled sunflower seeds

1 cup slivered, raw almonds

½-¾ cup raw pecans, walnuts, or hazelnuts (toasted, if desired, for extra flavor)

1½ teaspoon ground cinnamon

½ teaspoon ground nutmeg

½ teaspoon sea salt

3 tablespoons melted unrefined coconut oil

¾ cup maple syrup

½ cup brown rice syrup

¾ cup organic applesauce

4 tablespoons water

1 tablespoon vanilla extract

2 cups of your favorite dried fruits (raisins, cranberries, goji berries, cherries, chopped apricots or chopped figs work well)

1. Position a rack in the middle of your oven and preheat it to 300° F. Spray 2 baking sheets* (preferably with sides) with cooking oil to coat very well.

2. Mix the oats, seeds, nuts, spices, and salt in a large mixing bowl.

3. Heat the coconut oil over low heat in a heavy saucepan. Add the syrups, applesauce, water, and vanilla and whisk until blended and heated through (about 5 minutes).

4. Drizzle the syrup mixture over the oat mixture, and stir to coat.

5. Divide the granola mixture in two and spoon evenly over the prepared baking sheets.

6. Bake the granola for 45 -50 minutes, or until golden brown and clusters form.

7. As it bakes, stir granola very gently with a fork to evenly brown, every 15 minutes, taking care not to break apart the clusters.

8. Sprinkle the dried fruit evenly over the clusters and bake for an additional 10 minutes.

9. Set granola aside to cool. It will get crunchier as it cools. Store in airtight container for up to one month.

*(2 sheets save time, but no need to buy an extra for this recipe. Just work with half the granola and fruit mixtures at one time on one sheet. )

## STRESS EATING EXPLAINED

Why does the body want dense calories (high fat, high sugar, high salt) when we are under stress? It all started when we were hunters and gatherers and under stress from famine, predators, and the rigors of finding enough food. Our bodies needed a way to replenish our energy stores. When we're stressed the biochemistry of our blood changes.

When the brain perceives that something is wrong—some threat—chemical signals trigger the adrenal glands to flood the body with adrenaline and cortisol (stress hormones). Enzymes are then triggered, which turn on fat cells in the body to become fat-storing machines. Our body pours this cortisol into the blood and alerts the brain to look out for those sweet, high-fat foods. When cortisol has stimulated our appetite it is one of the strongest drives that we have – like the drive to seek a drug. The double whammy for Americans is that we are chronically stressed *and* we're constantly surrounded by an overabundance of the exact products that big-food marketers have created to feed that drive (and their cash registers).

Before reaching for food the following methods will help redirect your awareness about the habits you'd like to change and adjust your stress-eating behaviors.

### Eat Consciously and Mindfully

- ⌘ Identify stress triggers (schedules that are too tight, lack of sleep, anger and resentment about what is expected of you, feeling unsupported by spouse/boss/co-workers/children are common ones)
- ⌘ Have healthy foods within quick reach (prepared ahead of time)
- ⌘ Take ten deep breaths
- ⌘ Drink a big glass of water to feel full
- ⌘ Take a walk
- ⌘ Before you eat anything express gratitude for your food, the people whose labors have brought it into existence, and the benefits it will provide to your health
- ⌘ Eat slowly, carefully, and avoid gulping, rushing, or hurriedly chewing
- ⌘ Stock your kitchen, desk at work, and purse with high-value nutrient foods to help mitigate bio-chemical reactions in the body during times of stress, and which nourish all the body's systems for maximum coping ability.

### Include:

- ⌘ Chia/hemp seeds fight depression
- ⌘ Oatmeal/millet/buckwheat produce serotonin for calm, relaxed feelings
- ⌘ Walnuts contain chemicals that allow blood vessels to relax and lower blood pressure
- ⌘ Dark chocolate (at least 70% cocoa solids) has feel-good chemicals which calm the mind and lower blood pressure
- ⌘ Sweet potatoes boost serotonin levels and are high in antioxidants and beta-carotene
- ⌘ Kale/Brussels sprouts/orange juice are high in calcium which reduce PMS symptoms or even alleviate them altogether

- ⌘ Blueberries support the immune system and help to lower blood pressure
- ⌘ Asparagus/chickpeas stabilize moods

*Avoid:*

- ⌘ Caffeine overstimulates the adrenals which are already on overdrive due to stress
- ⌘ Alcohol spikes sugar levels in blood, bogs down liver function needed for the immune system, disturbs sleep patterns, causes depression, and reduces the ability to judge situations rationally—things feel worse than they really are
- ⌘ Salt triggers hypertension; a restricted salt intake allows the kidneys to remove stress hormones from the bloodstream at a faster rate
- ⌘ Sugar will exacerbate mood swings; it gets you high, then you crash
- ⌘ Trans fats in greasy fried foods will clog liver function, reduce circulation, and raise blood pressure
- ⌘ Animal proteins elevate brain levels of dopamine and norepinephrine, both of which are associated with higher levels of anxiety and stress

### Pumpkin No-Bake Energy Bites

This recipe for easy, on-the-go snacking will help fortify you against bouts of stress eating and provide sustained energy. Nutrient-dense, they are not just for big kids, but serve as a welcome treat in a lunchbox or as an after-school snack.

Pepitas (pumpkin seeds) have one of the highest amounts of iron in food. Their dense, chewy texture can take on added crunch by toasting them in a skillet for few minutes.

8 oz. (about 1 packed cup) chopped dates

¼ cup honey

¼ cup pumpkin puree

1 tablespoon golden, toasted flax seeds*

1 teaspoon ground cinnamon

½ teaspoon ground ginger

¼ teaspoon ground nutmeg

Pinch of salt

1 cup old-fashioned oats (dry, not cooked)

1 cup unsweetened coconut flakes

1 cup toasted pepitas (pumpkin seeds)*

1. Combine the dates, honey, pumpkin puree, flax seeds, spices, and salt in a food processor and pulse until smooth and combined.

2. Transfer the mixture to a large bowl and stir in the oats, coconut flakes, and pepitas until evenly combined. Cover and refrigerate for at least 30 minutes.

3. Once the mixture is cool (and easier to work with), line a small baking pan with parchment or wax paper and press the mixture evenly into the pan, let it cool, and then cut into bars.

4. Store tightly covered in the refrigerator for up to 2 weeks. Makes about 12 bars.

   *Golden flax seeds and pepitas are usually in the bulk bins at natural grocers or often found already toasted and packaged. Toasting brings out their flavor so when working with un-toasted seeds, simply stir a cupful in a skillet over medium heat, continuously, until you smell the aroma and hear the crackling of the seeds. It should take 3-4 minutes, tops.

### Hope's Cranberry Chutney

This is one of those recipes that gets passed from friend to friend, table to table wherever it appears. I've named it after my friend, Hope, who introduced it to me almost fifteen years ago. Subsequently, there hasn't been a holiday feast or party at which I've served it that it hasn't gone home scribbled on a napkin or grocery receipt by request. This creative treatment of the beloved berry will have you rethinking your approach to cranberry sauce for the Thanksgiving table.

1½ pounds fresh cranberries (two 12 oz. bags)

1 cup raisins

½ cup currants

2 cups sugar

1 tablespoon ground cinnamon

1 tablespoon ground ginger

1 teaspoon coarsely ground cloves

1–3 small to medium dried chipotle chilies, crumbled (depending on your level of heat preference)

Juice and rind (chopped) of a large lemon

2 tart apples, cored and coarsely chopped with skin on

1 onion chopped

2 cups celery with leaves on, chopped

1. Wash cranberries with 1½ cups of water. Bring to a boil with raisins, currants, sugar, cinnamon, ginger, cloves, chilies, and lemon juice. Simmer for 30 minutes.

2. Add everything else, simmer for 1½ hours (this amount of time really melds and deepens the flavors, so don't skimp).

3. Remove from heat, cool, mash some of the berries. This is a perfect make-ahead part of your holiday meal. You can refrigerate it and take it right to the table. It'll keep for up to a month in a tightly-covered container.

## Butternut Squash and Roasted Hazelnut Salad

There was an Old European tradition of baking ground hazelnut flour into special cakes to be eaten before bed for more prophetic dreams on All Hallow's Eve (October 31). In England, roasted hazelnuts were used to foretell romantic destinies on this night, as the nuts jumped around the roasting pans on the fire. It was correct to associate hazelnuts with the heart. They contain the second highest levels of Proanthocyanidin (PAC) of all superfoods. These antioxidants strengthen blood vessels, suppress platelet stickiness, reduce cardiovascular disease, and lower blood pressure. Hazelnuts also contain a slew of key minerals, B6, iron, and phosphorous.

3½ cups diced butternut squash

3 tablespoon extra-virgin olive oil

Sea salt and freshly ground pepper

½ cup blanched hazelnuts (without skins)

½ cup pomegranate seeds

3 cups salad greens of choice

1½ teaspoon snipped chives

2½ tablespoons balsamic vinegar

2 tablespoons hazelnut oil

1. Preheat the oven to 425° F. On a baking sheet, toss the squash with 2 tablespoons of the olive oil; season with salt and pepper. Roast for 20 minutes, until tender.

2. Spread the hazelnuts in a pie plate and toast for 6 minutes, until golden. Let cool, then chop.

3. In a large bowl, toss the greens, chives, hazelnuts, pomegranate seeds, and squash.

4. In a small saucepan, whisk together 1 tablespoon of olive oil with the vinegar and hazelnut oil and season with salt and pepper. On a very low heat, whisk the dressing until hot, 3–4 minutes.

5. Pour the dressing over the salad, toss well and serve immediately. Makes 2–3 portions.

### Roasted-Root Vegetables with Caramelized Fig Sauce

Figs are native from Afghanistan to Greece, and in the same family as the mulberry. Siddhartha Gautama (Buddha) is said to have become awakened after he sat under a large fig tree, which became known as the sacred Bodhi tree. In Ayurvedic medicine, figs balance more than just one dosha (mind-body physiological profile). They are used to treat sexual and reproductive issues in both men and women and are recommended after a hard childbirth. Ounce for ounce, figs contain more calcium than cow's milk.

This delicious fig sauce makes use of dried figs after their peak fresh season of late summer.

Paired with our seasonal all-stars of root veggies, this is one lip-smacking orgy of beautiful and healthy food, worthy of any Thanksgiving feast.

6–8 root vegetables of your choice*

Olive oil

Course sea salt

*Caramelized Fig Sauce (below)*

1. Pre-heat oven to 450° F.
2. Scrub and cut up vegetables in bite-sized pieces, leaving peels on, if desired.
3. Line a large baking pan with foil and arrange veggies on pan, then brush or spray generously with olive oil. Sprinkle with sea salt.
4. Roast for 20 minutes, then turn and adjust any sides of veggies that need more cooking. Check for doneness after 30 minutes. (Stick a fork in a couple pieces. The flesh should be very soft.)
5. Arrange cooked veggies on a serving platter and drizzle with warm Fig Sauce.

Makes 5–6 portions.

*Let yourself go wild with your selection of vegetables. Besides trying several varieties of potatoes, you could use yams, Japanese sweet potatoes, parsnips, beets, rutabagas, turnips, and carrots (orange or purple!). Choose medium sizes.

## Caramelized Fig Sauce

(adapted from *Veganomicon* by *Isa Chandra Moskowitz* and T*erry Hope Romero*)

1 tablespoon olive oil

1 clove garlic, chopped

1 small shallot, chopped

1½ cups dried mission figs, chopped

½ cup red cooking wine

½ teaspoon sea salt

½ cup honey

1 cup water

1 tablespoon Dijon mustard

2 teaspoon balsamic vinegar

1. In a small saucepan, sauté garlic and shallot until soft.

2. Add the figs and wine, cover, and bring to a simmer to evaporate most of the wine, approximately 3 minutes.

3. Add salt, water, and honey. Cover and simmer for another 3 minutes.

4. Turn off heat and stir in mustard and vinegar.

5. Transfer to blender and puree until smooth. Add water if mixture is too thick.

6. Serve warm over roasted vegetables.

## EXPLORING GRAINS AND GLUTEN-FREE EATING

Why is America so hooked on wheat? Why have we forsaken all the other wonderful, nutritious, and healthful grains available to us in favor of this one single plant?

Many experts point to genetic meddling that big agribusiness has done to create a "frankenwheat" that is intolerable for proper use by the body's digestive systems. But we also have an over-reliance on packaged and prepared foods containing wheat additives (malt, modified food starch, and dextrin are the most common) that dump more wheat into our systems and huge, entrenched government subsidies to wheat farmers which drive the production cycle that big-ag and big-food conglomerates rely on to flood the market with more wheat. Thus, the average American diet is stuffed with breakfast cereals, pancakes, bagels, donuts, pizza, pasta, subs, cakes, cookies, and snack crackers like a sub-prime mortgage is stuffed with a chain of dubious investors. Much as we invested all our capital in a faulty real estate bubble that popped and triggered the '08 economic meltdown, we've done the same with our food portfolio and it's making many of us sick.

As all good investment counselors will tell you, it's important to continually diversify your portfolio and the same can be said of grains. There are remarkable textures and flavors waiting to be discovered, as well as the great nutrition that alternative grains can provide when they are employed as part of a well-balanced diet. Quinoa, millet, farro, barley, and amaranth are but a few of the choices with which to begin experimenting. (Farro, spelt, kamut, and barley are distant cousins of wheat and as such are not recommended for celiac sufferers needing to completely eliminate all forms of wheat. For the rest of us, they contain a much lower gluten and glycemic load than whole wheat, so they can be viable choices for interesting grain cooking.)

If you are a baker you'll love what almond, coconut, and garbanzo bean flours can contribute to delicious and delicate pastries and breads. Whether you need to be gluten-free or want to reduce your wheat intake for the sake of diet diversity, learning to work with wheat alternatives is an excellent return on investment.

### Autumn Millet and Pomegranate Bowl

Many people believe that the true forbidden fruit mentioned in the story of Adam and Eve was not an apple, but a pomegranate. In the Seven Blessed Foods Ritual on Rosh Hashanah (Jewish New Year), it is wished that the number of good deeds you will do in the coming year are as plentiful as the seeds you find in the pomegranate when you cut it open. Nutritionally, pomegranates are a superb source of vitamin C (one fruit has 40% of daily requirement) and a good source of fiber, iron, phosphorus, calcium, magnesium, and potassium. They are extremely high in polyphenol antioxidants—far higher than oranges, blueberries, cranberries, green tea and red wine—and which fight the free radicals associated with the development of cancer.

Millet is best when cooked as you would a pasta—bring a large pot of water to a boil, then add the millet. After it is cooked, drain and rinse it.

1 cup millet

3 tablespoons brown rice or apple cider vinegar

3 tablespoons brown rice syrup

1 teaspoon fresh lemon juice

1 teaspoon sea salt

Ground black pepper to taste

¾–1 cup fresh pomegranate seeds

1 cup fresh persimmons, peeled, diced (choose fruit that is not too soft, but that will hold up to cutting)

½ cup chopped pistachios, toasted

2–3 cups mixed greens

Organic cruelty-free* poached egg (optional)

Finishing salt (optional; a nice, buttery Hawaiian red would be fantastic here)

1. Bring 2 quarts of lightly salted water to boil. Add millet and return to boil; reduce heat to medium, cover and cook for about 15 minutes, stirring once or twice. Drain the water from the millet, rinse and set aside to cool in a large bowl.

2. Whisk vinegar, syrup, lemon juice, salt and pepper together. Add fruits and nuts to millet bowl.

3. Toss the millet salad with the dressing to coat well. Serve on top of greens which have been placed in a clean serving bowl.

4. If desired, place hot poached egg on top of the millet mixture. Sprinkle with finishing salt and more pomegranate seeds.

Makes 2–3 portions.

* see page 304 for definition of cruelty-free eggs

## Manzana Chili Verde

Southwestern cuisine is an earthy mixture of ingredients cultivated by the Native Americans in the area (blue corn, squash, potatoes) with the spices of Mexican cooking bubbling up across the borders (chilis, cumin, cilantro, garlic). Green chili is a signature dish and as common as ketchup in New Mexico and Arizona, used almost as a condiment in every kind of dish imaginable from scrambled eggs and waffles to meatloaf and enchiladas. Its spicy, tangy mélange of flavors perfectly characterize what Southwestern cooking is all about.

Vegans and vegetarians long ago figured out how to substitute the meat in all their favorite recipes with beans and potatoes so as not to lose the heartiness inherent to them. This is especially important with stews such as chile verde, usually made with pork. I've adapted this recipe from *Veganomicon*, one of my favorite all-time cookbooks that takes meatless cooking to a whole new dimension. It makes clever and stylish use of seasonal tart green apples (*manzanas* in Spanish), and white wine for a superb dish on a cool autumn evening.

3 tablespoons olive oil

1 large onion, diced small

1–3 fresh jalapeño peppers, seeded and chopped into small pieces, for your preferred level of heat

2 large, fresh poblano peppers, seeded and chopped

4 cloves of garlic, minced

3 teaspoons ground cumin

1 teaspoon dried oregano

1 teaspoon sea salt

½ cup dry white wine

1 pound tomatillos, skin removed, washed, and chopped into small pieces

2 Granny Smith apples, cored and cut into small pieces

2½ cups vegetable broth

1 cup fresh cilantro, chopped, reserving ⅓ of this amount for garnish

½ cup chopped scallions, reserving ⅓ of this amount for garnish

1 pound Yukon Gold potatoes, cooked and cut in to bite-sized pieces

One 15 oz. can cooked, small white beans (lima, navy, or cannellini)

Juice of 1 lime

Avocado (optional)

1. Heat olive oil in a large pot over medium high heat.

2. Sauté onion, peppers, and garlic until soft, approximately 10 minutes.

3. Add cumin, oregano and salt and stir for one more minute. Add wine  tomatillos, and cook until soft, another 10 minutes.

4. Add apples, broth, cilantro and scallions, lowering heat to simmer and cooking for 20 more minutes, covered.

5. Turn off stove and use immersion blender to partially puree apple/tomatillo mixture. (If you use a standard blender or food processor in place of an immersion blender, transfer it back to cook pot after mixture is pureed.)

6. Stir potatoes, beans, and lime juice into tomatillo mixture and combine well.

7. Serve garnished with fresh cilantro, scallions, and avocado slices.

Makes 4–5 portions.

### No-Bake Salted Chocolate Pecan Bars

In Texas where I grew up, almost every yard had a producing pecan tree and every adult with a pulse had a favorite recipe (or a strong opinion about one) for Thanksgiving pecan pie. My grandmother's favorite adage was "you know you're a grownup when you can have pie for breakfast and nobody cares" applied year round since she kept a stash of pecans in her freezer for just such a purpose. Her version was certainly rich with loads of white and brown sugar, Karo corn syrup and tons of butter. Oh, the humanity.

I will not attempt to talk you out of your own Thanksgiving pecan pie experience, but in case you wanted something a little healthier and not so button-busting, you can slide these easy, no-bake goodies onto the dessert buffet and know you contributed something equally as satisfying that would turn any grandmother's head.

2 cups raw pecans

1¼ cup shredded unsweetened coconut

½ cup almond butter*

½ cup coconut oil, melted and cooled to room temperature

1 tablespoon coconut flour

¼ teaspoon salt

½ tsp cinnamon

4 large Medjool dates

1 tablespoon bourbon vanilla extract

1 cup high quality dark chocolate bar broken into small chunks

Coarse finishing salt, such as Maldon or Jacobson (the higher quality and crunchier, the better)

1. Prepare 9"×9" inch baking pan by lining with parchment paper, wax paper, or plastic wrap.

2. Add pecans to a food processor, pulse until coarsely chopped.

3. Add remaining ingredients, except for the chocolate chunks. Pulse until mixture comes together to form a dough.

4. Using a wooden spoon and your fingers, press and spread dough evenly in the pan.

5. Refrigerate until set, at least 2 hours.

6. Melt chocolate chunks by placing them in a heat-proof bowl; place this bowl over simmering water in a pot, taking care to make sure water doesn't touch the bottom of the chocolate bowl. Stir until completely melted, about 5 minutes.

7. Drizzle melted chocolate over the pecan base. Use the back of a rubber spatula to spread it out evenly.

8. Sprinkle finishing salt over chocolate. (Be Goldilocks here: not too much, not too little.)

9. Place pan in the refrigerator for one hour or until the chocolate sets a bit, then cut into bars.

10. Keep refrigerated until ready to serve.

Makes 12 bars.

*Make your own almond butter by processing 2 cups of roasted, unsalted almonds in a food processor. Alternate pulsing, processing at full speed, and scraping down the sides with a rubber spatula, until a smooth paste with a sheen forms. This could take 5–8 minutes of processing time. Makes about 8 ounces of almond butter. Store unused portion in glass storage container in fridge for up to one month.

# Chapter 18

## Autumn in Your Home and Family

. . . . . . . . . . . . . . . . . .

A utumn's activities naturally center on home, hearth, and family with the holidays and rituals during this season. Therefore, making your home environment a central component to you and your family's holistic wellness is a worthy undertaking. The effort is about uncovering the essence of your relationship to your home so that it is more than just a storage space for the current and future accumulation of all your stuff or a canvas on which to display your good taste or wealth.

We all know what it feels like to have people in our life who support, care, and look out for us. Your home's spaces can (and should) do the exact same thing. These intangibles have nothing to do with the size of a home or apartment or the cost of materials, but rather intention. Perhaps you've been in a very small and Spartan meditation room at a spa or retreat center and felt immediately at peace and yet felt very agitated and uncomfortable walking into a big house where no expense or design effort has been spared. Or within your own home, you might have certain rooms or parts of rooms that everyone always seems to congregate in, while others go unused.

### Environmental Psychology: A Home That Loves You Back

The cumulative effect of these experiences is known as *environmental psychology* and it can play a part in every type of structure, not just our homes. Attention paid to it has been proven to yield more productive and creative work, cut down on sick days and employee conflicts, and even workplace accidents when utilized properly in offices and factories, so imagine the effect it can have on you and your family. Treating your home as a sacred space, as your place of refuge and refueling and the protective womb that will nourish and support your dreams and goals is as vital as figuring out what foods to eat in order to stay healthy and ward off disease.

My friend Kim Colwell of the Shambhalla Institute here in Los Angeles, is a sustainable interior designer and second generation expert in the psychology of environmental design. She suggests asking some questions to help you change the relationship you have with your home, a particular room, or even an outdoor space.

- ⌘ How do you feel when you walk into your house or a particular room—confusion, overwhelm, dullness, or uplifted and comforted? If you feel overwhelmed then chances are your spaces are very cluttered. We spend more time, energy, and money managing our stuff than we ever have in probably the history of civilization. It's safe to say we all have too much stuff. Kim will cover a client's clutter with a sheet until it can be put in storage boxes and moved out of a room, just to immediately shift the energy. You'd be amazed at how much this can affect our brain processes and carry over into the rest of our lives.

- ⌘ Is a preponderance of stuff in the room from the past which no longer represents the now? Possessions can become security blankets for pain, trauma, upset and stress. Can these things be stored away or disposed of to help shift the energy in the room?

- ⌘ Are public and private spaces properly designated? Are there quiet, darker spaces for cocooning and recharging versus brighter, lighter, busier spaces to hold activity and action? Even one room apartments can have different corners of a room utilized for different purposes.

- ⌘ Is the purpose of the room and the furniture in it being used for what it was designed? In other words, are you using your dining table as a place to take nourishment, break bread and commune with others or for laundry storage and as a filing cabinet for tax records?

- ⌘ Is there a quality of light, color, texture, shape, and aroma in the room that reflects back to you a positive emotion, such as contentment, hope, love, peace, safety?

The answer to these questions can affect great change within our environment and subsequently, our lives. It can help break up a pattern of use in a house or room that could be contributing to depression, chaos, or inertia in our lives.

## SETTING UP A HOME ALTAR SPACE

Setting a specific intention for a space, which can be used for the sole purpose of meditation, prayer, or just quiet contemplation, is a great way to give you claim on the ability to create a home infused with conscious thoughts and habits.

The altar can be anything you want it to be. A bench, table, or couple of wooden crates gives you the starting place. You can drape fabrics over your altar, paint it, decoupage it—whatever moves you. On top you can put candles, incense, photos, knick knacks or tchotchkes—anything meaningful from your life. Children can contribute artwork, you can put money (for prosperity), specific herbs and aromatherapy oils for healing, seasonal food (autumn gourds are great), wine in chalices, beer in mugs, leftover birthday cake. Or nothing at all but a pretty leaf you found on your walk the other day.

This is the space in which to reflect, to take a time out, to re-gather your composure in a crisis, to mediate a family dispute, to memorialize departed loved ones, to mourn a pet, to celebrate a job promotion. A home altar gives you a place and the opportunity to mark the stuff of everyday life before it slips away into the ether. A dedicated space is a dedication to your home's own holiness.

# Chapter 19

## Autumn in Your Community and World

. . . . . . . . . . . . . . . . . . .

A s we begin to think about the seasonal ritual of a Thanksgiving meal and its true meaning of expressing gratitude for all we have, it is worthwhile to ponder the food we *don't* eat and instead, throw away. *Forty percent* of all our American food supply is wasted or thrown away from farm to fork. At the same time we are throwing away almost half of our food supply, we have an obesity epidemic (68% of adults and 32% of children), and *fifty million* people go hungry each night in America.

We have been able to harness technology to create a previously unimaginable bountiful and cheap food supply, yet it has paradoxically created one that is also wasteful and inefficient, one in which calories are cheap and nutrients are expensive. Our country wastes half again as much food as we did in the 1970s.

Environmental issues around food waste are enormous; food waste in our landfills decomposes into methane, a greenhouse gas that is twenty-three times more potent than carbon dioxide. Landfills are the second largest human-related source of methane emissions. Climate change is coming directly from our kitchens. When you add up the amount of oil needed to produce the food we throw away every year, it is seventy times the amount of oil that gushed into the Gulf of Mexico during the three months of the Deepwater Horizon spill.

Eliminating food waste is about changing our habits, as individuals, and as a society. If we could capture just thirty percent of the food that is getting lost we could feed all fifty million Americans who aren't getting adequate food right now. Cutting your food waste in half and giving the money to a soup kitchen would provide seven hundred meals for the hungry (based on the $1500 worth of food waste coming from the average American household per year).

Here are some ways you can manage your food so that less goes to waste:

⌘ Use the freezer; you can freeze cheese, milk, bread, and fruit

⌘ Plan your week's meals and make a detailed shopping list. This will help you to cut down on buying more food than you can eat before it goes bad

⌘ Order and cook smaller portions. Order one entrée at a restaurant and split it between two people

⌘ Always ask for doggy-bags when dining out and take home what you don't finish. The sooner you eat leftovers after the initial dish has been cooked, the less likely it will end up in the garbage several days later

⌘ Do not throw out food prematurely; sell-by and use-by expiration dates are guides for freshness *not safety*. This means that 20% of food waste in homes ($900 million each year) is due to misconception about sell-by dates

⌘ Compost your food scraps. You will be creating a usable soil amendment rather than methane, and you will be returning your food's nutrients to the soil

⌘ Donate prepared food you have left over from school, church, or office events to food pantries and homeless shelters. Every city has Good Samaritan laws to ensure you or your organization won't be held liable for the safety of potluck or catered dishes

We truly live in the land of plenty. *Abundance thinking* is about creating habits to bring others into this experience, connecting your everyday consumption with that of your fellow travelers on this journey. What better time to think about this than as you sit around your holiday table groaning with food?

### Work You Love Can Change the World

> *"Work is love made visible."*
>
> *– Kahlil Gibran*

Much of the focus of our adulthoods is given over to the knotty issue of how to make a living.

But what if we had the luxury of thinking about our jobs, our work with which we make a living, as an extension of our spiritual path in life? What would that look like? How could we begin to manifest that? More importantly, why think about work like that at all?

As the creator of a small eco-aware business, I've spent a lot of time talking with others, participating in discussions and conferences to soak up ideas about what it means to have a more conscious working life and how best to implement these ideas in the real world. The heart of the discussion is about revolutionizing old constructs of work, consumerism, and finally, how economies are actually formulated. Priorities such as work-life balance for the individual, sharing economies, bartering goods for services, worker ownership, collaboration over competitiveness, and social justice as integral to policy (people before profits) are a part of these goals.

The same can be said for how the individual approaches his or her own relationship to work. You don't have to believe or even care that your work will change the world, but you do have to believe and care that it will always change *you.* Do you want that change to be for the better or for the worse? As Henry David Thoreau pointed out with regards to weighing these kinds of decisions, "The price of anything is the amount of life you exchange for it." So your working life will undoubtedly affect your state of mind, which affects your day to day as well as long-term health. Your work is an extension of your most basic holistic living efforts.

Finding a new way of work which represents a spiritual path for you can be found in the least likely places. I hear many stories about how people found their work callings, the main theme being that it emerged out of something the person already liked to do. Sometimes what started out as a skill set related to a craft or hobby is turned into a full-fledged business. Volunteer work done initially as simple means of service turned into a paying position. Some always liked working in groups, so they were drawn to a community of like-minded people that gave birth to a business opportunity.

This season gives us the support and motivation to step fully into our adult selves, to harness our energies, talents, and life experiences toward creating a 2.0 version of ourselves. This is what it means to change the world through our work, and in turn, irrevocably change everything about ourselves.

*We must be willing to let go of the life we planned*
*so as to have the life that is waiting for us.*
**Joseph Campbell**

# Winter

**Element:** Air

**Human Aspect:** Mind

**Key Words:** Contemplate, Stillness, Release

**Season of Life:** Elders (Grandmother/Grandfather)

**World/Kingdom:** Animal

**Energy:** Receive

**Bodily Manifestation:** Breath, Lungs

**Time of Day:** Nighttime

**Heavenly Body:** Stars

**Earthly Manifestations:** Plains/Mesas/Winds

**Animal Totems:** Owl, Hawk, Eagles

**Human Manifestations:** Science and Math, Philosophy, Religion, Abstract Learning

**Self-Expression:** Wisdom, Knowledge, Contemplation, Harmony, Resonance, Alignment, Logic

# Chapter 20

## Themes of the Winter Season: Contemplate, Stillness, Release

. . . . . . . . . . . . . . . . . . . .

The Medicine Wheel makes the final quarter turn heading toward the longest night of the year: the winter solstice, December 21. This is the place of the wise elder within each of us—the grandmother and grandfather—that bestows clarity and patience. The winter is a time to understand and make peace with stillness and waiting, paying attention to the breath as it moves in and out of the lungs. Inside this deep contemplation is the seasonal practice of reviewing the year that has just passed. Nature provides the inspiration for going within, as the animals and plants begin their own hibernation. The north/winter is the place of the animal kingdom on the Wheel. It reminds us of the ancient and intimate role animals play in our lives, the inspiration and guidance they can provide us. Winter retreat is a time of pursuing mental activity and abstract thought, philosophy, knowledge, and logic. The alchemy of the north is about the energy of receiving—having an open mind and receiving information without first judging. Above all, it is a time of taking stock, releasing what is passed, and letting go of what is no longer needed in preparation for the new to come with the spring.

## ⌘ Stories and Rituals to Turn the Wheel

### The Winter Solstice: Summoning the Wise Elder

December 21 represents the winter solstice, that time in our Earth's relationship to the sun which creates the shortest day and longest night of the whole year. The ancients who were compelled to structure their lives around seasonal fluctuations of light and dark knew the secret to a dark midwinter's night—backbreaking outdoor labor must come to a halt; finally it was time to come inside to the fire and rest. They intuitively knew that their metabolisms were slowing down, that the human version of hibernation was built into our DNA, and that the worshipful thing was to recognize the very special magic of the hush of new fallen snow. These circumstances also made an excellent time for storytelling.

One of the West's most enduring and enchanting myths is that of Santa Claus, his elves and reindeer, which traces its roots back to 3000 B.C. to Sami culture and rituals. The Sami people, formerly known as Lapplanders, are from an area that combines parts of Finland, Norway, Sweden and Russia; a region so far north that it is often missing from weather maps on television. Their culture is rich with storytelling, teaching, poetry, and songs. Like Native Americans, the Sami's spiritual practices are based on Shamanism, the animistic belief system which holds that natural objects, natural phenomena, and the universe itself, possess souls. Shamans act as a medium between the visible world and an invisible spirit world; this can also describe Santa's essence.

### Santa Was a Shaman

Other details from the Sami creation myth emerge in Santa's story: he is drawn through the air behind his sacred, magical reindeer, whose antlers symbolize the surging force of life. The tall evergreen tree that became the center of the Christian holiday celebration is the world pole. Shamans all over the world ascend tent poles or trees when they make their astral journeys. Santa knows everything and visits us at night during our dreamtime when shamans do their best work. He knows if we've been good or bad and like karma itself, he gives us our just desserts. His attendants, the toy-making elves, were originally the old ones or elder gods (ancestors). His gifts are the gifts of the spirit-world made material.

The Sami's lives (and livelihoods) have traditionally been completely intertwined with those of their reindeer, so it is no surprise that reindeer are central to the story of Santa. The Sami word for "herd" is *eallu*; the word for "life" is *eallin*. Following the vast herds of reindeer seasonally along their migration routes, they use the reindeer for food, clothing (fur and leather), and in the old days, tools (from the bones)—nothing is wasted. The Sami regard their animals as possessing far more than an economic meaning. Animals represent a spiritual connection, and have been a vital component in helping humans integrate with the natural world around them. The Sami have known this and use the reindeer as one of their spirit guides—connecting them deeply to the Earth, while guiding them into the land of Spirit.

Summon your wise elder and work with him or her in this season. This is knowledge you've been accumulating from all the other seasons and from all your other experiences on the Medicine Wheel. Now is the time to look deep within yourself to tap into this guidance.

## FINDING YOUR ANIMAL SPIRIT GUIDE

It is universal practice in all shamanic healing to summon an animal to guide you on your way and keep you in touch with your true nature. For your non-shamanic, everyday purposes in navigating thorny and complex personal issues, seeking answers or solace in times of heartbreak and confusion, or simply to find a new way of problem solving, an animal guide can be just the right thing. An animal guide need not be your favorite animal or even one that you have previously had any contact with. But it is the one that has the lessons you need to learn and will, in some way, reflect a part of your nature.

I've adapted a basic creative visualization exercise from a 1987 classic, *Maps to Ecstasy: Teachings of an Urban Shaman* by Gabrielle Roth.

⌘ To begin calling in your guide, wrap up in a big, thick blanket and get comfortable lying on your back, on the floor, with your eyes closed (your choice of trance-inducing music playing softly), and begin breathing long, deep breaths. Feel the music entering your body, chest, shoulders, arms, hands, neck, face, hair, and then finally, your belly. When the music ends, let the breath go, and count down from ten to zero.

⌘ At zero, imagine yourself in a beautiful natural setting. In this beautiful place, find a comfortable spot and sit and wait. In your mind, call your spirit animal. Be patient. Within a few minutes your spirit animal will appear. Receive this animal with love. Ask what teaching it brings to you today. Accept any feelings or thoughts that come to you. When it seems time, let it go. But know that whenever you need it you can call out for it and the animal will return to guide and instruct. For now, let it go by taking a few deep breaths, slowly counting zero to ten, and on ten open your eyes.

Immerse yourself in a knowledge-base about your animal to become more familiar with it, and you'll really start to use your animal's qualities in your everyday problem solving. For instance, if your animal is a red fox, you'll learn that they are incredibly adaptable creatures, able to live in almost any habitat in wide temperature ranges. Perhaps this will inspire you to look at the parts of yourself that are inflexible and intractable and seek to find more ways to become adaptable outside your regular comfort zones.

The animal totems for the north on the Medicine Wheel—birds, especially Owl, Hawk, and Eagle—connect us to our higher knowledge and wisdom. Use them as a guide to find clarity with a problem or situation by using the powers of your mind. This can be especially useful if you are someone who tends to be overly emotional in moments that call for clear-headed thinking.

### Waiting Time: Live in the Changing Light of a Room

We reconnect to the richness of our interior lives, who we are when just hanging out with ourselves, perhaps using winter's weather excuse (or not) to cocoon inside. So much of our current form of existence is predicated on putting our energies and attentions outward to be heard above the noise and clatter always coming at us, straining to be seen and noticed separately from the hordes milling around us. Withdrawing our energies from these kinds of efforts is extremely challenging in our high-achievement-oriented culture, which defines success in any realm by measurable output. We are trained and conditioned to go, do, be. Very little emphasis is placed on quiet reflection, on solitude, on being alone, doing nothing. This is a very different relationship to self, even than prayer (often used for seeking solutions or absolutions) or meditation with its stated goal of "emptying the mind."

Waiting time, as we might call it, is its own thing. It actively puts the brakes on problem-solving and goal-setting. It is optimal to have exterior peace and quiet, yet it doesn't demand complete interior nothingness. It allows for mind wondering and daydreaming; it can be done in a body that is moving or still. Find waiting time on an ordinary day this winter, when staying in is a holiday gift or two that you give yourself.

Here is how May Sarton, in her classic book, *Journal of a Solitude* describes a day like this:

*January 18th*

*A strange, empty day. I did not feel well, lay around, looked at daffodils against the white walls, and twice thought I must be having hallucinations because of their extraordinary scent that goes from room to room. I always forget how important the empty days are, how important it may be sometimes not to expect to produce anything, even a few lines in a journal. I am still pursued by a neurosis about work inherited from my father. A day where one has not pushed oneself to the limit seems a damaged day, a sinful day. Not so! The most valuable thing we can do for the psyche, occasionally, is to let it rest, wander, live in the changing light of a room, not try to be or do anything whatever. Tonight I do feel in a state of grace, limbered up, less strained.*

To a person, I'm sure everyone reading this feels nothing is as premium as a day like May Sarton's "strange, empty day." But it is precisely the good thing we all need to have in our lives *every now and then*, even if only rarely, to make the important connections to our wise elder. That person exists within each of us no matter what our age. And she's got nothing but time on her side. She has stepped back from the hysteria of day-to-day life that permeates our younger selves. She knows that true wisdom, insights that will last and have resonance, don't show up unless they are bidden, invited, and waited for quietly and patiently.

## Owls in the Morning

I awake just before sunrise, around 5:30 a.m. Everyone else in the household is still sleeping and it is a bit chilly, maybe upper forties in temperature. I have been dreaming of my father; today would have been his birthday. My mother's would have been in a week. These dates bubble up from my subconscious every year at this time, since both of their deaths occurred around this time as well. My sense memory moves awareness of the dates into my body and I carry them around as an undercurrent of emotions and feelings for several weeks. It's a bad anniversary of sorts.

This winter the owls on my hill have been especially active. We have great horned owls around here and for the better part of November and December they became very vocal as soon as the sun went down each evening. Great horned owls look for their mates in early winter, in anticipation of nesting and breeding beginning in January and February. This early morning in February, it is owl talk I hear, a loud discussion and review of the night's hunting, right outside my window. I suddenly realize it was these two late-night stragglers who probably woke me up. I find myself compelled to see if I can actually spot them, so I slip out of bed and wander out on my back deck. There is a thin sliver of sky showing a weak streak of burnt orange in anticipation of the coming sun. I turn and look up at the tall junipers on the edge of my property about forty feet from my deck.

There they both are, on the uppermost tips where the junipers taper off into thinner, smaller fronds. The owls' weight make the tops sway precariously. The birds look down at me when I involuntarily gasp, not expecting to see them instantly and so close. My sound startles one of them, and it flies off, silvery and coppery in the cool morning light. I crane my head back to get the best view of the remaining one and hold my breath, knowing that my time with him (or her) is limited. We keep staring at one another until it hoots dismissively at me and flies off in a big whoosh, right over my head. The air around me is charged by the beating wings of the big bird.

### Desert Solitude

Late January or early February is my favorite time of year to visit the desert two hours away from Los Angeles, at Joshua Tree National Park, for hiking and hot mineral water soaks. It is quieter this time of year, the tourists from the holidays having all gone home. I decide it's my time to take off for a short trip out, anxious for some quiet that's *so quiet* it will make my ears ring.

There is also a greater likelihood at this time that some kind of winter storm will come along to dump snow on the mountains and rain on the desert floor. If this happens, the skies will get dramatic and quickly turn from deep blue to the roiling grays and blacks of the incoming storm. The natural hot springs burbling up all over the area are the place to be during these rare tempests. If you are extremely lucky, sometimes while sitting in a tub or pool smelling the sulfuric mineral water soaking into your bones and bloodstream, it will rain on you for a little bit. Or you can see the snow falling on the top of Mt. San Jacinto, as it muscularly juts up some 10,000 feet from the desert floor.

The desert holds a quiet allure to me and its beauty is subtle, rather than flashy. To appreciate it, you must get out and walk around. At first it seems an endless dry sea of brown, but soon you will start to notice other sorts of colors and textures that go beyond first perceptions.

⌘

On this particular visit, I take a hike toward an oasis. They are more common out in this area than you would think. The Native American desert dwellers knew all about them, for they were the sustaining sources of water. The fault lines that give California its earthquakes are the same geology that created all the hot springs as well as cold underground fresh water sources out here. The springs usually appear at the top inner walls of canyons through the fissures in the red and cream-colored canyons.

I find a large flat rock and lie down on it. The sun on the rock is soft and the complete quiet of my patch of the world in this moment is breathtakingly awesome. My breath seeps out of my body in great heaving sighs of relief, forcing me to let go of all my city tension. I feel the wound-up energy of my daily hamster wheel spinning to a halt in my body. I pull a little piece of sage off a nearby shrub and rub the leaf between my fingers. The aroma immediately reminds me of sitting in ceremonial circles washing the smoke over my body, giving thanks in humble gratitude for being alive.

## Making It Right:  The Ho'oponopono Prayer

I begin to try and sort through the dream I had about my dad and the emotions I've been carrying around for a few weeks. I feel fortunate to have had the owl sighting this morning. Besides being one of the totem animals for winter on the Wheel; owl-medicine in general is potent to Native Americans. Owl is honored as the keeper of spirits who have passed from one plane to another. Many myths refer to Owl as accompanying a person on his or her journey into the afterlife, winging its newly freed soul from the physical world into the realm of Spirit.

Beyond simply missing both my parents at this particular time of year, I've been fixated lately on my lack of vigilance in noticing the early signs and symptoms of my father's lymphoma that would be Stage 3 before it was finally discovered. I'm still wrestling with how much more comfort I could have provided him in his final months. I made the decision to power through some heavy-duty work commitments rather than put them off, as I should have, to spend more time with him through the roughest parts of his chemo treatments. He took a turn for the worse and I began making weekly trips up to the hospital in Portland.

One week I took a break to fly home to L.A. for a few days leaving my brother on duty. It was my dad's birthday and while he was sleeping, I left him a blanket and some slippers I had bought him. The next day he suddenly slipped into unconsciousness and although I made it back up to him before he drew his final breaths, I had to bid him my goodbyes hoping somehow he knew I had come back, that I was there in person. My bad timing has haunted me fiercely ever since.

Perhaps the owl I saw was a sign that my father had been safely escorted onward to the next place in his journey. A part of me already knows this, but I still blame myself for not having been a better guardian of his leave-taking. At the same time, I also suspect he didn't want me there keeping him from going, holding on too fiercely, when what he needed was for me to just let go. I search for some relief now, by just feeling my breath, trying to make it deep and slow.

Then I remember something haven't thought about in a while, but which gives enormous comfort. It's the *Ho'oponopono* mantra—a traditional Hawaiian prayer for reconciliation and forgiveness, originally used as a tool to help heal rifts in the community and in families.

*I'm sorry*
*Please forgive me*
*I love you*
*Thank you.*

Its basic tenet is that each person bears the responsibility for making things right with anyone with whom they have an issue or problem. It can also be used for self-forgiveness, sometimes the most challenging kind of forgiveness there is.

The beauty and power of this mantra is in its simplicity and directness. It's easy to remember, can be applied to any human relationship, and confers instantaneous results.

I start the chant in my mind and gradually let it be born outward on my breath. I croak out a small whisper and repeat it a dozen times, then I talk it conversationally, until I feel ready to project my voice up against the rust-colored boulders and into the canyon crevices with a shout of declarative energy: *I'm sorry, Dad. Please forgive me. I love you. Thank you.*

Over and over the words spill out. When I stop, utter silence. My ears strain to hear more than my own breathing. The wind has picked up a bit and it is shushing through the fronds of some nearby palms, as a parent would shush to comfort a child.

## Liberation and Release with Moksha

We now consider the true calling of this last phase of the Medicine Wheel and that is death. Death in the sense of a letting go, of release, of a dying off as an absolute necessity for allowing the regeneration of spring energy to begin.

If you've ever played with Tarot cards, you've understood the good fortune of getting the Death card in a reading. It portends an auspicious moment in your life when something must be allowed to die so that the next new phase can start to take root and grow. Life is richer when we no longer fear death of any kind—ours, others', or that of situations and phases. Understanding that everything must die gives everything more meaning. We are able to better separate the wheat from the chaff. When we are truly "working the Wheel" we know we will always move into another spring even after our last corporeal winter.

In Sanskrit there is a word with a similar concept of release called *moksha*. *Moksha* refers to liberation from the cycle of death and rebirth; it can also mean salvation, deliverance, freedom, and the natural state of the soul.

Voluntarily examining our attachments, as well as our feelings toward them, is important work to undertake from time to time. Just about every single spiritual discipline that I can think of teaches the value of non-attachment and the insight that is to be gained when one practices it.

Our culture places a premium on activities of acquisition and consuming, never more so than at this time of year with the holidays upon us. We can let our possessions or even our collection of certain friends define who we are as a person and define our self-worth. Whether you take the time to reconsider some of your material attachments and their meaning or whether you begin the process of non-attachment to those whom you most love, practicing *moksha* will definitely move you toward some worthwhile insights and toward your wise elder of winter.

## RITUAL TO CULTIVATE MOKSHA:
### RELEASING FEAR, CALLING IN PROTECTION

One of the stumbling blocks to letting go, to releasing attachment, is fear. We are afraid of what we don't know, and we can't know what's on the other side of letting go. Here's a ritual you can do for protection and releasing fear. Perhaps feeling safe helps dissolve fears and dissolving some of your fears is the first step in releasing your attachments on the way to *moksha*.

### The Durga Mantra

Goddess Durga is one of the most beloved figures in the Hindu pantheon and is referred to as the mother of the whole world and all nature; she protects her children from all troubles. The Durga mantra is the chant to Maa Durga, the Mother with whom we can have a soul talk about our sufferings and troubles and ask for help and guidance.

**Chant:** Om dum durgayei namaha

**Pronunciation:** Om doom door-gah-yay nahm-ah-hah

**Translation:** Om and Salutations to that feminine energy which protects from all manner of negative influences.

Dum is the seed mantra for energy of protection. A seed mantra is the quintessence of mantra, a distillation of sound containing infinite meaning in a single syllable. It is a vessel of self-generating power.

### Dissolving Fears Ritual

⌘ Place an ice cube, fifty-four drops of cypress essential oil, and a white carnation into a small silver or ceramic bowl. (The prettier and more decorative, the better).

⌘ Take a plain white pillar candle and with a toothpick scratch the symbol for protection that we used in our Autumn Hazelnut Divination (p. 165). This is the shield symbol (a circle with four dots placed where the four directions would be, with a fifth dot in the exact center of the other four). Light the candle.

⌘ Write your fears on a piece of paper, then burn the paper in the candle. You can drop the last burning bits into the bowl with the ice cube. The ashes should slowly be drowned by the melt of the ice cube.

⌘ Chant the Durga mantra fifty-four times (one each for the fifty-four letters in the Sanskrit alphabet and for the fifty-four intersecting *marma*, or energy points, in the body p. 27).

⌘ Blow out the candle and let the bowl remain as is until all the water from the ice cube has evaporated.

Besides being the color of north and winter on the Medicine Wheel, white also symbolizes truth, purity, trust, and innocence. Cypress is good for depression, calming fear, and generally imparts a soothing, tranquil effect on mental panic when used. White carnations are typically used to honor mothers.

# Chapter 21

## Essential Winter Health Practices

. . . . . . . . . . . . . . . . . .

On the Wheel, north/winter is the place of the mind and mental energy, and the bodily manifestation is represented by the breath and the lungs. Our emphasis is now on supporting lung health and cultivating a strong breath as antidotes to grief, which can settle in the lungs. Grief this time of year seems to go hand in hand with seasonal disorientation (lack of sunlight) and depression. This makes sense, as we are perhaps unconsciously grieving what we are preparing to let go of, what needs to die. Depression and sadness will suppress the immune system and winter is naturally a time of more flus, colds, and respiratory illnesses. Taking the information that comes from learning about the *Ho'oponopono* mantra, we can make critical connections into the mind body connection here, as a way to heal ourselves.

### Protecting the Immune System Through Mind-Body Connections

Nathan DeWall is a University of Kentucky psychologist and researcher in the field of social psychology. In studying the brain, he has found that physical pain and social pain share much of the same neural circuitry. The brain makes no distinction between a verbal or a physical insult. It has evolved to economically allocate its resources so that instead of creating an entirely new system to respond to social hurt, the brain has piggybacked the system for emotional pain onto that for physical pain. This dual role of the brain's pain network offers a powerful example of the connection between mind and body, and helps explain how emotional distress can make us sick, and human kindness sustains us in health.

This study sheds light on why depression, a kind of emotional-pain disorder, coexists so often in people who also have chronic or neuropathic pain disorders. It underscores the profound importance of social connection as an evolutionary imperative and the key to our survival as individuals and a society, as this system forces us to focus on the essential task of binding up torn social fabric, of nurturing our relationships with others after the immediate threat of expulsion from the group has passed. It has helped make us the uniquely social creatures that we are.

A 1949 discovery by Canadian neuropsychologist, Donald Hebb, found that each feeling, thought, or sensation a person experiences gets embedded in the brain's neurons and forms a network. Repeated experiences become increasingly embedded in this network, making it easier for the neurons to respond to the experience and more difficult to unwire them to respond differently. The axiom "what fires together wires together" describes this process.

Fighting off depression and anxiety, maintaining mental acuity into old-age and supporting general feelings of wellbeing at any age can be helped by understanding how important it is to continually feed the brain with positive thoughts and behaviors, new mental challenges that keep the brain from going to old pathways, and socialization with others who have our best interests at heart. Meditation and positive psychology techniques, including affirmations, are tools that have a proven track record for healthy brains.

## NEUTRALIZING WINTER DEPRESSION AND SAD

Seasonal Affectation Disorder (SAD) shows up in many people as the winter blues and manifests in mild symptoms of depression, although some people are severely affected and may need to seek out professional treatment. Men and women both report getting it, although women are more likely to develop it. Women appear particularly vulnerable during their reproductive years due to hormonal fluctuations.

### Coping Strategies
- ⌘ Get as much natural light as possible between 6:00 a.m. and 8:00 a.m.
- ⌘ Go for a walk or at least sit by a window

- ⌘ Open the curtains, pull up the shades, and spend time in the sunniest room in the house
- ⌘ Eat lunch outside, if possible. Even if it's cloudy, the natural light will do you good
- ⌘ Watch what you eat—the carbohydrate craving common in people experiencing winter depression, is thought to be caused by decreased levels of the brain neurotransmitter serotonin
- ⌘ Up your intake of vitamin D. It is thought to help elevate mood in those susceptible to SAD—sun exposure, oily fish (salmon, mackerel, tuna), tofu, egg yolks, and mushrooms are excellent sources. Other vegan sources include orange juice, soy yogurt, and almond milk
- ⌘ Keep your body clock in sync by rising and retiring at the same time each day, even on weekends or days off from work
- ⌘ Essential oils like peppermint, lemon, clary sage, bergamot, and geranium are all excellent mood elevators. Sprinkle a few drops on a tissue and hold directly under your nose, use in a room atomizer, or find in a high quality candle

### Depression, Nutrition, Dreams

I had a naturopath once tell me that "depression isn't the mind crying out in pain but the body crying out for nutrition". This stands to reason, as the brain is mostly fat, so foods that are high in the "good fats" (essential fatty acids/omega 3s) can keep the brain functioning properly. Nutrient deficiencies are now believed by some medical professionals to be responsible for the epidemic of depression we are seeing in America and countries that have adopted our way of eating. A diet consisting of fried and processed foods full of hydrogenated oils and no fresh, pure sources of omega 3s is not only bad for the heart and increases the risk of cancer, but is bad for the brain, too. Could this epidemic also be a reflection of anti-fat diet fads for the last decade? Is the mostly female obsession with low-fat, no-fat food labels reflected in the staggering numbers of American women who are now on antidepressants?

Spanish researchers conducted a study on twelve thousand adults for six years and found that those who favored healthy fats of olive oil, fish, nuts, and seeds in their diets had a *30% reduced risk* of depression. Those whose diets had high levels of trans-fats had a *48% increased risk* of depression. Trans-fatty acids cause a decrease in the correct transmission of the nervous response and a decrease in neuroprotection and neuronal regeneration.

---

### WOMEN AND ANTIDEPRESSANTS

⌘ Nearly one in four American women are taking anti-depressants (only 15% of men take them)

⌘ The popular anti-depressant Paxil has been newly implicated in studies linking its users to higher risk of breast cancer

⌘ In 2011, American pharmacists filled 264 million prescriptions for antidepressants, up more than twenty-five million since 2007. The number of prescriptions written for antidepressants has seen a 300% increase in the last twenty years

⌘ A review of thirty years of data by the *Journal of the American Medical Association* (JAMA) found that SSRIs (the class of drugs most prescribed antidepressants are in), work little better than a placebo for people whose depression is simply mild to moderate

⌘ People who use anti-anxiety medication have a 36% increased mortality risk

---

In another study, Canadian researchers found that depressed patients taking 1200 mg of fish oil a day had about *the same level* of relief as they'd likely get from pills. (Vegans and vegetarians can get adequate levels of essential fatty acids from plant sources such as flax, chia and hemp seeds, avocado, walnuts).

Without sufficient quantities of the amino acids tyrosine and tryptophan the body can't manufacture serotonin and dopamine, the mood boosting neurotransmitters that are the target of most antidepressants. A well-balanced brain also requires zinc to enhance the receptors' ability to interact with the neurotransmitters, and B6 and B12 to maintain healthy nerve cells. A dietary deficiency of vitamin B6 may result in low serotonin levels.

In addition, several dietary, lifestyle, and health factors reduce the conversion of tryptophan to serotonin, including cigarette smoking, high sugar intake, alcohol abuse, excessive consumption of protein, hypoglycemia, and diabetes. Low serotonin levels are associated with depression, anxiety, irritability, impatience, impulsiveness, inability to concentrate, weight gain, overeating, carbohydrate cravings, poor dream recall, and insomnia.

### Using a Dream Journal for Winter Mental Health

Marred dream recall as a side effect of improper nutrition is particularly alarming to me. Having a vital and ongoing relationship to your dreams is essential to balanced wellbeing. Every single Native American teacher and elder with whom I've ever come in contact emphasized this point; especially vital, since the shaman's journey is launched in the unconscious mind. Each dream is a potential source of insight and change. When you can remember your dreams, you gain increased knowledge, self-awareness, and self-healing. Dreams are an extension of how you perceive yourself; a source of inspiration, imagination, and creative problem solving.

Your ability to access your own wise elder while working this section of the Wheel can be through your dreams. The winter has perhaps brought the gift of staying in, napping more, and sleeping more. Let your first stop on the road to wellness this season be through connecting your daily nutrition to the ability to remember your dreams. Keep a dream-wellness journal by your bedside to jot down your dreams immediately upon waking.

Every fragment, every sensation, every image is an offering of nourishment and healing that has been given especially to you. Honor these gifts as you would the blessings of good, healthful food to put in your mouth.

## ⌘ Yoga, Meditation, and Breath Work for Winter

### Breath and Pranayama: Winter Survival

In winter, the breath is clearly visible as the hot air from our lungs condenses on the cold air of the atmosphere around us. Winter gives us the visual reminder of the magic of our breath. The breath is a perfect metaphor for the one thing in life which doesn't change, which remains the same as long as we are alive. In our most intense periods of upheaval, drama, and change, the breath, *your* breath, is the tangible, consistent thing that is always there for you.

By practicing *pranayama* you are helping to energize your life force through your breath. The stronger the breath, the stronger the *prana* or life force. I've given you specific *pranayama* to support the particular themes of each season. In this season we connect to the essentials of the breath, to the lungs, and the whole of the respiratory system that supports the breath.

Both Hatha and Kundalini yoga provide a superb series of poses and breath work to parallel our wellness goals during winter season—a Circulation Set, which raises internal heat and creates warmth, and a series of poses that will provide comfort and security to offset the intensity of the letting-go and releasing-of-fears work you are doing this season. Called *restorative poses*, these poses celebrate and accentuate slowing down the body and mind. Their function is to repair and nourish you during the quiet break you will be giving yourself.

### A Kundalini Yoga Circulation Set to Warm Up, Keep up

These exercises focus on generating warmth in the body—perfect for those cold winter days when it's a little hard to get going. They also stimulate energy around the heart and thymus gland. Opening up energy around the heart helps to release fear. The thymus helps regulate the immune system, as well as the circulation and respiration systems. This set is only about fifteen or twenty minutes from start to finish: a quick and efficient way to kick start your day. Don't forget to start this set with the Adi Mantra and upon completion of this Kundalini set, chant "Sat Nam," described on page 181.

**Warm Up:** Hold hands in prayer in front of chest—heart area, then rotate wrists so fingers are facing out away from body, thumbs are facing up to ceiling. Rub hands together vigorously, holding elbows up and out to the side. Do for two minutes.

**Stretch Pose:** Lying on your back, arms by your side, lift head, torso, arms, and legs off floor. Palms face the floor as you press your low back against the floor and pull you belly toward your spine. Try to hold yourself up with the strength of your abdominal muscles, not your neck or upper back muscles. Pull chin down toward chest. Look at your toes. Do Breath of Fire (page 47) for one minute. Rest for fifteen seconds, and do a second set for one more minute.

**Lifting Bridge Pose:** Squat down, then place the palms flat on the ground behind the buttocks. (1A) Inhale and pull the hips up into a modified bridge pose. The spine is arched way up. (1B) In this position, begin swinging the head up and down as fast as you can with Breath of Fire. Continue for fifteen seconds. Then, continuing Breath of Fire, alternately raise and lower the buttocks rapidly and powerfully (1A, 1B) for one minute. Try to work up to two minutes as you get used to this exercise.

**1A**               **1B**

**Frog Pose:** Sit down in a squat position on the floor with your buttocks resting on your lifted heels. Feet are about hip distance. Your fingertips are resting on the floor in front of you with your bent knees angled out to each side. Inhale and straighten legs, keep looking at the floor in front of your feet. Exhale bend and sit back down on heels. Repeat up and down, lifting on inhales bending on exhales. Keep your fingertips on the floor as you straighten and bend the legs. Tight hamstrings may mean you don't straighten your legs all the way just yet. Keep going up and down as rapidly as you can for two minutes.

Bonus: Frog pose also helps to combat depression. It brings blood flow to the adrenals, located at the root chakra (base of the spine) in the pelvis. Over-taxed adrenals from unmanaged stress can manifest in depression and anxiety.

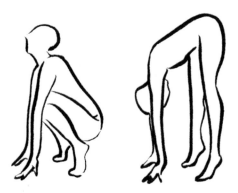

### Restorative (Suptas) Poses:  Quiet Time for Healing

The alchemy of the north on the Medicine Wheel is to receive with the mind. Holding with the mind (inflexible thought) or determining with the mind (pre-determined judgment) promotes imbalance. The Wheel counsels that living in balance means cultivating an open, flexible mental state which allows your innate wisdom to flourish. Restorative poses provide your body with quiet time and space so that your mental energies can be directed toward receiving your wise elder guidance. This is an excellent time, therefore, to be ready to receive problem-solving ideas and inspirations.

These Hatha poses come from a class of poses known as *supta* (reclining) and are traditionally done at the end of a vigorous yoga practice session to help the body cool and slow down before engaging back out in the world again. In beginner classes they can be supported versions of more challenging poses and make use of props to help the spine, for example, or hamstrings or hips to open and release without strain.

Many yoga studios have created specialty classes using *suptas* and prop intensive poses called Restorative Yoga Classes. They are commonly held on Sunday afternoons or evenings as a way to align with the slower, easier energy of that day of the week. Some are enhanced by candlelight and perhaps a live musician playing harmonium. I urge you to replicate a similarly soothing atmosphere by making sacred your home practice space with all the mood lighting, candles, fabrics, and music you can muster.

Because you will be arranging your body in the poses specifically to minimize any strain or strong effort on your part, you will need to gather a few props to help facilitate this goal.

You'll need:

⌘ A yoga bolster or thick, firm couch cushion or pillow about three to four feet long and 18"–24" inches wide. You want something here that is without give, sturdy not cushy, similar in feel to a futon.

⌘ Two or three yoga blankets or thick, heavy blankets with a dense weave.

⌘ Two yoga blocks or two large, heavy dictionary-sized books (at least six inches thick)

⌘ One eye pillow or eye mask

Because there is no movement in the restorative posture sequence, it's a good idea to wear clothing that will keep you warm and cozy, especially if practicing on a cold day. Wear socks to keep your feet warm and it's most advisable to practice on top of a warm blanket on a rug, if you don't have carpeting underneath you. Stay as long as you'd like in each pose; generally five minutes is considered to be very therapeutic, but feel free to stay longer.

Other tips:

⌘ Practice deep, full breathing. Breathe in spaciousness. Breathe out anything that you are grasping, clinching, or holding onto. Try to notice where you might be holding tension in your body. Use your exhales to help dislodge that tension and breathe it out.

⌘ Meditate on your heart opening, full, and free of worry.

⌘ Allow yourself the relief of surrendering to the forces of gravity; let gravity do all the work here of opening up your body.

⌘ Keep letting go of any thoughts that arise that will take you out of the practice in this moment.

## Child's Pose (Supported Balasana)

This becomes a counter-pose to Camel (page 110) when practiced right after. It moves the spine into a neutral position as it releases the whole of the back body. Hips open up as well. This pose confers deep feelings of safety.

Tips for Practice:

⌘ The bolster should be pressing right in under the belly, close to the pubic bone so you are fully supported with an option to put a block under the top part of the bolster for even more elevation.

⌘ Place an extra blanket on top of the bolster if needed as the head often appreciates a little support.

⌘ Spend equal time with your head turned in each direction. Or if the neck does not like being turned, place the hands on the bolster and rest the head on the hands, facing down.

## Legs Up the Wall (Supported Viparita Karani)

This posture reverses daily effects of gravity on circulation, legs, and internal organs and as a result helps soothe anxiety, upset, and agitation. Anytime the head is lower in space than the feet, the brain is enlivened by extra blood flow. This surplus of oxygen is a mood lifter.

Tips for practice:

⌘ Place a bolster alongside a wall, a couple of inches out, and sit sideways on the bolster. Swing the legs up the wall and shuffle in so the buttocks are fairly close to the wall.

⌘ The legs can be comfortably apart for this version.

⌘ If the lower back is sensitive you may like to practice the simpler Legs Up the Wall Pose without the bolster under the hips.

⌘ If you are very tight in the back of the legs, come off the bolster and allow the buttocks to move away from the wall, so the legs will be at an angle.

### Corpse Pose (Savasana)

Yoga has given us the gift of letting us pretend to be dead through this pose. To relax to the point of leaving behind our awareness of the world around us and surrendering to a state of nothingness is exquisite. By residing in the state between fully awake and fully asleep, the brain produces alpha frequency waves. It is the gateway to your subconscious mind and lies at the base of your conscious awareness. *The voice of the alpha state is your wise elder, which becomes clearer and more profound the more you slow down the brain frequency.*

Tips for practice:

⌘ Lie on your back on the floor, head resting on only a thin layer of blanket or nothing at all (avoid propping up the head with a thick cushion or pillow as this can strain the neck).

⌘ If your lower back feels pinched in this position, roll up one of your blankets and put it under your knees. Put another blanket on top of you, to keep warm.

⌘ Let your feet and legs drop open and away from one another, let your arms drop open, palms face up. Let your breath slow down and become soft and shallow.

- ⌘ Do not allow yourself to fall asleep. Likewise, try to avoid thinking about your day or the grocery list or how much you need to repaint the bathroom. This may take some practice, but the in-between state is the place you want to keep getting to.
- ⌘ When you are ready to come out of the pose, start first by deepening your breath. Then wiggle your fingers and toes before moving your arms and legs.
- ⌘ Roll to one side before slowing sitting upright. Make a clear transition between being a corpse and being reanimated to honor the sacredness of this time for yourself.

### *Breath Work*

### *Deergha Swasem: Slowed Down Breathing*

One of the most effective and profound ways to connect with the functioning of your lungs, the transporters of your *prana*, your life force, is through conscious breathing. The foundation of learning yogic *pranayama* is *Deergha Swasem* or three-part breath.

Easy to practice, easy to master, *Deergha Swasam* is breathing slowly and deeply. Envision filling your lungs from bottom to top—first by expanding the abdomen, then the middle rib cage, and finally the upper chest. When exhaling, envision the breath emptying in reverse, from top to bottom, pulling in the abdomen slightly at the end to empty the lungs completely.

Studies have shown that you can take in and give out seven times as much air—that means seven times as much oxygen, seven times as much *prana*—in a three-part deep breath than in a shallow breath. Remember, more oxygen in the body also means more oxygen in the brain. When the brain is flushed with oxygen, its functioning increases on all levels. Think of extra oxygen as nature's Prozac.

### *Hand Mudras for Prayer and Meditation*

If you've ever seen a statue of the Buddha, you will have seen a *mudra*. It's the position in which he's holding each of his hands.

Every beginner yoga student learns about *mudras* (Sanskrit for *sign* or *seal*) the moment he or she steps into a class for the first time. Hand mudras are symbolic gestures whose essence is devotion, as each mudra is an offering, a gift to the Divine. Mudras are an ideal tool for calling up the internal state with which you want to approach your yoga practice or any other life task. A mudra quickly seals the energy around you and helps to create sacred space.

The **atmanjali mudra** (reverence to the heart seal) is the most familiar, also known as the praying hands position.

When you place your hands together, leave a little hollow space between the palms. By placing your hands in the *atmanjali mudra* in front of your heart, this supports and creates harmony, balance, repose, silence, and peace. This gesture also coordinates left and right brain hemispheres

Another is the **jnana** (knowledge or wisdom) **mudra**, which has the index finger (representing your individual consciousness) touching the thumb (universal or world consciousness). Unifying your individual consciousness with that of the world is the spiritual goal of yoga.

Traditionally, in yoga classes the two hands hold *jnana mudra* and rest on the knees in *sukasana,* easy cross-legged sitting pose.

The **dhyana mudra** is the classical gesture of meditation and contemplation. This mudra forms the shape of a bowl, symbolizing inward emptiness, free and pure to receive everything we need on our spiritual path.

My friend Kiki, engaged in a regular Zen Buddhist-style sitting meditation practice for many years now, advises one to hold a pressure between the thumbs in *dhyana* that would be strong enough to hold a piece of paper, but not strong enough to crush an ant. The right palm rests lightly on the left and together the hands are held lightly on the lap, close in to the lower belly, as Buddha does.

# ⌘ Healing Bodywork for Winter

### *Thymus Tapping to Ignite the Immune System*

In the case of the ailments that are emphasized in this winter chapter, those involving the immune system, respiration, and circulation are affected by the thymus. The thymus sits right above the heart, just left of center at the sternum or breastplate. This is also where the heart chakra is located. An Ayurvedic technique called *tapping* is a simple and easy way to activate the energy of the heart chakra, which stimulates the thymus, and helps to kick start it if it is particularly sluggish or if you are fighting off a cold or flu.

With the first three fingers of your right hand, tap briskly and succinctly on the thymus. Tap for two to three minutes while taking deep breaths. Take care to avoid striking on the sensitive tissues of your breast and nipple area; stay on the hard bone of the sternum. You can hear the difference, as the bone gives off a distinct *thump*, like that of a ripe melon.

You are literally rapping on the door of the sternum, on the door to this pocket of energy, asking it to open up. If your system is down, this area will feel tender to the touch, so be gentle. While you are tapping, you can close your eyes and visualize the color green, as this is the fourth color of the spectrum, which corresponds to the heart chakra.

When you have finished your tapping session, lay your hands over this thymus-sternum-heart chakra area. Bless yourself ("I bless myself" is all you need to say here), bless your body, bless your health. Amen.

# CHAKRAS AND ENDOCRINE SYSTEM GLANDS: PARTNERS IN WELLNESS

In Ayurveda, the chakras play an integral role in mapping elements of wellness as well as disease. Chakra (*wheel* in Sanskrit) refers to one of seven energy centers in the human body. The chakras comprise an energy system and function as pumps or valves regulating the flow of energy throughout the system. The chakras interact with the physical body through two major vehicles, the endocrine system and the nervous system. Each of the seven is associated with one of seven glands of the endocrine system as well as the seven colors on the spectrum.

The endocrine system and the hormones they release influence almost every cell, organ, and function of our bodies. The endocrine system is instrumental in regulating mood, growth and development, tissue function, and metabolism, as well as sexual function and reproductive processes. The foundations of the endocrine system are the hormones and glands. As the body's chemical messengers, hormones transfer information and instructions from one set of cells to another. Hormone levels can be influenced by factors such as stress, infection, and changes in the balance of fluid and minerals in blood through nutrition or lack of it.

Chanting, bodywork, diet, emotional, and mental balance all affect and support harmony in the chakras, and in turn, holistic health and wellness.

| Gland/Function | Chakra Point | Color |
|---|---|---|
| Adrenals - Stress responders | #1 Base of Spine | Red |
| Ovaries/Testes – Reproduction, fertility | #2 Lower Belly | Orange |
| Pancreas – Digestion, regulates blood sugars | #3 Solar Plexus | Yellow |
| Thymus – Respiration, Circulation, Immune System | #4 Heart | Green |
| Thyroid – Metabolism (energy usage) | #5 Throat | Blue |
| Pituitary – "Master Gland" regulates all others | #6 Third Eye | Indigo |
| Pineal – Sleep control, sexual function | #7 Crown | Violet |

### Reflexology: The Feet as Portals to Healing

Reflexology is a specific type of massage technique for the feet that focuses on stimulating reflex points. It's an ancient holistic therapy practiced by the Egyptians and Chinese as early as 2300 B.C. Each reflex point is said to act as a mirror which corresponds to a particular organ or system in the body. Stimulation of these points in the feet, helps release blockages to rebalance the energy flow in the body. There are seven thousand nerves and twenty-six bones in the feet making them incredibly sensitive and intricately designed by nature.

Our feet tend to get ignored during winter, simply because we are covering them up so much to keep them warm. But there is value in uncovering them to explore the richness of their contributions to your wellness. At the same time, I know many women tend to heap abuse on their feet in their unholy fixation on fashion no matter what the season. Inevitably there is a reckoning when it's time to step out of the six-inch stilettos and kick off the sky-high booties. Taking care of your feet with reflexology is one of the few massage techniques that you can effectively give to yourself in your quest to become a more practiced self-nurturer.

## Foot Reflexology Chart

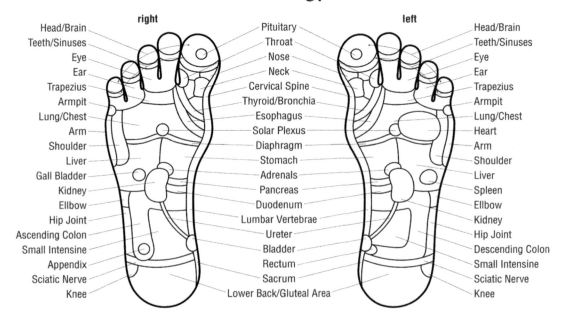

Refer to the chart I've included while you are enjoying your massage time. The layout of the feet in reflexology is meant to reflect the various areas and zones of the body, more or less. The lower body and its systems are in the heels, while the head and its aspects are in the toes. You'll see that all the systems that we've been focusing on for winter—circulation, respiration and immunity—are located in or near the toe pads at the top of the foot.

You can treat yourself to a massage by pressing on the areas shown on the chart with your thumbs or the knuckle of your index finger while you breathe deeply. Press for twenty seconds and follow that by making small circles all over these points. Use a little lotion or massage oil if your fingers need some glide. Don't forget the rest of the foot—sometimes just a little loving attention on these very sensitive and often mistreated parts of the body can make a huge impact on your outlook for a dreary winter's day. And of course, for a more expert experience of reflexology consult with a trained professional.

## ⌘ Plant Healing for Winter: Aromatherapy, Herbs, Teas, and Tonics

### Aromatherapy

*If we surrender to earth's intelligence we could rise up rooted like trees.*

*–Rilke*

The central challenges of the winter season are keeping the immune system and lungs strong (to combat colds, flu and other respiratory infections), managing depression, and letting the natural process of grieving at the end of this cycle run its course.

Native American traditions have ceremonies and rituals that connect with trees and forests and refer to trees as "The Standing Nation," stalwart, proud, enduring. In Japan, going for a therapeutic walk in the woods is known as *shinrin-yoku*, or "forest bathing," which is a short leisurely walk to soak up the atmosphere and scents of the forest. It is a recognized practice in their culture for the release of stress and depression. A large percentage of the Earth's ancient forests are made up of coniferous (evergreen) trees—pine, redwood, cypress, cedar, fir. The coniferous forests are as important to the planet's overall living ecology as the tropical rainforests.

In the cold, wind, and snow of winter they're real survivors. Their essential oils can revive one's energies, promoting strength, motivation, warmth and stamina. At the same time they tend to refresh, clarify, and open up space (in every sense of the word). This makes these oils valuable in wintertime, which places extra demands on our reserves of energy, endurance, and warmth. In the often emotionally draining or confusing holiday times of the winter season, conifer oils can help pull us through.

⌘ **Cypress** (*Cupressus sempervirens*) essential oil is especially comforting and restores feelings of security and stability. Cypress helps ease the feeling of loss and has been called the *funeral oil* for this reason. It also provides mental structure and the collection of thoughts for absent-mindedness, lack of concentration, squandering of energies, and uncontrollable sobbing. It can help counteract negative emotions of grief, sorrow, lethargy, and fear. Cypress encourages the positive emotions of strength, comfort, understanding, balance, inner peace, purity of heart, patience, and trust. In other words, all the qualities one would wish for in a wise elder. Medicinally, cypress is used to jumpstart sluggish circulation and act as a decongestant. It unclogs and moves out mucus from the sinuses and bronchial tubes. It also unclogs pores in the skin that have become congested. Placing a few drops of this oil on a tissue and inhaling several times an hour will help on your worst, stuffy days, as will five to seven drops into a steaming hot bath.

⌘ **Pine** *(Pinus sylvestris)* is probably inextricably intertwined with Christmas and its powerful sense memories for those of us raised in that tradition. Pine bark and needles contain vitamin C, which means they are loaded with beneficial antioxidant compounds. The extract of the coastal pine tree's (*Pinus maritima*) bark and needles mixed with water has been patented as Pycnogenol—which has been used as a jet lag remedy. Pine also provides great relief for colds and congested sinuses. My grandmother made a "pine steam" by soaking needles and bark in a stove-pot filled with hot water. When the water began steaming, we were instructed to stand over the pot with a towel over our heads and hold it out to capture the steam. Deep breaths through the mouth and nose worked to loosen the mucus and open up the stuffiness. You can use five to seven drops of pine essential oil in place of the needles and bark.

⌘ **Peppermint** *(Mentha piperita)* is a cross between watermint and spearmint and is often referred to as the world's oldest medicine. For colds, sinus congestion, and respiratory problems it is unparalleled. It stimulates the mind and has a warming effect on and in the body from its principle component of menthol. Because it works into the hippocampus part of the brain, like rosemary, it stimulates mental activity and is excellent for mental fatigue, memory loss, and the inability to concentrate. It clears the head and refreshes the spirit. It also is good for dizzy spells, nervous tension, rapid heartbeat, depression, and headaches caused by mental overexertion. When rubbed on the chest, it will act as an expectorant to loosen mucus. Make a chest rub by combining one tablespoon of solidified coconut oil with five to ten drops of peppermint oil. Massage all over the chest and lung area. This same mixture can be dabbed under a stuffy nose to help it open.

## Forgiveness Aromatherapy Blend: Help with Letting Go

5 drops of melissa (lemon balm)

3 drops of frankincense

3 drops of geranium

2 drops of bergamot

1. Blend in a 4 oz. spray bottle filled with distilled or purified water.
2. Spray around your heart chakra, as well as your aura (the energetic space that encircles your entire physical being head to toe) and pulse points. As you spray, inhale the scent with your eyes closed. This is good to use with the *Ho'oponopono mantra* (page 236). Spray before and after the chant.

Melissa, or Lemon Balm, has traditionally been used as a remedy for melancholia and as a strengthener of the brain and nerves. Frankincense is known as an expectorant (metaphorically forgiveness is about releasing what is caught up or congested). It has an elevating, warming, and soothing effect on the mind and emotions. Geranium is cleansing, refreshing and is both sedative and uplifting, like bergamot, so it is useful for anxiety.

### Herbs, Teas, and Tonics

The scourge of winter, forever and always, is the common cold. Nothing has been proven to cure the common cold so what is the holistic self-care approach? Other than daily prevention (proactive nutrition, exercise, adequate sleep, regular hand washing) the goal is to find a way to reduce symptoms safely and perhaps shorten the duration of the suffering.

You'll perhaps notice that many of the recommended winter herbal remedies are roots of some sort, as they were in autumn. When considering how a living thing such as a plant imparts its healing properties, first remember that the roots of the plant are responsible for the growth and wellbeing of the entire plant.

⌘ **Garlic** (*Allium sativum*) has medicinal properties recognized for centuries—specifically for lung and respiratory ailments as well as for treating colds—in addition to being a very tasty thing to eat. Garlic has strong antibiotic, anti-fungal, and antiviral properties with the active ingredient being allicin, a sulfuric compound that attacks invaders in the body. It has been shown to be effective in lowering high-blood pressure and preventing heart disease. My all-purpose cold remedy is garlic syrup. Take one pound of peeled, minced organic garlic cloves and put them in a jar. Cover with 1 cup of apple cider vinegar and ⅓ cup distilled water. Shake well and let stand for four hours. Strain and add equal amounts of raw, organic honey (about ½-¾ cup). Cap the jar and keep in a cool place. Take one tablespoon 3–8 times daily for bronchitis, coughs, colds, mucus, sore throat, and chills.

⌘ **Ginger** (*Allium sativum*): Ginger contains high amounts of iron, calcium, paradol, and gingerol—a powerful antioxidant. The volatile oils in ginger also stimulate the circulatory and respiratory systems, lower cholesterol, deter blood clots, and purify the blood. It's great for colds and chills that often come with winter ailments, as it has an internal warming effect on the body. I prefer fresh, organic ginger to capsules containing the powdered version. The easiest delivery method is to make tea with it (grate a tablespoon of fresh ginger into one mug of hot water or milk, add a dollop of honey), or by adding it to a smoothie. It gives even the blandest concoction a pleasant kick. For people who have sluggish circulation, particularly on chilly days, drinking a mixture of hot water with lemon, honey, and ginger will bring up your internal temperature and give you a much needed flush. Having it on hand, like fresh garlic, and regularly adding to your food on an everyday basis is easy: grating an inch long bit into rice, lentils, stir-fry dishes, and even salad dressings, is all you need.

⌘ **Marshmallow** *(Althaea officinalis):* is a medicinal herb most commonly used to treat sore throats and dry coughs. The marshmallow plant, especially the leaves and roots, contains polysaccharides that have antitussive, mucilaginous, and antibacterial properties. Because of this, marshmallow has a soothing effect on inflamed membranes in the mouth and throat when ingested orally, specifically a sore throat. The antitussive properties help reduce dry coughing and prevent further irritation. The easiest way to take marshmallow root is in a supplement or in a prepared tea. As a cough and respiratory agent, a cold-brewed marshmallow root tea is wonderful and tastes delicious (yes, the ancestors of our jet-puffed marshmallows were originally made from this plant). Soak a thumb-sized piece of root in one cup of cold water overnight. Add the sweetener of your choice and gargle the mixture.

⌘ **Mushrooms** have been used for three thousand years by humans the world over to promote good health and fight illness. In the world of natural health, medicinal mushrooms are known as some of the most potent boosters for the immune system. About a dozen varieties are being studied for their ability to destroy cancer cells. Found in shiitake, reishi, agaricus, blazei, murill, and cordyceps varieties, among others, the beta glucan they contain stimulates and mobilizes immune cells. (Seek out the fascinating work of Paul Stamets, mycologist, author, and advocate of bioremediation and medicinal mushrooms.) The conventional wisdom from mushroom authorities is to eat a combination of fresh, whole mushroom species for the best effect and to make sure they are organic. Mushrooms absorb and concentrate the qualities of whatever they grow in (soil) or on (trees, other plants), so you are getting those nutrients as well. If you use a supplement, be sure you are getting the entire mushroom—the fruit body parts, the mycelia (similar to a plant's root system), and growth media extract (base substances used to grow mushrooms.) All three parts have greater medicinal benefit when used together versus only using one part by itself. Also be sure it is a Certified P-Value, which assures that medicinal mushrooms are always at their highest quality and retain nutritional integrity.

# Chapter 22

## Healing Beauty Rituals for Winter

. . . . . . . . . . . . . . . . . . . .

The particular conditions of winter are such that between the drying heat inside our homes and the cold dry air outside of them our skin can begin to suffer. In addition, the overindulgence of alcohol, sugar, and rich fatty foods from the holidays can also wreak havoc on skin and hair, problems that we are literally covering up day after day in order to stay warm.

### Blessed Refuge:  The Beauty of Quiet Pamper Time

I see being forced indoors during winter to be a blessed refuge, an opportunity to indulge in some serious pampering time. Taking care of yourself holistically means employing tactics to address your emotional, spiritual, and mental states *together* with your physical state. There is a direct result, a specific connectivity between these components, when you are actively engaged in taking care of yourself *by yourself*. It's completely different than when you pay someone else to give you a massage or body scrub or have a partner give you a foot rub. Those can be amazing and important moments and you should have them regularly in your life. But making it a priority once in a while to do it for yourself can be monumentally shifting—especially when it comes to depression, sadness, and even existential disconnection—some of our seasonal challenges.

There is a particular agency in finding solace when you are alone with yourself. This is a mature love of self and it means you have tuned in to your wise elder. You gather the ingredients, you administer them, you receive them; they are the holy sacraments of your faith in your own abilities. The space and time that you've collected are the temple walls for the duration.

The recipes for winter beauty are meant to reflect the aromas and other sensory delights of the season: chocolate, sugar, spices, peppermint, and citrus all play a part in our seasonal memories. But instead of putting all of them in our mouth, we'll put just a little and then put the rest on our bodies in sacred ritual.

### ChocoCocoMint Facial Cleansing Scrub:  Winter Moisturizing Mantra

"Moisturize, moisturize, moisturize." Let this be your winter mantra. And there is no better ingredient than coconut oil for this purpose. At room temperature, coconut oil is solid. So you can just scoop out a spoonful and go to town. As it warms to your skin's touch it will dissolve nicely. Massage gently into face, neck, décolletage, knees, elbows, and hands for a fast and easy skin quencher. Because it has antimicrobial properties (seemingly counter intuitive because it is *oily*) it is also good for healing blemishes and breakouts.

For a more sensuous and uplifting face cleanser, this recipe plays off the smooth glide of coconut oil with the course texture of brown sugar, the heavenly aroma (and antioxidants) of the chocolate, and the aroma therapeutic qualities of peppermint.

½ cup of medium-high heat coconut oil (do not use raw coconut oil as it can burn easily in the melting process)

1½ cups of organic turbanado raw cane sugar (small granules preferred)

½ cup of organic brown sugar

2 tablespoons organic cocoa powder

5–7 drops peppermint essential oil

1. Melt the coconut oil. (Best method is to run hot water over the outside of the jar. Otherwise, heat in microwave in 20-second increments. Take care not to overheat. )

2. Fill medium-sized bowl with the sugar and cocoa.

3. Pour the jar of oil over the dry ingredients and mix well, making sure the sugar is completely dissolved.

4. Add the peppermint oil to the bowl and continue to mix.

5. Scoop a small palm-sized amount out of the jar and gently massage into face in a circular motion with fingertips. Rinse with lukewarm water. Pat dry.

6. Store in an airtight glass jar. Does not need to be refrigerated. Good for up to three months.

## CocoMint Toothpaste: Natural Pearly Whites

This is a terrific, non-toxic version of a tooth- and gum-care product that will cost you pennies on the dollar. Coconut oil kills mouth germs that can cause plaque buildup, gingivitis, and cavities, as well as bad breath.

2 tablespoons coconut oil

2 tablespoons baking soda

10 drops of peppermint essential oil

1. Mix baking soda and coconut oil in a small bowl, until it forms a paste like consistency.

2. Add the peppermint oil and mix.

3. Dip toothbrush into mixture and brush teeth as usual. At least one minute, 3 times a day is recommended by dental hygienists for maximum results.

## Nutmeg and Milk Facial Soother

This is a recipe well known in Ayurvedic beauty traditions as a remedy for curing acne and breakouts. Whether or not you need to treat acne, this recipe will leave your face feeling exceedingly soft and supple. The smell of nutmeg to me is evocative of a warm winter's day spent indoors baking holiday treats; deeply relaxing and pleasurable.

Nutmeg is revered in India for its all-purpose medicinal benefits ranging from treating asthma, toothaches, and rheumatic joint pain to curing myriad digestive issues. It has a strong antibacterial component. In general homeopathy, nutmeg is used to treat anxiety and depression.

This paste is made using milk, which offsets the inherent oiliness of the nutmeg and neutralizes the warming qualities of the spice.

2–3 whole, fresh whole nutmeg pods

1 tablespoon cold, whole organic milk or cream

1. Grind the nutmeg pods to a very fine powder in a coffee bean grinder (or you can use a mortar and pestle if you prefer).

2. Put the nutmeg powder in a glass bowl. Add the milk to make a paste.

3. After washing your face with warm water, pat it dry, and then spread the nutmeg paste evenly over your face.

4. After 10–20 minutes, use lukewarm water to remove the paste, followed by cold water to close the pores.

NOTE: you might feel a slight tingling or light burning sensation from the paste. This is not harmful or indicative of any particular skin sensitivity—some people with thin, fair, and very sensitive skin *never* experience this, and others with olive, oily, or darker skin *do* report this sensation. However, using whole cow's milk or cream rather than non-dairy milks (soy, almond, rice) seems to mitigate the tingling sensation.

## *Coffee and Black Tea Remedies*

The beautifying benefits of both coffee and tea are undisputed, if slightly different. Coffee is a strong anti-inflammatory and diuretic so it will help ease puffiness in the face. Black tea is known for its skin soothing properties and for healing and repairing skin cells as well as dark circles under the eyes.

⌘ **Facial Exfoliator:** Mix 2 tablespoons wet coffee grounds or the contents of one green or black tea bag that has been brewed, with enough flaxseed or grapeseed oil to moisten and turn into a spreadable paste. Spread on clean dry face and then rinse with lukewarm water. Pat dry.

⌘ **Face Mask:** In a blender, combine 2 tablespoons coffee grounds, 2 tablespoons cocoa powder, 3 tablespoons milk (whole), heavy cream or plain, unsweetened yogurt and 1 tablespoon honey. Blend until smooth, then apply all over face. Let mask set for 15–20 minutes. Rinse with lukewarm water. Pat dry.

⌘ **Eye Treatment**: For tired, puffy eyes or dark circles under the eyes, take two black tea bags that have been steeped, squeezed out, and chilled in fridge. Place over eyelids and lie down to rest for 20 minutes.

## Vitamin C Ginger Sugar Body Scrub: Winter Dull Skin Brightener

This exfoliating scrub will eliminate dull, flaky, dead skin, while the vitamin C from the orange boosts skin repair. Ginger is warming and revitalizing. The olive oil moisturizes and creates a smooth, silky skin texture (like "buttah").

Make it ahead and store in the fridge. Heat the mixture for 20–30 seconds in the microwave for a warm scrub on a cold winter's day. Conversely, take directly out of the fridge and use for a cool body treat on a hot day.

1 cup course cane sugar

1 thumb-sized piece of fresh ginger, peeled and grated fine

Juice of one orange, freshly squeezed

Extra virgin olive oil

3–5 drops orange essential oil

1. Mix the sugar, ginger and orange juice together in a small bowl. Add enough olive oil to make a consistency similar to damp sand for sensitive skin or a drier consistency for thicker, less sensitive skin. Add the orange oil.

2. Massage all over body in gentle, circular motions then rinse off with warm water in the shower or bath.

For a cracked heel skin and foot conditioner substitute 1 cup coarse sea salt for the sugar. (If using Dead Sea salts, grind larger granules into smaller ones.) Mix in the juice of half the orange or one lemon. Omit the ginger. Add enough olive, almond, or coconut oil to make a spreadable paste, like cake icing. Add 3–5 drops orange or lemon essential oil to match whichever juice you used. Heat in microwavable dish for 30 seconds. Massage warm mixture vigorously into feet. Pull thick woolen socks over feet. Leave on overnight, then rinse mixture off feet in the morning.

## Cappuccino Milk Bath Indulgence

Milk and oats have been staple skin beautifiers for everyone since Cleopatra's day. The fats and enzymes in the milk do pretty amazing work on the skin. (Unfortunately there is no comparable vegan substitute, insofar as the effect it has on the skin, but you can use rice milk powder or potato milk powder for texture and still enjoy the other elements of the bath soak. Both can be found in natural food grocers and online.) Oats, you will recall, address skin that is irritated, stressed, and now in winter, overexposed to cold and wind.

This recipe is pure, me-time indulgence, as foamy and as delicious to smell as it feels. This is definitely a reward for the stresses of the holidays. I would recommend sinking slowly into the hot bath with a wee crystal glass of chilled champagne at the ready, and with a large heavy bolt across the door if you have children.

¼ cup baking soda

1 cup whole milk powder

1 cup of oat flour

2 tablespoons cocoa powder

½ oz. vanilla essential oil or fragrance oil*

Optional: 1 tablespoon Dendritic Salt**

1. In a medium sized mixing bowl, combine all the dry ingredients well. Then add the vanilla essential oil and stir thoroughly to disperse the oil evenly throughout the dry mix.

2. Store in an airtight glass jar. Use a handful dropped into the running water of your bath to get the foaming cappuccino-effect from the milk powder.

Oat flour can be made by giving regular oatmeal a whir in a food processor or blender for 30–45 seconds. You want to end up with the same kind of texture as wheat flour—soft and powdery.

*Pure vanilla essential oil is somewhat expensive. If you don't have the budget to spring for it, then vanilla fragrance oil will work just as well and is much less expensive. They are both usually sold online through the same web retailers.

**Dendritic Salt is a very fine grain salt which gives it high absorption qualities, making for a bath mixture that has less clumping, greater fragrance retention, and dissolves quickly in water. It, too, can be sourced easily online.

# Chapter 23

## Winter Kitchen Rituals: Food, Nutrition, Recipes

. . . . . . . . . . . . . . . . . . .

Citrus is the quintessential fruit for winter. What is more cheerful to see on a gray and cold winter's day, than perfectly round orbs of yellow and orange sitting on your kitchen counter? I think the sunny, bright, and vivacious energy that citrus fruits impart are nature's impeccable antidote to the winter blahs, as if it were known we humans would need something to stand in for the sun. Their scent pierces through stale heavy indoor air as you cut them, with bursts of sweet astringency. That these fruits would also hold a substance (vitamin C) specific to helping our immune systems at their most vulnerable during this time is the winning bonus.

Using food this season for our wellness means keeping our temperature and moods elevated. Working with roots began in autumn, and continues to be relevant in winter. Soups, hearty carbs, and winter greens keep us balanced and sated, nourishing a strong and vital constitution to combat winter's health assaults. Chocolate, a known mood elevator, can be used to great benefit now.

### The Green Motini Vegetable Cocktail

Part of getting caught up in the holiday spirit often involves celebrating with alcohol, from the tickly fizz of a great champagne to the warmth of a hot toddy on a cold night after caroling. My inspiration for a healthier alternative is the current exciting cocktail culture devoted to artisanal concoctions made from fresh vegetables and fruits. This non-alcoholic *mocktail* blends the flavor profiles of the mojito and appletini, and takes full advantage of the abundance of winter greens in season right now for a huge lift on a gray winter's day. Cheers!

1 small handful of kale

1 small handful of chard

1 small handful of spinach

5 fat mint leaves

Juice of 1 lime

½ cucumber, peeled

½ green apple, cored but with skin on

1. Put all in blender with 1–2 cups filtered/purified water, depending on your preference of consistency.

2. Blend until smooth.

3. Pour into a chilled martini glass and garnish with an apple slice on the rim.

### Winter Smoothie with Blood Orange, Fig, and Ginger

Colorful, naturally sweet, and packing heat from the ginger, this beauty is a great antidote to a cold, a stuffy nose, or otherwise *blah* feeling on a damp, bone-chilling day.

Blood oranges have a raspberry edge to their flavor, in addition to that incredible hue. The red color in blood oranges is the result of anthocyanin, which develops when these citrus fruits ripen during warm days tempered with cooler nights (almost the entire U.S. crop is grown in California and harvested in winter there because of these perfect Mediterranean conditions). Anthocyanin is a high value antioxidant (slowing and even preventing the growth of cancer cells) and is found all over the plant kingdom as the red in cherries and red cabbage, the blue in blueberries, and the purple in eggplants.

⅓ cup fresh carrot juice (about 4 medium sized carrots)

⅓ cup of fresh blood orange juice (1 med to large orange)

½ banana, roughly chopped

1–2 small dried figs, finely chopped

1 teaspoon fresh ginger, peeled and finely grated

1. Blend until smooth.

2. Drink at room temperature or over ice.

3. To get fancy with it, shake over ice and strain into a chilled martini glass. Garnish with a slice of blood orange on the rim.

### Winter Greens and Tangerines with Miso Dressing

Do you know about Sumo tangerines? They are butt-ugly and drop-dead delicious, the sharpeis of the citrus world. Huge and bumpy and shaped exactly like a Sumo wrestler, they even sport a topknot. This seedless fruit is a cross between a Satsumo mandarin and an orange. Unbelievably juicy and sweet, at their worst they blow away the very best tasting naval orange on its good day. They're in season from mid-February to early April so do your best to score some during that time if you can. Otherwise, use any kind of tangerine you can find to pair with the most crisp, freshest greens available.

I love this tasty miso dressing (adapted from Martha Rose Schulman, *New York Times*) as it incorporates our winter healing herbs (ginger and garlic) and a fermented product (the miso) with beneficial probiotics. This is an easy way to work more of all those healthful items into your diet.

*Salad*

6 cups fresh winter greens (kale, chard, spinach, red-leaf lettuce, washed and torn into bite-sized pieces)

2–3 peeled Sumo tangerines with sections separated

½ cup walnut pieces, toasted

*Miso Dressing*

2 rounded tablespoons white or yellow miso

2 tablespoons rice vinegar

½ teaspoon grated fresh ginger

1 small garlic clove, minced or put through a press

Pinch of cayenne (optional)

2 tablespoons dark sesame oil

2 tablespoons grapeseed oil

Method:

1. Combine the miso and vinegar in a small bowl and whisk together with a fork. Add the remaining ingredients and whisk until amalgamated.

2. Toss dressing with greens, citrus and walnuts in a large salad bowl.

## Kale Potato Soup

(adapted from *Fields of Greens* cookbook)

I always credit these series of books from the famed San Francisco restaurant of the same name for helping me understand how discerning and sophisticated a vegetarian cooking repertoire could be. This recipe is one that I make over and over every winter as my talisman against cold and flu season. It is simple, precise, and a breeze to prepare if you are under the weather.

I have adopted it as my vegan version of Mom's Chicken Soup since it is the perfect antidote for a lousy head cold, what with all the garlic and the red pepper. Everything in it is pure, unadulterated comfort and goodness for flushing out those nasty germs. It's health in a bowl. It slurps when you need to slurp and it's got enough substance to feel hearty when your soul needs propping up in a certain way. It truly is the loving arms of your mother wrapped tightly around you in a big bear hug.

1 onion, chopped into small pieces

6–8 cloves of garlic, minced

2 tablespoons olive oil

½ teaspoon red pepper flakes (more if you like spicy heat)

2–3 tablespoons nutritional yeast

6–8 cups of water or vegetable broth

6–8 medium sized Yukon Gold and new potatoes cut into small chunks

1 bunch of kale, torn into bite-sized pieces (I prefer Dino or Tuscan kale for this one)

Salt to taste

Method:

1. Sauté the onions and garlic in the olive oil until soft and translucent. Add the red pepper flakes, the nutritional yeast, the broth, and the potatoes. Bring to a boil, then turn down the heat and simmer until the potatoes are soft, 15 – 20 minutes. Add the kale and salt and simmer for another 10 minutes.

## Red Lentil and Coconut Spice Soup

Dal, a thick stew made from split lentils, is a traditional common comfort food of the people on the Indian Subcontinent. There are black, green, and yellow lentil dals, all with their own particular flavors and then there is mansoor dal, made from red lentils. These lentils have a lighter, more buttery taste to me; they cook more quickly and do not require presoaking as the other lentils do. But the real reason I prefer red lentils? They make a final result that is a beautiful shade of yellow-orange, the color I see when I close my eyes and turn my face toward the sun.

This recipe is based on ingredients common to a traditional South-Indian mansoor dal with spices that make it a tridoshic dish or one that benefits all doshas in Ayurvedic wellness. The warm perfume of the coconut oil, combined with the toasty fragrance of the curry spices, give a complexity of flavor that will surely transport you on any winter's day when the sun is in short supply.

½ large red onion, finely chopped

2 teaspoons coconut oil

1 teaspoon red pepper flakes

1-inch fresh ginger, peeled and minced

1 clove garlic, peeled and minced

1 cup red lentils, rinsed and sorted

1 teaspoon ground coriander

1 teaspoon paprika

1 teaspoon cumin

Pinch of cinnamon

One 15 oz. can light coconut milk cream (this is the Thai-style cooking milk, not the coconut non-dairy milk beverage)

3 cups filtered water

1 teaspoon vegan bouillon cube or powder

½ teaspoon sea salt

Black pepper to taste

Juice of 1 lime

1. Heat the coconut oil in a heavy based saucepan. Add the onion and sauté on a medium low heat until softened and translucent.

2. Add the chili, garlic, and ginger to the onion and stir well. Cover and cook for a few more minutes until the flavors begin to marry.

3. Add the red lentils to the pan along with the ground coriander, paprika, cumin, and cinnamon. Mix thoroughly and then pour in the coconut milk and water.

4. Sprinkle in the vegetable bouillon salt and freshly ground black pepper.

5. Cover, bring to a boil and then lower to a gentle simmer for forty minutes, stirring frequently.

6. Juice the lime and set aside.

7. When the lentils have softened and almost disintegrated and formed into a thick, creamy soup, take off the heat.

8. Stir in the lime juice to finish.

## Winter Grain Bowl with Shitaki and Carrots

The term *meaty* gets thrown around a lot when we talk about mushrooms, but shii-takes, more than any other, embody a satisfying umami you can't really get from any other plant-based food. May-be it's because wild ones grow on fallen logs, that these fungi are uniquely imbued with a smoky, rich flavor. Shiitake are  known to reduce cholesterol and contain chemicals that contribute to a strong immune system.

This dish, with the shiitake, bulgur and carrots, is meant to be a hearty, stick-to-your-ribs one-bowl meal, perfect for extra, yet tasty, fortification against blustery winter evenings.

1 tablespoon olive oil

2 tablespoons minced shallots

1½ cups shiitake (or any other mushroom you have available), small dice*

½ cup dry white wine (substitute unsweetened apple juice if you cook without alcohol)

2 cups vegetable broth

¾ teaspoon sea salt

1 cup medium-grind bulgur

½ cup peeled, small-dice carrots

2-3 cups mixed greens of choice, tossed with Miso Dressing (p. 272)

Crunchy raw vegetables such as jicama or daikon radish, cut into small matchsticks

1 poached, organic cruelty-free egg (optional)

Finishing salt (optional; a nice, smoky *sel gris* would be fantastic here)

1. Heat oil in a medium saucepan over medium heat. When it shimmers, add shallots and cook until just beginning to soften, about 2 minutes. Add mushrooms, season with salt and freshly ground black pepper, and cook until moisture released is almost evaporated, about 4 to 5 minutes.

2. Increase heat to medium high. Add wine and cook until almost evaporated, 3 minutes. Add water and bring to a boil. Stir in salt and bulgur and cover.

3. Reduce heat to low and simmer for 10 minutes. Stir in carrots and simmer until fork tender, 5 more minutes. Turn off heat and let stand covered for 5 minutes. Fluff with a fork.

4. To serve: place mixed greens in serving bowl and spoon bulgur/mushroom mixture on top. Place raw veggies to one side of the bowl. Place hot egg on top of bulgur mixture, if using. Sprinkle with finishing salt, if using.

* When using fresh shiitakes, don't throw out the stems if you happen to find them too woody in taste or texture to eat. Cut them off, toss them in a freezer bag and put them into your next vegetable stock. It will make it taste richer and heartier than any vegetable stock you've ever made.

### Winter Borsht with White Beans

I was introduced to a version of borsht on a cold winter's night at my friend Mamie's *Trivial Pursuit* parties that were all the rage among newly minted college graduates back in the day. We were also all cooking our way through the *Silver Palette* and *New Basics* cookbooks by the brilliant Sheila Lukins and Julee Rosso. Mamie made their borscht and it was something I've tinkered with every winter since. Over the years I've evolved a vegetarian version but I think it has stood the test of time. Besides adding a unique flavor profile, the kraut and the caraway seeds are excellent support for healthy functioning of the digestive system.

Beets belong to the chenopod family which includes chard, spinach, and quinoa and are high in iron, antioxidant, and anti-inflammatory properties. Beets contain betaine, the same substance that is used in certain treatments of depression. It also contains tryptophan, which relaxes the mind and creates a sense of wellbeing, similar to chocolate. (I have a beet and chocolate cake recipe I will share if you twist my arm.)

2 lbs. beets, peeled and cut into small chunks

1 teaspoon salt

2 tablespoons olive oil

1 medium onion, peeled and diced

3–4 whole cloves, coarsely ground

4 cloves of garlic, peeled and minced

3 cups of high quality old-world style sauerkraut, drained of liquid*

2 cups white beans (Great Northern, navy, cannellini or baby lima), cooked or 1-15 oz. can

2 carrots, peeled and cut into small dice

2 tablespoons tomato paste

4 cups low sodium vegetable broth

2–3 teaspoons caraway seeds

½ cup chopped fresh dill (if available)

Sea salt and freshly ground black pepper to taste

1-20 oz. can tomatoes, drained and chopped

¼ cup fresh squeezed lemon juice

Plain, unsweetened yogurt (regular or vegan) for garnish

1. Place beets in a large saucepan, cover with cold water, and add the salt. Bring to a boil, reduce the heat, and cover. Simmer until the beets are just tender, about 35-40 minutes. Remove the beets with a slotted spoon. Strain and reserve the cooking liquid.

2. Heat the oil in soup pot and sweat the onions, then add the garlic, and cook for another 5 minutes at medium heat, taking care not to scorch garlic.

3. Add the cabbage, beans, carrots, tomato paste, stock and 2 cups of the reserved beet liquid. Partially cover and bring to a boil, then reduce heat and cook 15 minutes.

4. Add the caraway seeds, chopped dill, salt and pepper, tomatoes, and cooked beets. Simmer, uncovered, for 15 minutes longer.

5. Add the lemon juice, stir and cook for another couple of minutes.

6. Serve garnished with a drizzle of good quality, organic yogurt (optional).

Serves 10–12.

*Avoid using canned sauerkraut made with vinegar and instead go for raw, naturally fermented kraut in the refrigerated section of your health food store or try shopping at an ethnic grocery.

## Double Chocolate Cherry Cookies

My friend, Barri, is a devoted wheat-flour baker and couldn't get over the gluten-free goodness of these cookies so she sent me the recipe, pronto. I'm grateful that she did. The double dose of dark antioxidant-rich chocolate along with almond flour (rich in cholesterol-lowering omega fatty acids) makes these cookies a heart-healthy treat, a mood lifter, and a superb indulgence from the Christmas/Hanukkah holidays all the way through to Valentine's Day.

2¾ cups blanched almond flour*

½ teaspoon sea salt

½ teaspoon baking soda

¼ cup unsweetened cocoa power

½ cup grapeseed oil (or coconut oil for a hint of that extra flavor)

¾ cup maple syrup or brown rice syrup

1 tablespoon vanilla extract

1 cup coarsely chopped dark chocolate (73% cacao, fair-trade, organic)

1 cup dried Bing cherries

1. Preheat oven to 350° F. Line 2 large baking sheets with parchment paper.

2. In a large bowl, combine the almond flour, salt, baking soda, and cocoa powder.

3. In a medium bowl, whisk together the oil, sweetener, and vanilla extract.

4. Fold the wet ingredients into the almond flour mixture until thoroughly combined.

5. Fold in the chocolate and cherries.

6. Spoon the dough 1 heaping tablespoon at a time onto the prepared baking sheets, leaving 2 inches between each cookie.

7. Bake for 10 to 15 minutes, until the tops of the cookies look dry and start to crack; be careful not to overcook. Let the cookies cool on the baking sheets for 20 minutes then serve.

*You can purchase almond flour at any specialty or health food grocer. Or you can cleverly make your own much more cheaply: simply pulverize raw almonds in your blender at high speed or food processor on pulse. Do half cups at a time so that you don't over process and turn the almonds into almond butter. If you want to get fancy and use blanched almonds without the skin, then your flour will be whiter and finer, but won't really change the dynamics of this recipe much.

# Chapter 24

## Winter in Your Home and Family

. . . . . . . . . . . . . . . . . . . .

O f course, it's the supreme irony that our modern holiday season coincides with the naturally occurring time out we've been discussing in this winter chapter. It comes with its own practically perfect kind of stress. The tradition we have is one of a consumer fest (orgy, really) of unmitigated shopping, spending, and accruing of debt. (I'm including all non-Christians who, despite their best efforts, still get swept up within the framework of Christmas during the month of December.) We engage in an almost psychotic rushing about with ten million things to do: gifts to buy, parties to go to, family obligations, travel in overcrowded planes, and a propensity to overeat and over imbibe. We turbo charge through the ice and sleet and snow and come skidding into the holiday table full of resentment, a migraine, and gunning for a grudge match with every single member of our family. Joy to the freakin' world, indeed.

### Killing Christmas (But in a Good Way)

What if it doesn't have to be that way? What if by approaching it all with a different sensibility, we could alter our relationship to the madness, if not opt out of it altogether? In looking for new ways to find a "reason for the season," perhaps *ahimsa* can be the idea we keep coming back to. This Sanskrit word translates as *nonviolence,* but most teachings on it agree this concept denotes a dynamic peacefulness that is prepared to meet all situations with a loving openness. It can be the touchstone of our approach to the holiday madness and help us to open up to possibilities of experiencing it in ways that perhaps we haven't before.

*Ahimsa* as "non-violence" is *the* choicest behavioral expression of eco-awareness. It's the very embodiment of making as small a footprint as possible on Earth. Simply put, this means to simplify, reduce, and simplify some more. It takes real guts to opt out entirely of shopping and gift gifting. Children who are used to getting boatloads of gifts will take this the hardest. Your friends and relatives might accuse you of being a Scrooge and trying to "kill Christmas." But actually, you wouldn't be helping to destroy Christmas as a concept, you'd just be killing your participation in overconsumption. Market forces (and the institutions that exist to perpetuate them) would have you believe that your sacred duty is to shop and spend or without it the capitalist economy would collapse. It's not likely that the entire population of America will quit consuming all in the same moment, but little by little maybe a shift will occur over time to the creation of a newer, more sustainable economy. And your part in that can begin with little courageous shifts in your own behavior.

In this new system, you wouldn't be letting material objects represent your true character and values. The emphasis would shift from spending money to spending time. Making and eating wonderful feasts with loved ones (or helping to prepare them for the less fortunate), lighting candles, telling stories, taking long walks together—those rituals are the most important part of the season, aside from any religious expression your family might have. They can add up to new habits, new traditions, and less stress.

Ideas for an alternative holiday experience:

⌘ If you can, don't buy stuff at all: make donations to environmental groups or humanitarian charities in the name of your giftees

⌘ Forego sending traditional holiday greeting cards. The 2.65 billion Christmas cards sold each year in the U. S. could fill a football field ten stories high. Almost nine hundred thousand trees are cut down to make all those cards. Less than 20% of the world's remaining forests are believed to be intact. Email your greetings or better yet, pick up the phone and call

⌘ Don't decorate with store bought things: Try browsing at flea markets, cleaning out the kids' toy chests and game closets, and visiting your neighbor's garage sales for components with which to make your own and practice recycling. More plastic products from China does not a happier holiday make

If you do need to exchange gifts, try these suggestions. Re-imaging the way we all perceive money and spending is a fundamental way to practice *ahimsa* and helps us circle back to smarter and more sustainable ways of living.

- ⌘ Make gifts yourself (bake, knit, sew, create potted plants, make teas, potpourris)
- ⌘ Create gift certificates of your time or skill sets (two hours of babysitting or dog-walking; organize closets/garage for your recipient, plant a small herb garden, build a bookshelf)
- ⌘ If you must shop, choose craft fairs for unique handmade items in support of local artists. The loving energy that gets transmitted through an artisanal product versus one that came off an assembly line, is simply immeasurable. You can also seek out small, local owner-operated boutiques

So let's say the shopping-gifting component of your holiday experience is actually a cinch, it's the human component (i.e., your family, friends, co-workers) that is the time suck and stress trigger. Some tips to help ease your way:

- ⌘ Engage others to *really* help you with meal planning and execution: potlucks are one of humankind's greatest inventions. You have to trust that the world will keep spinning even though you haven't made every single dish yourself from scratch
- ⌘ Plan a simple getaway for yourself or your family to a quiet, isolated vacation spot. Or go on a yoga or meditation retreat instead. Opting out of traditional family visits and doing your own thing for one year may create more appreciation for the next time you are all together
- ⌘ Have honest discussions with all the folks with whom you are in an obligatory gift exchange and agree to strict spending limits that honor everyone's budget

# FUROSHIKI AND MOTTAINAI:
## JAPANESE CONCEPTS FOR WASTE-FREE HOLIDAYS

Americans have a habit of throwing away 25% more trash during the Thanksgiving to New Year's holiday period than any other time of year. The extra waste amounts to twenty-five million tons of garbage or about one million extra tons per week. If every family got in the habit of reusing just two feet of holiday ribbon, the thirty-eight thousand miles of ribbon saved could tie a bow around the entire planet. If every American family wrapped just three presents in reused materials, it would save enough paper to cover forty-five thousand football fields.

*Mottainai* is a Japanese word that means "too good to waste." It is a word *and* a way of thinking in Japan that is used almost every day—reduce, reuse, and recycle—all in one.

This is beautifully demonstrated in *furoshiki*—any kind of wrapping cloth used to transport gifts or other items. It fell out of favor when plastic bags became ubiquitous after World War II, but has been at the forefront of a renewed national consciousness in Japan about everyday environmental practices. Modern *furoshiki* makes use of any fabric or textile that would ordinarily be thrown away; instead it is used to wrap a gift. Like the aesthetic in all Japanese traditions, using furoshiki is as much a part of the experience as the act of giving itself.

Here are other ways to gift wrap creatively:

⌘ Try using colorful pages from magazines, old maps, or the Sunday comics

⌘ Avoid using paper entirely by using reusable decorative tins, baskets, or boxes

⌘ If you do buy wrapping paper, look for those made of recycled paper

⌘ Reusable, cloth ribbons can be used in place of plastic bows

⌘ Finally, unwrap gifts carefully and save wrappings for reuse next year

Remember, it's all *mottainai.*

# Chapter 25

## Winter in Your Community and World

. . . . . . . . . . . . . . . . . .

W e turn to this final mindful consideration of community in conjunction with the larger overriding theme of winter: letting go and releasing, death as the last stage before rebirth, and death as it connects to life. Only now we'll be discussing literal death, not metaphorical death. What is supposed to happen to us, our remains, when we die? Here's why this is an important question.

### Conscious Green Burials

American funerals are responsible each year for the felling of thirty million board feet of casket wood (some of which comes from rare and endangered tropical hardwoods extracted from rainforests), ninety thousand tons of steel to line caskets, 1.6 million tons of concrete for burial vaults, and 5.3 million gallons of embalming fluid. Embalming fluid contains potent carcinogens which can leach into the ground and possibly contaminate underground water sources used for agriculture and drinking. Cremation is also an environmental horror story, with the incineration process emitting many noxious substances, including dioxin, hydrochloric acid, sulfur dioxide, and climate-changing carbon dioxide.

Traditional cemeteries must constantly incorporate new acreage and cut down existing trees to make room for more burial plots. The maintenance involved uses more chemicals in the form of pesticides and herbicides, not to mention water resources, to keep the lawn and landscaping to an aesthetic that is surely at odds with the local ecosystem (think of golf courses in Las Vegas).

An urban version of timber clearcutting, huge swaths of tree-rich land are shaved down to the dirt, then replaced with a carpet of all-season sod and speckled with the granite headstones of its newest inhabitants.

It is clear that nature has intended that our bodies be reunited with the earth. All organisms that have ever lived on the earth, have died and returned to the soil to be recycled into new life. In nature there is no waste, since constant microbial activity in the soil breaks everything down and turns it into something useful in order for more organisms to survive. This incredibly efficient system is a perfect incarnation of the Divine that flows through all life cycles. Why wouldn't we humans want to include ourselves in this vision of everlasting life? There is no better tribute to any person than to convey them on their journey to the arms of Mother Earth.

Green burials promote natural burial sites and allow the growth of native trees, shrubs, and wildflowers to flourish, which in turn bring birds and other wildlife to the area. No attempt is made to control the natural habitat, instead, allowing nature to take its course. Oftentimes habitat restoration is involved, as conservation easements are granted for the burial sites. Burial containers are made of recycled materials which will break down quickly in the soil. No embalming fluid is used. Loved ones can visit the site and pay tribute to the deceased by contributing plantings for the area in keeping with the habitat. Everyone involved in the equation stands to gain from the experience, including the surrounding community which has an inviting natural resource within its midst.

### The Logic of Distance: Finding Compassionate Origins of Chocolate, Diamonds and Gold

Three of the most prevalent ingredients on gifting lists in this season between Christmas and Valentine's Day are chocolates, gold, and diamonds. Our habits to consume and purchase them are deeply ingrained. These products are sourced almost exclusively from African and South American nations which are some of the poorest on the planet. These three little luxuries have been dubbed *dirty gold*, *blood diamonds*, and *blood chocolate*. This means the resource is harvested or mined through the abuse and slavery of the people forced to work the extraction, with local middleman profits used to finance wars and civil anarchy.

The first-world companies who sell us our luxuries must operationalize according to a *logic of distance* between producer and consumer as a way to maximize their profits. This logic assumes that the further removed a consumer is from the conditions under which a producer labors, the less likely he or she will have awareness and, ultimately, motivation to protest the horribly inhumane conditions that brought the product to their table or jewelry box.

Environmentally, mineral mining of any kind, especially gold and diamond mining on the scale at which it is conducted, is very detrimental. Mining enough gold to produce one simple wedding band produces twenty *tons* of waste, leaching toxic chemicals (mostly mercury and cyanide) into the earth and water around it. Typical commercial production of diamonds devastates the riverine ecosystems where diamonds are typically found. After tons of riverbed are removed, the diamonds are usually handpicked from the sand and gravel by women and children.

About seventy percent of the cocoa used in the one hundred billion dollar global chocolate market is grown in West Africa, with the Ivory Coast accounting for about forty percent of that. Just as blood diamonds helped finance some of Africa's most brutal wars in Angola, cocoa helps subsidize political instability and bloodshed in these parts of Africa. But chocolate's bitter aftertaste comes from the fact that the industry is a magnet for child slavery.

One way to be socially conscious is to get into the habit of seeking out fair-trade chocolate. You can visit http://www. fairtradeusa.org/ to download an app on where to find fair-trade-certified products, as well as donate to help further the cause of ending child labor in the cocoa trade. Be assiduous about learning where your chocolate comes from and don't buy chocolate from a brand that can't verify their source as fair trade. Be aware that many smaller, artisanal brands are owned by one of the big three—Nestle, Hershey's, and Mars (for example, Scharffen Berger and Dagoba are owned by Hershey), which can make the efforts to trace their dirty origins more difficult.

As for gold and diamonds, look to companies such as Green Karat and Brilliant Earth, which use certified recycled diamonds and gold and help consumers become more educated about where their jewelry comes from. You can also buy antique jewelry or even take it to a jewelry designer to repurpose and custom design so that your pieces are new to you and your giftee.

Your buying habits as a consumer will close the distance between you and the producer. The closer the distance, the more ethical a world we will live in, and the more your gifts of these luxuries will truly be given with love in the largest sense of the word possible.

# Chapter 26

## Coming Full Circle

. . . . . . . . . . . . . . . . . . . .

Now we've come to the end of our year together. We've concluded an action-packed, full, and, hopefully, fulfilling experience of exploring seasonal living from the inside out, holistically and habitually, in order to create a beautifully realized quality of life that spirals around our hearts and souls, as well as our families, our communities, and the world at large.

The Wheel can continue to be your compass on your journey through every season to come. The process of creating a conscious lifestyle isn't about doing any one thing in particular, but consists of paying attention to all the interlocking parts (mental, physical, emotional, and spiritual) that make up our human experience. We can look to nature once again for clues about how complex interdependency of all life in an ecosystem is necessary for its healthy functioning.

A beautiful example is in the studies in Yellowstone National Park, of wolves being reintroduced back into the park in 1995, after having been absent for seventy years and hunted to local extinction. The deer population had exploded in those years and grazed away all the vegetation, despite the best efforts of wildlife management (and hunters). The reintroduced wolves started naturally preying on the deer and then the deer began avoiding certain parts of the park. In these places, the vegetation started rebounding, turning back into forests with some trees quintupling their height in just six years. This caused songbirds and migratory birdlife to increase greatly, and beaver populations who eat the trees. Their dams began providing renewed habitats for ducks, otters, muskrats, reptiles, and amphibians. The wolves also killed coyotes, and the mice and rabbits increased as a result which meant more hawks, weasels, foxes, badgers. Ravens, bald eagles, and bears fed on the carrion the wolves left and their populations rose because they also fed on berries from the shrubs that had regenerated. Then the rivers and creeks began to change course and flow more properly and meander less. With reduced erosion, more pools formed, which is good for wildlife habitats. Regenerating forests began to stabilize the river banks so they became more fixed in their course, maintaining a healthy geography of the land. Scientists call naturally occurring effects such as this a *trophic cascade.*

In humans, overall states of health and wellbeing are the results of many components—genetics, environment, circumstance, and habits. But we also create *trophic cascades* for ourselves, in both positive and negative ways. For the vast majority of us, our habits trump all else as the determiner of our good or ill health, premature death or vibrant longevity.

Older people living vibrantly into their eighties and nineties, (called *super seniors*) appear to be applying brakes to the aging process, defying the usual expectations of old age by remaining extremely active, sharp, and healthy. Longevity studies on these seniors show results consistent with researchers' established data, but it also reflects what the super seniors have been practicing almost their whole lives. This includes physical activity almost every day, balanced diets consisting of real food prepared simply and freshly, positive mental outlook which cultivates a sense of progress through life relative to current time and place (no comparing today with yesterday) and daily habits and rituals that keep predictable schedules for all health practices.

So, let's say you've become aces at building a lifestyle around good health and wellbeing habits. Science seems to think this will get you far down the road toward a great old age. My hope is that you develop your practices also because they help you to live your life with more joy and happiness *now* filled with a loving family, rewarding adventures, close friends, and creative work. The reward is in the doing, each day, starting now.

My wish for you is that you will come to regard your life and lifestyle the way gardeners come to regard their gardens. As any organic gardener will tell you, the key to successful gardening is soil management. The quality of the stuff in the ground underneath determines how viable and succulent the stuff up top will be. Think of this book as a manual for your soil management. Your life, as the garden, is not a static thing. It is ever-changing and malleable, responsive to the amount you fertilize it, prune it, and simply spend time pulling weeds. The end result of being able to walk among gorgeous flowering specimens, lush-leaved and crowding toward the sun is a wonderful and gratifying reward for the hard work that produces all of it. But at some point the pleasure of seeing the blossoms becomes equal to the pleasure of the work that produces them. The doing is also the prize. The joy comes when you are sitting in the dirt, digging your hands into the loamy, fertile soil, and inhaling its musky, fresh-earth smell. Here, all is well.

*I am restored in beauty*
*I am restored in beauty*
*I am restored in beauty*
*I am restored in beauty*
*In beauty may I walk*
*All day long may I walk*
*Through the returning seasons may I walk*
*On the trail marked with pollen may I walk*
*With grasshoppers about my feet may I walk*
*With dew about my feet may I walk*
*With beauty may I walk*
*With beauty before me, may I walk*
*With beauty behind me, may I walk*
*With beauty above me, may I walk*
*With beauty below me, may I walk*
*With beauty all around me, may I walk*
*In old age wandering on a trail of beauty, lively, may I walk*
*In old age wandering on a trail of beauty, living again, may I walk*
*It is finished in beauty*
*It is finished in beauty*

**traditional Navajo prayer**

# Appendix

# Basic Tips to Get the Most Out of
# Your Essential Wellbeing Practices

. . . . . . . . . . . . . . . . . . .

### Yoga

Hatha Yoga *asanas* (postures) were designed to affect the subtle body for the purpose of insight and higher consciousness. Created over three thousand years ago, they were originally meant to prepare the adherent for the discipline of a rigorous spiritual practice. This included a codified series of daily habits, such as breath work, diet, meditation, chanting, and study of sacred texts, in order to lay the groundwork for spiritual transformation. So even though our modern twenty-first century yoga may sometimes look very different, the primary focus of yoga is still the inner life of the body, making it key to the mind-body relationship.

If you have an established practice of yoga already in your life, then you'll be more than familiar with all the material, in which case, my hope is that my interpretation of the postures and exercises, and this thematic arrangement of them, will provide new insight and connections for you. If you are new to yoga my hope is that you'll use your time with the postures to better understand the concepts of each season, but know that your understanding of the postures themselves will be better served with supplemental in-person instruction with an experienced teacher at your local studio.

⌘ If you are a beginner, it is important to emphasize there is a level of complex body awareness that Hatha Yoga demands, which requires patience, dedicated practice, and excellent guidance best given by an experienced instructor.

⌘ You should have respect and compassion for your limitations *as they exist each day*, just as you would when confronted with a mountain to ski down, a boulder to climb on, or an ocean to swim in.

- ⌘ Pain and discomfort exist to help us tune in to our bodies more meticulously. They should not be ignored and are not always a sign that more tenacity is required.

- ⌘ If you can't breathe easily and deeply while performing a particular pose, then you need to pull back out of it enough to do so, or stop completely.

I've included Kundalini yoga exercise sets (*kriyas*) that support a couple of season's themes because Kundalini's emphasis on vigorous movements are a nice counterpoint to the more arranged and aligned postures emphasized in Hatha Yoga. Their straightforwardness and timed repetitiveness are a great way to immediately get the adrenaline flowing and blow the cobwebs out of the brain. (I do want to stress that I have never been trained to teach Kundalini. I've only studied it from the perspective of being a Hatha teacher and it is still a part of my ongoing yoga practice. My instruction has come from Gurmukh Khalsa at the Golden Bridge Yoga Studio here in Los Angeles, as well as from other teachers she has trained.)

### Healing Bodywork

Therapeutic bodywork can be found just about anywhere these days. Yoga studios, gyms, and health food stores abound with referrals for freelance practitioners. Many therapists form practices together or can be found through chiropractors, acupuncturists, and other alternative health care providers. The specialized massage techniques highlighted in this book, and their practitioners, can be found online through their accreditation organizations.

- ⌘ Make sure you know the qualifications of your therapist. Do a little homework beforehand and find out about their training, experiences, and specialties before you book a session.

- ⌘ Many therapists who work at busy day spas or massage chains are human and will be most tired at the end of the day or their work week. It's a rule of thumb that therapists who regularly perform more than four sessions a day more than four times a week will be approaching burnout. See if you can find out what your therapist's typical work load is.

- ⌘ Don't eat just before a massage session. Let your body digest your meal first.

- ⌘ Be on time. If you arrive in a frenzied, rushed state it may take longer to relax.

- ⌘ Communicate with your massage therapist. Before the session, give accurate health information and let the massage therapist know your expectations and reasons for the massage.

⌘ Give feedback to the massage therapist during the massage on the amount of pressure, speed of hand movement, etc. Help them do their best work by participating in your healing process.

⌘ Some people like to talk during a massage, while others remain silent. Tell your massage therapist what you prefer. At the same time, if *you* are busy chatting, you'll not allow your mind to relax and your body to integrate the work.

⌘ Allow for some open, quiet time after your massage session. If you're dizzy or light headed after the massage, do not attempt to get up and walk out or drive your car home. It may take a little time to integrate or absorb the results of the massage session.

## Plant Healing: Aromatherapy, Herbs, Teas, and Tonics

Humans have co-evolved their relationship with plants over the past few million years. Some compounds perform the same functions in plants that they do in the body. Our bodies know the substances that occur in plants and they possess sophisticated mechanisms for metabolizing plant materials.

Fully eighty-five percent, or 5.1 billion people worldwide currently use natural plant-based remedies for both acute and chronic health problems. Although drugstore shelves in the United States are stocked mostly with synthetic remedies now, as recently as the early 1950s many of the larger pharmaceutical companies still offered a broad variety of plant-based drugs in tablet, liquid, and ointment forms. In fact, the replacement of herbs with synthetic drugs is a relatively new phenomenon, less than a century old.

To be clear, modern medicine has real value and saves millions of lives day in and day out. But for everyday minor ailments, phytotherapy offers a huge range of alternative options which are safe and effective with little to no side effects.

Please consult with your health care professional before using any plant remedy suggested in this book if you are concerned about its potential effects and efficacy.

### Essential Oils (Aromatherapy)

Aromatherapy has been used for therapeutic purposes for nearly six thousand years around the globe. Each oil contains its own mix of active ingredients and this mix determines what the oil is used for. Some oils are used to promote physical healing—for example, to treat swelling or fungal infections. Others are used for their emotional value—they may enhance relaxation or help with depression.

The essential oils used in aromatherapy have a different composition compared to other herbal products because the distillation process used in aromatherapy recovers the lighter phytomolecules of the plant. The efficacy of essential oils is in the speed at which they are absorbed into the bloodstream. When inhaled through the nose, this happens almost instantly; through the skin in as little as fifteen minutes. The oils' fragrances are believed to activate nerve cells in the nasal cavity sending impulses to the limbic system, which is the area of the brain associated with emotions and memory. When applied topically (on the skin) they activate thermal receptors and destroy microbes and fungi, since many essential oils are antiseptic and some are antibacterial. Internal application may stimulate the immune system (generally in prescribed form).

⌘ Pregnant women, people with high blood pressure, severe asthma, or with a history of allergies should use caution and consult with their health care professional prior to working with the oils.

⌘ People with estrogen-dependent tumors (such as breast or ovarian cancer) should not use oils with estrogen-like compounds such as fennel, aniseed, sage, and clary-sage.

⌘ People receiving chemotherapy should talk to their doctor before trying aromatherapy.

⌘ Never take essential oils by mouth unless you are under the supervision of a trained professional. Taking some oils by mouth could be harmful.

⌘ Avoid using near your eyes.

⌘ Essential oils are highly volatile and flammable so they should never be used near an open flame.

⌘ Animal studies suggest that active ingredients in certain essential oils may interact with some medications. Researchers don't know if they have the same effect in humans. Consult with your health-care professional to be sure.

## Herbs, Teas, and Tonics

⌘ It is always wise to consult with a trained herbalist to get the best advice about which herbs to take, when, and for what purposes. Local herbalists can be found through referrals from natural food grocers, naturopathic M.D.s, homeopaths, and other alternative health practitioners.

⌘ Perhaps even more important than with your food, source organic versions of your herbal choices and research your purveyors so that you can be assured of getting the highest quality herbs procured by the most ethical means possible.

⌘ If you are currently taking prescription drugs or other supplements/vitamins prescribed by a doctor, make sure you consult with him or her before taking the herbal remedies listed in this book in case any are contraindicated by your situation.

## *Personal Care Products*

Unregulated chemicals in cosmetics and body-care products have been linked to cancer, hormone disruption, chronic allergies, and a host of other problems. For example, there are common beauty products that contain the same ingredients found in car wash degreasers and oven cleaners. The average American woman who wears conventional lipstick on a regular basis, will swallow about ten pounds of petroleum by-product in her lifetime and possibly lead exceeding recommended doses from certain brands.

The FDA does not test the dozens of dyes used in cosmetics or set their allowable amounts of heavy metals in them; it outsourced that job years ago to the Cosmetic Ingredient Review, an organization established in 1976 by a cosmetics-industry-aligned trade and lobbying group. Over the years, the US has banned twenty-two chemicals outright. By comparison, the EU currently bans more than thirteen hundred chemicals. All personal care products (defined by anything we put onto our face, hair, body) are absorbed by our skin into our blood stream and end up in the same places as the food we eat—stored in our organs, fat cells, and soft tissues.

Environmental biologists are also finding that some synthetic beauty ingredients end up polluting the environment in very specific ways. An example of this is with micro-plastics, identified as micro-beads in beauty products, which are tiny bits of plastic used in facial exfoliants and body washes. There can be approximately 330,000 micro-beads per tube of face scrub. They are not biodegradable or easily removed by wastewater treatment plants and so are washed into the world's oceans and lakes and enter the food chain. Along the way they sponge up other toxins and chemicals (like motor oil and insecticides), then are consumed by shellfish and fish and subsequently eaten by humans.

While both men and women are certainly affected by chemical overloads in our personal care and beauty products, women are by far the biggest users of these products and, therefore, have the highest exposure.

All of this means our entrenched American beauty habits have far-reaching consequences that can negatively affect our health, the environment, and our wallets. Here are some ways to protect yourself and your loved ones when purchasing your personal care and beauty products:

⌘ Learn to read labels and educate yourself about ingredients.

⌘ Helping you to identify and understand all the ingredients you are putting on your body is the goal of the Environmental Working Group. They maintain the Cosmetic Safety Database which organizes seventy-five thousand products by name and rates ingredients by toxicity levels. (They have a mobile app for reference while shopping at www.ewg.org/skindeep/.)

⌘ Choosing to make your purchases from small, local, or owner-operated businesses using chemical-free, responsibly-sourced ingredients is a huge step toward sustainable beauty care. You will also be contributing to the local economy, rather than sending your dollars overseas.

⌘ Farmer's markets and artisan craft fairs have an increasing number of vendors showcasing their handmade beauty products: face creams, skin tonics, body butters, soaps, and bath elixirs. Many of them grow some, if not all, of the ingredients used in their products or they are sourcing from other local suppliers.

Here are some guidelines when purchasing homemade beauty products:

⌘ Ask detailed questions from the vendor regarding ingredients and processes, and when it was made. Find out how long your product is made to last and the recommended storage procedure.

⌘ Smell Test: natural herb and flower scents will always be much more subtle than fragranced commercial grade brands. The handmade product will most likely contain the herbs/flowers not just for their smell but for their efficacy—their ability to achieve results. Homemade products will be preserved with salts, alcohols such as bourbon/brandy, honey, or maple syrup. Their main moisturizing ingredients will be aloe vera gel or carrier oils, such as olive, apricot kernel, grapeseed, coconut, avocado, and hemp. Fragrances will come from essential oils. So do the smell test every few days at home, to see how your product is holding up.

⌘ The textures will also be a bit different as the ingredients are not being put through an assembly line process with chemical additives included to keep the ingredients from separating. That's okay. Give it a good shake or stir to blend before using.

⌘ Keep it in the fridge to prolong life of product. At a minimum, store in a *dark*, cool, dry cabinet.

⌘ A lot of times ingredients won't be listed as *certified organic,* which is okay. Certification can be a time consuming (expensive) process that a small mom and pop vendor cannot afford to undertake. If they are sourcing high quality ingredients that haven't been compromised with chemicals then it should be fine.

⌘ Hopefully, you'll happen upon a seller who packages his or her products in re-usable containers: once you've finished using it, you can bring it back for a re-fill. It's a great suggestion to impart to your favorite vendor if they are not yet selling this way.

## Food

Buying local, seasonal, and organic food is one of the most important wellness habits you can create for yourself, with repercussions for your community as well as the world at large. Here are some reasons why organic is essential:

⌘ You eliminate exposures to a dangerous class of insecticides known to disrupt neurological development in infants and children.

- ⌘ Organic food isn't irradiated. Cats fed a diet of irradiated food developed multiple sclerosis within three to four months.

- ⌘ Organic farming standards prohibit the use of antibiotics and genetically modified vaccines in farm animals. Consumption of hormone-laced beef and dairy is correlated with increased rates of breast, testis, and prostate cancers.

- ⌘ Organic farmers do not contribute to air and water pollution. Widespread testing of municipal water systems across the U.S. has shown that the principal sources of drinking water for more than half the population have been contaminated. The main suspect is runoff from conventional farms containing pesticides, herbicides and other toxic chemicals.

- ⌘ Farm workers in this country are exposed to the highest concentrations of agricultural poisons of any segment of the population and the devastation to them and their families is well documented. These are the people who tend and harvest our food and they can be protected by organic farming methods.

- ⌘ By buying organic, you are supporting small scale, local farmers. You are keeping local farms viable; you are not contributing to the environmental and social costs of the worldwide transport of foods or supporting a system based on the exploitation of third-world labor. You are helping your community attain food security.

- ⌘ Many organic farmers incorporate alternative and renewable energy sources into their farming/homesteading systems which will help to wean us off petroleum dependency.

- ⌘ Sourcing organic eggs and milk products from small, independent family farms who care for their animals compassionately is recommended over sourcing from large-scale, industrial agriculture. Eggs sourced from people raising backyard chickens are the most cruelty-free, since the chickens are considered pets and will likely be kept until the end of their natural lifespan.

# Select Bibliography

· · · · · · · · · · · · · · · · · · ·

## Books

Agnon, Shmuel Yosef. *Days of Awe: A Treasury of Jewish Wisdom for Reflection, Repentance, and Renewal on the High Holy Days.* New York: Schocken, 1948.

Albertson, Kathleen. *Acupuncture and Chinese Herbal Medicine for Women's Health: Bridging the Gap Between Western and Eastern Medicine.* Seattle: CreateSpace, 2009.

Alexander, Leslie M., and Linda A. Straub-Bruce. *Dental Herbalism: Natural Therapies for the Mouth.* Rochester, VT: Healing Arts Press, 2014.

Ashley-Farrand, Thomas. *Healing Mantras: Using Sound Affirmations for Personal Power, Creativity, and Healing.* New York: Wellspring/Ballantine, 1999.

———. *Mantra: Sacred Words of Power.* Louisville, CO: Sounds True, 2004. Audiobook, compact discs.

Atreya. *Ayurvedic Healing for Women.* York Beach, ME: Samuel Weiser,1999.

Bach, Edward, and F.J. Wheeler. *The Bach Flower Remedies.* New York: McGraw-Hill Education, 1998.

Baillie-Hamilton, Paula. *Toxic Overload: A Doctor's Plan for Combating the Illnesses Caused by Chemicals in Our Foods, Our Homes, and Our Medicine Cabinets.* New York: Avery, 2005.

Ballentine, Rudolph. *Diet and Nutrition: A Holistic Approach.* Honesdale, PA: Himalayan Institute Press, 2007.

Barnett, Cynthia. *Blue Revolution: Unmaking America's Water Crisis.* Boston: Beacon Press, 2012.

Beach, Hugh. *A Year in Lapland: Guest of the Reindeer Herders.* Madison, WI: University of Wisconsin Press, 2001.

Benjamin, Patricia J. *Tappan's Handbook of Healing Massage Techniques.* 5th ed. New York: Prentice Hall, 2009.

Bloom, Jonathan. *American Wasteland: How America Throws Away Nearly Half of Its Food: and What We Can Do About It.* Boston: De Capo Lifelong Books, 2010.

Bopp, Judie, Michael Bopp, Lee Brown, and Phil Lane Jr. *Sacred Tree: Reflections on Native American Spirituality.* Twin Lakes, WI: Lotus Press, 1984.

Brady, Catherine. *Elizabeth Blackburn and the Story of Telomeres: Deciphering the Ends of DNA.* Cambridge, MA: MIT Press, 2009.

Brown, Edward Espe. *Tomato Blessings and Radish Teachings.* New York: Riverhead, 1997.

Buettner, Dan. *The Blue Zones: Lessons for Living Longer from the People Who've Lived the Longest.* Washington, DC: National Geographic, 2009.

Buhner, Stephen Harrod. *The Lost Language of Plants: The Ecological Importance of Plant Medicines for Life on Earth.* White River Junction, VT: Chelsea Green Publishing, 2002.

———. *The Transformational Power of Fasting: The Way to Spiritual, Physical, and Emotional Rejuvenation.* Rochester, VT: Healing Arts Press, 2012.

———. *Herbal Antibiotics, 2nd Edition: Natural Alternatives for Treating Drug-resistant Bacteria.* North Adams, MA: Storey Publishing, 2012.

Caldecott, Moyra. *Myths of the Sacred Tree.* Rochester, VT: Destiny Books, 1993.

Calvert, Robert Noah. *The History of Massage: An Illustrated Survey from Around the World.* Rochester, VT: Healing Arts Press, 2002.

Chai, Makana Risser. *Na Mo'olelo Lomilomi: The Traditions of Hawaiian Massage and Healing.* Honolulu, HI: Bishop Museum Press, 2005.

Colbin, Annemarie. *The Whole-Food Guide to Strong Bones: A Holistic Approach.* Oakland, CA: New Harbinger Publications, 2009.

Desikachar, T. K.V. *The Heart of Yoga: Developing a Personal Practice.* Rev. ed. Rochester, VT: Inner Traditions, 1999.

Dev, Acharya Keshav. *Mudras for Healing.* New Delhi, India: Acharya Shri Enterprises, 1995.

Dillard, Annie. *The Writing Life*. New York: HarperCollins, 1989.

Dull, Harold. *Watsu: Freeing the Body in Water*. 4ᵗʰ ed. Middletown, CA: Watsu Publishing, 2008.

Eaton, Evelyn. *The Shaman and the Medicine Wheel*. Wheaton, IL: Quest Books, 1982.

Eddy, John A. "Medicine Wheels and Plains Indian Astronomy." In *Native American Astronomy*. Edited by Anthony F. Aveni. Austin, TX: University of Texas Press, 1977.

Erhart, Shep, and Leslie Cerier. *Sea Vegetable Celebration: Recipes Using Ocean Vegetables*. 3rd ed. Summertown, TN: Book Publishing Company, 2001.

Farmer-Knowles, Helen. *The Healing Plants Bible: The Definitive Guide to Herbs, Trees, and Flowers*. New York: Sterling, 2010.

Farrer-Halls, Gill. *The Aromatherapy Bible: The Definitive Guide to Using Essential Oils*. New York: Sterling, 2005.

Fife, Bruce. *The Detox Book: How to Detoxify Your Body to Improve Your Health, Stop Disease, and Reverse Aging*. 2d ed. Colorado Springs, CO: Piccadilly Books, 2001.

——— . *Coconut Cures*: Preventing and Treating Common Health Problems with Coconut. Colorado Springs, CO: Piccadilly Books, 2005.

Fitzgerald, Randall. *The Hundred-Year Lie: How to Protect Yourself from the Chemicals That Are Destroying Your Health*. New York: Plume, 2007.

Frawley, David. *Yoga & Ayurveda: Self-Healing and Self-Realization*. Twin Lakes, WI: Lotus Press, 1999.

——— . *Neti: Healing Secrets of Yoga and Ayurveda*. Twin Lakes, WI: Lotus Press, 2005.

——— . *Mantra Yoga and Primal Sound: Secret of Seed (Bija) Mantras*. Twin Lakes, WI: Lotus Press, 2010.

Gibbons, Euell. *Stalking the Wild Asparagus*. Chambersberg, PA: Alan C. Hood & Co., 1962.

Gimbutas, Marija. *The Civilization of the Goddess: The World of Old Europe*. San Francisco: Harper San Francisco, 1991.

Gladstar, Rosemary. *Herbal Recipes for Vibrant Health: 175 Teas, Tonics, Oils, Salves, Tinctures, and Other Natural Remedies for the Entire Family*. North Adams, MA: Storey Publishing, 2008.

Graedon, Joe, and Terry Graedon. *The People's Pharmacy: Quick and Handy Home Remedies.* Washington, DC: National Geographic, 2011.

Green, Miranda. *Celtic Goddesses: Warriors, Virgins and Mothers.* New York: George Braziller, 1996.

Greenberg, Paul. *Four Fish: The Future of the Last Wild Food.* New York: Penguin Books, 2011.

Hanh, Thich Nhat. *A Guide to Walking Meditation.* Nyak, NY: Fellowship Publications, 1985.

Harris, Mark. *Grave Matters: A Journey through the Modern Funeral Industry to a Natural Way of Burial.* New York: Scribner, 2008.

Hatt, Emilie Demant. *With the Lapps in the High Mountains: A Woman among the Sami, 1907–1908.* Edited by Barbara Sjoholm. Madison, WI: University of Wisconsin Press, 2013.

Hawken, Paul. *Growing a Business.* New York: Simon & Schuster, 1988.

———. *Blessed Unrest: How the Largest Movement in the World Came into Being and Why No One Saw It Coming.* New York: Viking Penguin, 2007.

Hirschi, Gertrud. Mudras: *Yoga in Your Hands.* York Beach, ME: Samuel Weiser, 2000.

Hobbs, Christopher. *Medicinal Mushrooms.* 3d ed. City: Botanica Press, 1995.

Hoffman, David. *The Herbal Handbook: A User's Guide to Medical Herbalism.* Rochester, VT: Inner Traditions, 1989.

———. *Holistic Herbal: A Safe and Practical Guide to Making and Using Herbal Remedies.* 4th ed. London: Thorsons Publishing Group, 2003.

Hollender, Jeffrey, Geoff Davis, and Reed Doyle. *Naturally Clean: The Seventh Generation Guide To Safe & Healthy Non-Toxic Cleaning.* Gabriola Island, BC: New Society Publishers, 2006.

Honore, Carl. *In Praise of Slowness.* New York: Harper One, 2004.

Israel, Toby. *Some Place Like Home: Using Design Psychology to Create Ideal Places.* East Sussex, UK: Design Psychology Press, 2010.

Iyengar, B.K.S. *Light on the Yoga Sutras of Patanjali.* London: The Aquarian Press, 1993.

———. *Light On Yoga: Yoga Dipika.* New York: Schocken, 1995.

Jung, C. G. *The Undiscovered Self: With Symbols and the Interpretation of Dreams.* Translated by R. F.C. Hull. Princeton, NJ: Princeton University Press, 2010.

Katz, Sandor Ellix. *The Art of Fermentation: An In-Depth Exploration of Essential Concepts and Processes from around the World.* White River Junction, VT: Chelsea Green Publishing, 2012.

Kaza, Stephanie. *Mindfully Green: A Personal and Spiritual Guide to Whole Earth Thinking.* Boston: Shambhala Publications, 2008.

Khalsa, Karta Purkh Singh, and Michael Tierra. *The Way of Ayurvedic Herbs: A Contemporary Introduction and Useful Manual for the World's Oldest Healing System.* Twin Lakes, WI: Lotus Press, 2008.

Khalsa, Darma Singh. *Food as Medicine: How to Use Diet, Vitamins, Juices, and Herbs for a Healthier, Happier, and Longer Life.* New York: Atria Books, 2004.

Kilham, Chris. *Tales from the Medicine Trail.* New York: Rodale Reach Books, 2000.

Knaster, Mirka. *Discovering the Body's Wisdom: A Comprehensive Guide to More Than Fifty Mind-Body Practices.* New York: Bantam, 1996.

Kolster, Bernard C., and Astrid Waskowiak. *The Reflexology Atlas.* Translated by Nikolas Win Myint. Rochester, VT: Healing Arts Press, 2005.

Koren, Leonard. *Undesigning the Bath.* Berkeley, CA: Stonebridge Press, 1996.

———. *Wabi-Sabi for Artists, Designers, Poets & Philosophers.* San Francisco: Imperfect Publishing, 2008.

Lad, Vasant. *The Complete Book of Ayurvedic Home Remedies.* New York: Harmony, 1999.

Levine, Andrew S. and Valerie J. Levine. *The Bodywork and Massage Sourcebook.* Los Angeles: Lowell House, 1998.

Lappe, Frances Moore. *Diet for a Small Planet.* New York: Ballantine Books, 1991.

Lawless, Julia. *The Illustrated Encyclopedia of Essential Oils: The Complete Guide to the Use of Oils in Aromatherapy & Herbalism.* Boston: Element Books, 1995.

Lehner, Ernst, and Johanna Lehner. *Folklore and Symbolism of Flowers, Plants and Trees.* Mineola, NY: Dover Publications, 2003.

Lilienfeld, Robert and Rathje, William. *Use Less Stuff.* New York: Ballentine Books, 1998.

Louv, Richard. *The Nature Principle: Human Restoration and the End of Nature-Deficit Disorder.* Chapel Hill, NC: Algonquin Books, 2011.

Macnaughton, Ian, ed. *Body, Breath, and Consciousness: A Somatics Anthology*. Berkeley, CA: North Atlantic Books, 2004.

Malkan, Stacy. *Not Just a Pretty Face: The Ugly Side of the Beauty Industry*. Gabriola Island, BC: New Society Publishers, 2007.

Mann, A.T. *The Sacred Language of Trees*. New York: Sterling Ethos, 2012.

Mascaro, Juan, trans. *The Upanishads*. New York: Penguin Classics, 1965.

McCall, Timothy. *Yoga As Medicine: The Yogic Prescription for Health and Healing*. New York: Bantam, 2007.

McGaa, Ed. *Mother Earth Spirituality: Native American Paths to Healing Ourselves and Our World*. San Francisco: HarperSanFrancisco, 1990.

Middleburgh, Charles, and Andrew Goldstein. *High and Holy Days: A Book of Jewish Wisdom.* Norwich, UK: Hymns Ancient & Modern Ltd., 2010.

Monaghan, Patricia. *Encyclopedia of Goddesses and Heroines*. Westport, CT: Greenwood Publishing Group, 2009.

——— . *Goddesses in World Culture.* Westport, CT: ABC-CLIO, 2010.

Moskowitz, Isa Chandra, and Terry Hope Romero. *Veganomicon: The Ultimate Vegan Cookbook*. Boston: De Capo Press, 2007.

Murphy, Sallyann J. *The Zen of Food.* New York: Berkley Trade, 1998.

Murray, Colin, and Liz Murray. *The Celtic Tree Oracle: A System of Divination.* London, UK: Connections Book Publishing, 2015.

Myss, Caroline. *Anatomy of the Spirit: The Seven Stages of Power and Healing.* New York: Harmony Books, 1997.

——— . *Sacred Contracts: Awakening Your Divine Potential.* New York: Harmony Books, 2003.

Newton, Anna. *Herbs for Home Treatment.* Devon, UK: Green Books, 2009.

Ni, Daoshing, and Dana Herko. *The Tao of Fertility: A Healing Chinese Medicine Program to Prepare Body, Mind, and Spirit for New Life.* New York: William Morrow, 2008.

Ni, Maoshing. *The Tao of Nutrition.* rev. and exp. Los Angeles: Sevenstar Communications, 1993.

——. *Secrets of Longevity: Hundreds of Ways to Live to Be 100.* New York: Avery, 2006.

——. *Second Spring: Dr. Mao's Hundreds of Natural Secrets for Women to Revitalize and Regenerate at Any Age.* New York: Atria Books, 2009.

Norris, Susie. *Chocolate Bliss: Sensuous Recipes, Spa Treatments, and Other Divine Indulgences.* Berkeley, CA: Celestial Arts, 2009.

Perlmutter, David. *Grain Brain: The Surprising Truth about Wheat, Carbs, and Sugar—Your Brain's Silent Killers.* New York: Little, Brown and Co., 2013.

Peterson, Lee Allen, and Roger Tory Peterson. *A Field Guide to Edible Wild Plants: Eastern and Central North America.* Peterson Field Guides. New York: Houghton Mifflin Harcourt, 1999.

Pollington, Stephen. *Leechcraft: Early English Charms, Plant-Lore and Healing.* Little Downham, UK: Anglo-Saxon Books, 2000.

Prelitz, Chris. *Green Made Easy: The Everyday Guide for Transitioning to a Green Lifestyle.* Carlsbad, CA: Hay House, 2009.

Rätsch Christian, and Claudia Müller-Ebeling. *Pagan Christmas: The Plants, Spirits, and Rituals at the Origins of Yuletide.* Rochester, VT: Inner Traditions, 2006.

Richmond, Lewis. *Aging as a Spiritual Practice: A Contemplative Guide to Growing Older and Wiser.* New York: Gotham, 2012.

Rosenthal, Norman E. *Winter Blues: Everything You Need to Know to Beat Seasonal Affective Disorder.* New York: The Guilford Press, 2005.

Rosso, Julee, and Sheila Lukins. *The New Basics Cookbook.* New York: Workman Publishing, 1989.

Roth, Gabrielle, and John Loudon. *Maps to Ecstasy: Teachings of an Urban Shaman.* Novato, CA: New World Library, 1989.

Ruppenthal, R. J. *Fresh Food from Small Spaces.* White River Junction, VT: Chelsea Green Publishing, 2008.

Ryan Thomas. *The Sacred Art of Fasting: Preparing to Practice.* Woodstock, VT: Skylight Paths, 2005.

Sams, Jamie, and Linda Childers, illustrator. *Sacred Path Cards: The Discovery of Self through Native Teachings.* New York: HarperCollins, 1990.

———. David Carson, and Angela C. Werneke, illustrator. *Medicine Cards: The Discovery of Power Through the Ways of Animals.* New York: St. Martin's Press, 1999.

Sarton, May. *Journal of a Solitude.* New York: Norton, 1977.

Scaravelli, Vanda. *Awakening the Spine.* 2d ed. New York: HarperOne, 1991.

Schnaubelt, Kurt. *Advanced Aromatherapy: The Science of Essential Oil Therapy.* Rochester, VT: Healing Arts Press, 1998.

Scott, David, and Tom Pappas. *Three Bowl Cookbook: The Secrets of Enlightened Cooking from the Zen Mountain Center.* North Clarendon, VT: Tuttle Publishing, 2000.

Shaw, Miranda. *Passionate Enlightenment: Women in Tantric Buddhism.* Princeton, NJ: Princeton University Press, 1995.

Shealy, C. Norman. *The Illustrated Encyclopedia of Healing Remedies.* New York: Harper Element, 2009.

Shearer, Alistair. *The Yoga Sutras of Pantanjali.* Translated and introduced by A. Shearer. New York: Bell Tower/Random House, 1982.

Siegel-Maier, Karyn. *The Naturally Clean Home: 150 Super-Easy Herbal Formulas for Green.* North Adams, MA: Storey Publishing, 2008.

Simeona, Morrnah Nalamaku. *Self I-dentity Through Ho'Oponopono.* Honolulu: The Foundation of I, Inc. Freedom of the Cosmos, 1989.

Smith, Bruce, and Yahiko Yamamoto. *The Japanese Bath.* Salt Lake City: Gibbs-Smith, 2001.

Somerville, Annie. *Fields of Greens.* New York: Bantam Books, 1987.

Sompayrac, Lauren M. *How the Immune System Works.* 3d ed. Hoboken, NJ: Wiley-Blackwell, 2008.

Stamets, Paul. *Mycelium Running: How Mushrooms Can Help Save the World.* Berkeley, CA: Ten Speed Press, 2005.

Stauffer, Kathrin A. *Anatomy & Physiology For Psychotherapists: Connecting Body and Soul.* New York: W.W. Norton, 2010.

Sternberg, Esther M. *Healing Spaces: The Science of Place and Wellbeing.* Cambridge, MA: Belknap Press, 2010.

Teeguarden, Iona Marsaa. *Acupressure Way of Health: Jin Shin Do*. Taos, NM: Japan Publications/ Redwing Book Co., 1978.

Teish, Luisah. *Jambalaya: The Natural Woman's Book of Personal Charms and Practical Rituals*. San Francisco: HarperSanFrancisco, 1985.

Tierra, Michael. *The Way of Chinese Herbs*. New York: Gallery Books, 1998.

Wells, D. *The Penguin Dictionary of Curious and Interesting Numbers*. London: Penguin Group, 1987.

Vasey, Christopher. *Natural Remedies for Inflammation*. Rochester, VT: Healing Arts Press, 2014.

Weil, Andrew. *Natural Health, Natural Medicine: The Complete Guide to Wellness and Self-Care for Optimum Health*. Boston: Mariner Books, 2014.

Wigginton, Eliot, ed. *The Foxfire Book: Hog Dressing, Log Cabin Building, Mountain Crafts and Foods, Planting by the Signs, Snake Lore, Hunting Tales, Faith Healing, Moonshining, and Other Affairs of Plain Living*. New York: Anchor Books, 1972.

Williamson, Ray F. *Living the Sky: The Cosmos of the American Indian*. Norman, OK: University of Oklahoma Press, 1984.

Winter, Ruth. *A Consumer's Dictionary of Cosmetic Ingredients: Complete Information about the Harmful and Desirable Ingredients Found in Cosmetics and Cosmeceuticals*. 7th ed. New York: Harmony, 2009.

Wood, Rebecca. *The New Whole Foods Encyclopedia: A Comprehensive Resource for Healthy Eating*. New York: Penguin Books, 2010.

## Articles

Chikly, Bruno. "Lymph Drainage Therapy." *Massage & Bodywork* (June/July 2001).

Cooney, Elizabeth. "Secrets of the Narwhal Tusk." *Harvard Gazette* (18 March 2014).

Cousteau, Jean-Michel. "The Truth about Sunscreens and Coral Reefs." *Diver* (June 2012).

Crawford, Amanda McQuade. "Hormones Demystified." *Yoga Journal* (May–June 1997).

Gourley, Leah. "Marine Biology Mystery Solved." *Harvard Gazette* (2007).

Harrar, Sari. "Omega-3 Fatty Acids and Mood Disorders." *Today's Dietitian* (January 2012).

Leviton, Alex. "Thalassotherapy—the Power of the Sea." *Healing Lifestyles & Spas* (March 2005).

Lu, Stacy. "How Chronic Stress Is Harming Our DNA." *American Psychological Association Newsletter* (October 2014).

Marris, Emma. "Rethinking Predators: Legend of the Wolf." *Nature* (7 March, 2014).

Mayrhofer, Pat. "The History of Hot Stone Massage." *Massage Magazine* (May, 2010).

Mondragon, Tamara. "History of Lomilomi." *Massage Magazine* (July 2000).

Prilutsky, Boris. "Lymph Drainage for Detoxification." *Massage & Bodywork* (June/July 2006).

Rao, T. S. Sathyanarayana, et. al. "Understanding Nutrition, Depression and Mental Illnesses." *Indian Journal of Psychiatry* (April–June 2008).

Sánchez-Villegas, Almudena, et. al. "Dietary Fat Intake and the Risk of Depression: The SUN Project." *PLOS One* (January 2011).

Weir, Kirsten. "The Pain of Social Rejection." *American Psychology Association Newsletter*, vol. 43, no. 4 (April 2012).

Young, Simon N. "How to Increase Serotonin in The Human Brain Without Drugs." *Journal of Psychiatry and Neuroscience* (November 2007).

## Other Resources

"10 Reasons to Care Where Your Jewelry Comes From." Brilliant Earth. (Additional webpages listed as "Conflict Diamond Issues," and "Gold Mining Issues.") Accessed on March 20, 2013. http://www.brilliantearth.com/top-ten-jewelry-issues/.

"42 Ways to Trim Your Holiday Wasteline." UseLessStuff.com. Accessed on Nov. 3, 2012. http://www.use-less-stuff.com/ULSDAY/42ways.html.

"Bone Health Basics." National Osteoporosis Foundation. Accessed on Oct. 12, 2013. http://nof.org/learn/bonebasics.

"Chemicals in Cosmetics." Breast Cancer Fund. (Additional webpages listed as "Research Methods," and "Reduce Your Risk.") Accessed on May 11, 2012. http://www.breastcancerfund.org/clear-science/environmental-breast-cancer-links/cosmetics/.

"Child Labor and Slavery in the Chocolate Industry." Food Empowerment Project. (Additional webpage listed as "Food Justice: Know the Issues.") Accessed on March 22, 2014. http://www.foodispower.org/slavery-chocolate/.

"Conflict Diamonds." Global Witness Project. (Additional webpage listed under "About Us.") Accessed on Jan. 12, 2015. https://www.globalwitness.org/campaigns/conflict-diamonds/.

"Deodorants, Antiperspirants and Your Health." Control Your Impact. Accessed on March 4, 2012. http://www.controlyourimpact.com/articles/deodorants-antiperspirants-and- your-health/.

"Holiday Waste Program." Stanford University. Accessed on Nov. 3, 2012. http://bgm.stanford.edu/pssi_holiday_waste.

"Polybrominated Diphenyl Ethers." Breast Cancer Fund. (Additional webpage listed as "Chemicals and Radiation Linked to Breast Cancer.) Accessed on May 11, 2012. http://www.breastcancerfund.org/clear-science/radiation-chemicals-and-breast-cancer/polybrominated-diphenyl-ethers.html.

"Skin Cancer Statistics." Centers for Disease Control and Prevention. (Additional webpages listed as "Rates by Race and Ethnicity," and "Rates by State, Trends, and Behavior Rates.") Accessed on Feb. 26, 2013. http://www.cdc.gov/cancer/skin/statistics/index.htm.

"Sunscreen Guide and Annual Report." Environmental Working Group (2013). Accessed on Apr. 5, 2013. http://www.ewg.org/2013sunscreen/.

"The Truth about Sunscreens and Personal Care Products." Organic Consumers Association (2004). Accessed on Aug.1, 2013. https://www.organicconsumers.org/old_articles/bodycare/sunscreen.php. Originally posted in the Terressential newsletter, *Exposure*. http://www.terressentials.com/exposure.html#TiO2.

"Twelve Simple Tips to Improve Your Sleep." Division of Sleep Medicine, Harvard Medical School. (Additional webpages listed as "Why Sleep Matters," "The Science of Sleep," and "Getting The Sleep You Need.") Accessed June 6, 2013. http://healthysleep.med.harvard.edu/healthy/getting/overcoming/tips.

"What Is Green Burial?" Green Burial Council. (Additional webpages listed as "History of GBC," "Mission of GBC," and "Education." Accessed on Dec. 20, 2012. http://greenburialcouncil. org/home/what-is-green-burial/.

Adams, Lynn, et. al. "Blueberry Phytochemicals Inhibit Growth and Metastatic Potential of MDA-MB-231 Breast Cancer Cells." NCBI, National Institutes of Health, PMC articles (May 1, 2010). http://www.ncbi.nlm.nih.gov/pmc/articles/PMC2862148/.

Braun, David Maxwell. "Overfishing Leaves Much of Mediterranean a Dead Sea." *National Geographic Voices* (March 2, 2012). http://voices.nationalgeographic.com/2012/03/02/overfishing-leaves-much-of-mediterranean-a-dead-sea-study-finds/.

Emmons, Robert. "Why Gratitude is Good." *Greater Good,* UC Berkeley (Nov. 16, 2010). http://greatergood.berkeley.edu/article/item/why_gratitude_is_good.

Hanson, Rick. "How to Grow the Good in Your Brain." *Greater Good*, UC Berkeley (Sept. 24, 2013) http://greatergood.berkeley.edu/article/item/how_to_grow_the_good_in_your_brain.

Kestenbaum, David. "Mottainai Grandma Reminds Japan, 'Don't Waste'" *Adaptation,* NPR special series (Oct. 8, 2007). http://www.npr.org/templates/story/story.php?storyId=14054262.

Ledesma, Natalie. "Nutrition and Breast Cancer." *Women's Health Matters*, University of San Francisco Medical Center. Accessed on July 15, 2013. http://cancer.ucsf.edu/_docs/crc/nutrition_breast.pdf.

Lu, Stacy. "Visionaries: Elissa Epel on Why Toxic Stress Is Public Health Enemy #1." TEDMED (blog), *Visionaries* series, (March 13, 2013).

http://blog.tedmed.com/visionaries-elissa-epel-on-why-toxic-stress-is-public-health-enemy-number-one/.

Rogers, Kara. "The Legend and Mystery of the Narwhal." *Science Friday* (March 16, 2011). http://www.sciencefriday.com/blogs/03/15/2011/the-legend-and-mystery-of-the-narwhal.html?series=2.

Sifferlin, Alexandra. "How Exercise May Lower Breast Cancer Risk." In Healthland, *Time* (May, 8, 2013). http://healthland.time.com/2013/05/08/how-exercise-may-lower-breast-cancer-risk/.

# Recipe Index

. . . . . . . . . . . . . . . . . .

## Main Dishes and Bowls

## Sweets

## Condiments and Snacks

# Index

. . . . . . . . . . . . . . . . . .

Digestion, 48, 58, 79, 80, 134, 135, 139, 276

Dissolving Fears Ritual, 239

Divination Ritual, 163–66

Dry brushing, 36–37

# E

Earth Day, 84

Emotional health, 46, 48, 50, 52, 92–93, 97–99, 115–16, 132, 135, 182, 192–93, 242, 259

Endocrine system, 255

Energy, 9, 50, 97, 116, 117, 118, 246, 256

Environmental psychology, 219–20

Environmental sustainability, 14, 75, 83, 151–54, 282–84, 285–88, 289–90

Equinox, 41; autumnal, 159-60; vernal 21

Essential oils, 50–52, 116–17, 127

Ethical consumerism, 286–88

Euell Gibbons, 53

# F

Fasting, 72–73

Fear: banishing of, 117, 166-67, 191; holding in body, 109-10, 115-16, 177; releasing of, 238-39, 246

Feet, care of, 60–61, 115, 125, 198, 256, 257

Fermented foods, 39–40, 59

First aid kit, 148

Food preparation as ritual, 63–64

Food waste, 123–24

# G

Garlic, 260

Geranium, 117, 243, 259-60

Ginger, 260–61

Gluten-free, 212–13

Gratitude, importance of, 171–73

# H

Hair care, 129, 197

Heart, health of, 65, 82, 134, 138, 173, 193, 194, 209, 258, 259, 260, 278

Helicrysum, 51

Herbs; for healing, 10–11, 78–81, 118–19; growing, 78; how to preserve, 81

Hormones, 118, 191, 255

# I

Immune system, health of, 38, 40, 49, 51, 79, 80, 119, 132, 182, 193, 194, 241, 246, 254, 257, 261, 269, 275

Impact on planet, 84

Inflammation, decreasing of, 40, 51, 52, 54, 118, 134

Insect: bites, 80, 118, 127; repellent, 79

Intuition, 162–63

# J

Jin Shin Do, 115–16

Juniper Berry, 61–62

# K

Kidneys, health of, 175-78

# L

Lavender, 80, 116, 127, 199

Lemon, 3, 59, 76-77, 243, 261

# Permissions

. . . . . . . . . . . . . . . . . .

Grateful acknowledgment is made to the following authors for kind permission to reprint previously published material:

From *A Guide to Walking Meditation*, by Thich Nhat Hanh (Nyack, NY: Fellowship Publications, a division of Fellowship of Reconciliation) 1985, with permission courtesy of Parallax Press, Berkeley, CA.

"Song for the Salmon" excerpt, by David Whyte from his book, *River Flow: New and Selected Poems*©, 2012 (p. 146). Printed with permission from © Many Rivers Press, www.davidwhyte.com, Langley, WA, USA.

"Prayer for Autumn" by Sun Bear. Printed by permission of Honor the Earth and Winona LaDuke, Callaway, MN.

*Rilke's Book of Hours: Love Poems To God*, by Rainer Maria Rilke, translated by Anita Barrows and Joanna Macy. Excerpt reprinted with permission by Penguin Group, New York (USA)

# About the Author

· · · · · · · · · · · · · · · · · ·

Holistic wellbeing expert Randi Ragan is the founder and owner of the award-winning GreenBliss EcoSpa, celebrating its ten-year anniversary in 2016. Prior, Randi was a yoga and meditation teacher at Los Angeles' top studios for 12 years, during which time she created programs for children, seniors, corporations, Hollywood celebrities, production studios and talent agencies, and private addiction recovery centers. She has led yoga and spiritual retreats in California, Mexico, and Hawaii, and formed The Blessing Works, which specialized in the creation of customized healing ceremonies and rituals for its clients.

Randi's work has been featured on television (NBC's *Your LA,* ABC/Channel 7 *Morning Show* and CBS/Channel 2 *News At Noon*); in magazines (*Martha Stewart's Whole Living, Organic Spa Magazine, Vegetarian Times, Healing Lifestyles and Spas*); blogs (*Daily Candy, The Huffington Post, She Knows, The Beauty Exchange, Spa Addicts*); and podcasts (*The Bourbon Lounge, What Really Matters, Earth Train Radio, and LA Stories*).

Randi was the inaugural Editor, Health and Wellness for CocoEco Magazine, and columnist for Natural Child World Magazine. Her writing can be found online at her blog, The Mindful Living Almanac (randiragan.com). She is also a frequent speaker at conferences, schools, and businesses, and regularly produces salons, workshops, and retreats about holistic living and conscious wellness.

Randi lives in Los Angeles with her husband and 14–year–old daughter.

Printed in Great Britain
by Amazon

17613334R00194